SOJOURNER

PREPARING FOR THE JOURNEY OF A LIFETIME

BIBLE STUDY

Leader's Guide

Richard Kuenzinger

Published by Innovo Publishing, LLC
www.innovopublishing.com
1-888-546-2111

Publishing quality books, eBooks, audiobooks, music, screenplays & courses for the Christian & wholesome markets since 2008.

SOJOURNER
Preparing for the Journey of a Lifetime
-Bible Study Leader's Guide-

Copyright © 2023 by Innovo Publishing
All rights reserved.

No part of this publication may be reproduced, stored in a retrieval system, or transmitted in any form or by any means electronic, mechanical, photocopying, recording, or otherwise, without the prior written permission of the Publisher.

Scripture was taken from a variety of versions, including the Berean Standard Bible, English Standard Version, International Standard Version, King James Version, New American Standard Bible, New International Version, New King James Version, and New Living Translation. Copyright attributions can be found on pages 146–147.

Library of Congress Control Number: 2023947141
ISBN: 978-1-61314-967-6

Cover Design & Interior Layout: Innovo Publishing, LLC

Printed in the United States of America
U.S. Printing History
First Edition: 2023

Has God called you to create a Christ-centered or wholesome book, eBook, audiobook, music album, screenplay, or online course? Visit Innovo's educational center (cpportal.com) to learn how to accomplish your calling with excellence.

CONTENTS

Introduction & How to Use the Leader's Guide 9

1: *The Creation Era* 10
- Week 1: Creation 11
- Week 2: Adam and Eve 14
- Week 3: Sin 17
- Week 4: The Flood 21
- Week 5: The Tower of Babel 24

2: *The Patriarch Era* 27
- Week 6: The Abrahamic Covenant 28
- Week 7: Isaac 31
- Week 8: Jacob 34
- Week 9: Joseph 37

3: *The Exodus Era* 40
- Week 10: Moses 41
- Week 11: The Passover 44
- Week 12: The Red Sea 47
- Week 13: The Ten Commandments 50

4: *The Conquest Era* 53
- Week 14: Jericho and Rahab 54

5: *The Sin Cycle/Judges Era* 57
- Week 15: Failure to Keep the Law 58
- Week 16: Ruth 61

6: *The Kingdom Era* 65
- Week 17: Samuel 66
- Week 18: Saul 69
- Week 19: David's Obedience to the Covenant 72
- Week 20: David's Prophecies 75
- Week 21: Solomon 78
- Week 22: Proverbs (or Christmas) 82

7: *The Divided Kingdom Era* 85
- Week 23: The Kingdom Splits 86
- Week 24: The Fall of Israel and the Promised Redemption 89

8: *The Captivity Era* 92
- Week 25: The Fall of Judah 93
- Week 26: Jeremiah 97
- Week 27: Ezekiel 100
- Week 28: Daniel's Prayer 103

9: *The Return Era* 106
- Week 29: Ezra 107
- Week 30: Nehemiah 111

10: *The Silent Era* 114
- Week 31: Malachi 115

11: *The Gospel Era* 119
- Week 32: Jesus' Birth Announced 120
- Week 33: John the Baptist 123
- Week 34: Love Your Enemies 126
- Week 35: Fishers of Men 129
- Week 36: The Beatitudes 132

    Week 37: Jesus Calms the Storm 135
    Week 38: Feeding the 5,000 (Optional: Use Easter lesson) 138
    Week 39: The Promise of a Helper 141
    Week 40: Jesus Walks on Water 144
    Week 41: The Good Samaritan 147
    Week 42: The Prodigal Son 150
    Week 43: The Greatest Commandment 153
    Week 44: Judas Betrays Jesus 156
    Week 45: The Last Supper 159
    Week 46: Good Friday/Crucifixion 163

12: *The Church Era* 166
    Week 47: Pentecost 167

13: *The Mission Era* 170
    Week 48: Paul and Barnabas Sent 171
    Week 49: The Antioch Meeting 175

14: *The End of Time Era* 178
    Week 50: The Revelation 179
    Week 51: The Gospel in Christmas 183
    Week 52: The Gospel in Easter 186

Scripture Citation Index 190

INTRODUCTION & HOW TO USE THE
Leader's Guide

Dear Sojourner Leader,

Welcome! The lessons contained in this **Sojourner Bible Study (SBS)** are based on the fourteen eras of the Bible. These eras are taken from the Chronological Bible Study and lessons that have been used in English as a second language (ESL) classes. The lessons were chosen because they guide you from Creation to the Cross and then into the Church Era. The last lesson is from the Revelation of John, with a glimpse of the goal, Heaven.

These lessons are designed to allow the leader flexibility in preparation and discussion of the lesson. Each lesson has a theme, a verse and questions designed to direct the student's focus. Each lesson will also have some ideas of how to serve based on what is learned.

There are fifty-two lessons. In a normal church calendar, you will find one or two weeks without Sunday school meetings. These lessons are based on the assumption that the new Sunday school year begins on the first Sunday of June, or the first Sunday of August. Therefore, use your discretion on how to handle Christmas and Easter lessons. We have placed Christmas and Easter at the end, lessons 51 and 52.

The theme of each lesson will build on the foundation laid in the previous lesson—the objective being to build a knowledge base of the Bible, which will encourage continued learning. The verse of each lesson should guide the student to the theme. The student should be encouraged to memorize the verse.

Bible study without application is meaningless. You as a leader should help the students find ways to apply what they are learning. We have offered some thoughts in the So What? sections. The leader should make each lesson missional. Encourage the student to share the lesson with family and friends today. Encourage the student to serve this week in a way that will allow the student to live out the lesson.

You will see some repetition built into the lessons. For example, when you "Connect the Gospel," you will notice the same format. This also applies to the section, Talk. The repetition in these areas will help any student be a Bible study leader by using these ideas.

Please don't feel that these lessons are rigid. Use them as a guide in developing your own lessons. You know your students better than we do. You may never cover everything in a lesson. That's okay. Encourage your students in their faith walk. If you only read one verse in the lesson and then spend the rest of the time talking, don't worry. Try to emphasize the point of the lesson as you close and pray.

Finally, although you can complete this study on your own, it is designed to be completed with other students in a group setting (like a Bible study class or Sunday school class), with a Sojourner leader who can help lead discussions about each lesson and provide additional feedback.

May our God and Father, in the power of the Holy Spirit, give you wisdom and discernment in teaching your students. We hope you will teach them with the idea that one day they too will teach others.

Scan the QR code to download a PDF version of this workbook:

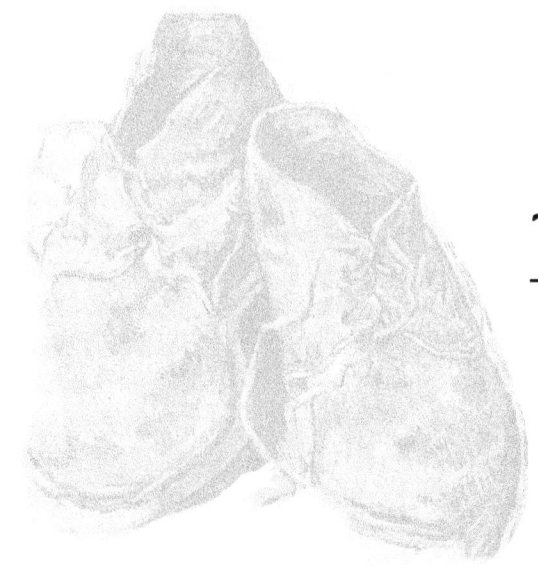

1: The Creation Era

Week 1: Creation
Genesis 1:1-31

Key Verse: "In the beginning God, created the heavens and the earth." (Genesis 1:1)

LEADER'S NOTE

As you prepare for this lesson, focus on the fact that we have a Creator. Feel free to show the work of God through His words. Look at the progression of Creation. Each event occurred in the order necessary to sustain the next. Notice there is order and not chaos. Everything was created after its kind. Pears don't grow on grape vines. Everything was created in its mature state. At the end of the lesson, does the student know Genesis 1:1?

CONTEXT

The Genesis account was written by Moses, even though the last of the Genesis events takes place over 400 years before Moses was born. How did he do it? The ability to write dated back to the days of Abraham. God enabled His Word to be passed down through oral and written form, and He equipped His people to record it.

OPEN UP

Ask the students if they made anything this week.

- Did you make your bed or a sandwich?
- Did you create anything this week?

THINK ABOUT

What's the difference between making something and creating something?

READ

Verse 1: This is our memory verse. Why is this so important? If we do not believe in a Creator God, then we have no absolute standard. (An absolute standard does not change regardless of what is happening around us. Jesus is the same yesterday, today and forever—Hebrews 13:8.) If we were not created in God's plan, then nothing really matters. The entire Bible hinges on acceptance of this verse.

Verses 2-3: The Spirit of God is in action. The darkness is changed.

Verses 4-25: What did God do? How did He do it? How did He feel about it?

Verses 26-31: What did God do? Why did He create man and woman? In verse 28 God "blessed them." Did He bless any other part of creation?

FOCUS

In the beginning God, created the heavens and the earth. (Genesis 1:1)

The focus of this lesson is that all things were created by God. They were created in an order and with a purpose. "For God is not a God of confusion but of peace, as in all the churches of the saints" (1 Corinthians 14:33).

LEADER'S GUIDE—SOJOURNER BIBLE STUDY

TALK
- What is this teaching me about God?
- What is this teaching me about people?
- Why is this important to me today?

CONNECT THE GOSPEL

This is the Gospel: "For what I received I passed on to you as of first importance: that Christ died for our sins according to the Scriptures, that he was buried, that he was raised on the third day according to the Scriptures" (1 Corinthians 15:3-4). Everything that God created was good and for a purpose. God created us in His image and He gave us a job. Do we look like God today? If so, how so? If not, why not? Our sin separates us from God and His perfection. The Gospel is the "good news" that the God of Creation has come into a fallen world and made a way for us to be new again.

Is it possible to bear His image today? He gave us His Son so that we could be made new. A new creation (2 Corinthians 5:17). If we have been made new, are we being obedient to the job He has given us?

SO WHAT?

Daily we hear about evolution or evolutionary ideas. People speak of fossils and resources being billions of years old. Some scientists continue to search for a "missing link" that will connect apes to humans. How can we share what we know from Genesis 1 with the people around us? Can we speak in grace and truth and talk about what we believe without it leading to an argument?

View the "Is Genesis History?" video to learn how science supports Genesis:

SERVE

How can I serve based on Genesis 1? God created the universe and He put Adam and Eve in the Garden to be caretakers. Has that job changed? No, it hasn't. We've just relocated. We are still caretakers of God's creation. This week, look around your school, your neighborhood, and even the church parking lot, and find ways to take care of what God created. Pick up trash, help someone—even taking care of yourself with good hygiene, eating right, and sleeping, are ways to be focused on God's creation.

DIG DEEPER

In the beginning God, created the heavens and the earth. (Genesis 1:1)

The foundation of any religion has a creation story. The genesis, the beginning, of the Christian faith, is the foundation of a Creator. If someone does not believe in a Creator, it will be difficult to talk to them about sin and salvation. Genesis chapters one and two help people see the work of the Creator.

"In the beginning God…" The entire Bible is God-centered, from the beginning in Genesis until the end of Revelation.

He who testifies to these things says, "Yes, I am coming soon." Amen. Come, Lord Jesus. The grace of the Lord Jesus be with God's people. Amen. (Revelation 22:20-21)

God has revealed Himself in creation. He spoke the word, and there was light. David said in Psalm 119:130, "The unfolding of your words gives light; it gives understanding to the simple." The Word of God also guides us to an understanding of Him.

The first verse of the Bible is so rich and deep, so, if we are going to dig deeper, we need to explore some of the words. *Beginning, God, created,* and *heavens and earth*, are all words we need to investigate.

"Beginning." When was this beginning? The point in time when God spoke first is the "beginning." We do not have a date to point to and say, "this is day one." It is from this beginning point that we begin our study of God and His creation. Nothing existed before the beginning. God exists outside of nature, space, and time.

"God." The Hebrew word is Elohim, which is the plural form of El, so we see the plurality of God. He is One God, and He exists in three distinct natures as Father, Son and Holy Spirit. The name "El" shows that He is all powerful. "For in him all things were created: things in heaven and on earth, visible and invisible, whether thrones or powers or rulers or authorities; all things have been created through him and for him" (Col. 1:16).

"Created." God made something out of nothing. The Latin phrase is "ex nihilo." This is the idea that nothing was in existence prior to God creating, or bringing it into existence. Again, God exists and works outside of the laws of nature. Of course, He can create something from nothing. If He could not, would He be God Almighty the Maker of Heaven and Earth?

Which brings us to our last words in Genesis 1:1, "The heavens and the earth." When you look up into the sky, you see the creation of God. When you look around at grass, trees, mountains, and rivers, you see the creation of God. When Paul was in Athens speaking to the philosophers, he put creation in their cultural context.

> *The God who made the world and everything in it is the Lord of heaven and earth and does not live in temples built by human hands. And he is not served by human hands, as if he needed anything. Rather, he himself gives everyone life and breath and everything else. From one man he made all the nations, that they should inhabit the whole earth; and he marked out their appointed times in history and the boundaries of their lands. God did this so that they would seek him and perhaps reach out for him and find him, though he is not far from any one of us. For in him we live and move and have our being. (Acts 17:24)*

Our lesson showed us that God created everything, and it was good. We know that our world is not good today. God did not change. He is the same yesterday, today and tomorrow (Hebrews 13:8). The Bible tells us that a day is coming when the earth will be made new.

> *Then I saw "a new heaven and a new earth," for the first heaven and the first earth had passed away, and there was no longer any sea." (Revelation 21:1)*

We are living in a time between the Perfect Creation and the Perfect Re-creation. With this in mind, how now should we live? If you have experienced new life in Christ, you know that this world is temporary. We need to help people around us see that eternal hope that is in Christ alone.

Notes

LEADER'S GUIDE—SOJOURNER BIBLE STUDY

Week 2: Adam and Eve
Genesis 2:4-25

Key verse: *"For this reason a man shall leave his father and his mother, and be joined to his wife; and they shall become one flesh." (Genesis 2:24)*

LEADER'S NOTE

As you prepare for this lesson, remember that we have a God who created us for a purpose. It was His design that we should not be alone, and in that design, He created marriage. One man and one woman. At the end of the lesson does the student see a plan developing between Genesis 1:1 and 2:24?

CONTEXT

When we discuss context, it is important to help the students understand the danger in taking a verse by itself. Encourage the students to read the before and after of the verses they like.

The events in the opening chapters in Genesis take place more than 2,500 years before Jesus was born. They were not recorded until the time of Moses, approximately 1440 B.C. The Genesis account preserves the story of God's people that would be passed down to generations and provides a source of hope in God's perfect plan. It was important to understand that God had a plan for men and women. It began perfectly with the man and the woman as co-laborers.

OPEN UP

- What is marriage today?
- What do people think of marriage?
- What do you think about marriage?

THINK ABOUT

What does the marriage of a man and woman represent?

READ

Verse 4: Moses is giving us more definition to the Creation story from chapter 1.

Verses 5-9: Notice the Lord working. Take note of what He is using in His work. He caused the mist to water the earth, He used dust to create the man, and He used His own breath to give life to the man. The Lord causes the growth. What is the purpose of the two trees in the midst of the garden?

Verses 10-14: We have a geographical location for the Garden. The Tigris and the Euphrates rivers are still in existence.

Verses 15-17: The Lord provides direction and guidance for Adam. To whom did the Lord give the command?

Verses 18-25: The Lord created a "helpmate" for the man. They had a perfect union. This union is a reflection of the perfect relationship they had with God. Their "nakedness" symbolizes the purity of their image. Remember that they were created in the image of God. In a perfect relationship there is no shame (1:27).

1: THE CREATION ERA

FOCUS

> *For this reason a man shall leave his father and his mother, and be joined to his wife; and they shall become one flesh. (Genesis 2:24)*

The focus of this lesson is that God created man and woman in a perfect union in a perfect plan. The woman is a helpmate for the man, a partner, not a servant. This perfect union, which we can see daily, is an image of how our relationship with God should be. The Father and the Son are in perfect union, and likewise the man and woman should be as well.

TALK

- What is this teaching me about God?
- What is this teaching me about people?
- Why is this important to me today?

CONNECT THE GOSPEL

This is the Gospel: "For what I received I passed on to you as of first importance: that Christ died for our sins according to the Scriptures, that he was buried, that he was raised on the third day according to the Scriptures" (1 Corinthians 15:3-4).

The Gospel is the picture of God doing the work to restore our perfect union with Him. Do men and women live in perfect union today? Why did Jesus have to die for our sins? What did our sin do to our relationship with our Creator? Adam and Eve were in a perfect relationship with their Creator, and we can have that same relationship. Just as our sin separates us from God, our faith in His work restores that relationship.

SO WHAT?

Right now, you are not married. However, as a follower of Christ, you are in a relationship. You can live as if you are married to your Creator. The most important relationship in our life will be with our Creator.

God created man and gave him a job. Then God brought him a partner.

Let's do what God has created us to do and wait for Him to bring us our partner. You can begin praying for who that will be. Also pray that you will remain faithful to the Lord along the way.

SERVE

There are so many broken relationships around us. This week, let's pray for our friends, neighbors, and other people we know who are struggling in a relationship. It may be a marriage, or just friends who are not speaking to each other. Find a way to encourage them this week. Point out that God created us for relationship, and the best relationship is being right with Him.

DIG DEEPER

> *For this reason a man shall leave his father and his mother, and be joined to his wife; and they shall become one flesh. (Genesis 2:24)*

"For this reason…" What is the reason? We need to look deeper into verse 23, and we need to understand what is happening in the Garden of Creation. "The man said, 'This is now bone of my bones and flesh of my flesh; she shall be called "woman," for she was taken out of man.'"

God had put the man in the Garden, and God gave him the animals, but there was not a suitable helper for the man (Genesis 2:20). This woman was a helper, not a servant, nor a leader, but a helper. God designed her to help the man rule over God's creation. The only difference between the two people was their sex. Male and female.

Marriage was designed to be "one flesh," not a multiple relationship. One man for one woman equals one flesh.

> *Has not the one God made you? You belong to him in body and spirit. And what does the one God seek? Godly offspring. So be on your guard, and do not be unfaithful to the wife of your youth. (Malachi 2:15)*

The wording in Malachi shows us again the "oneness" of the relationship. One man and one woman. The Bible gives us examples of men who had multiple wives, and in every example of multiple wives you will find problems. The purpose of this relationship is to serve as a pattern for us to follow in our relationship with God in Christ Jesus.

> *For we are members of his body. "For this reason, a man will leave his father and mother and be united to his wife, and the two will become one flesh." This is a profound mystery—but I am talking about Christ and the church. (Ephesians 5:30-32)*

When we follow Jesus, He is our "husband." We know this sounds weird, and it's probably why Paul called it a "mystery." We, as the church, are the "wife" or the "bride" of Christ. Christ has given Himself for us, and we are in perfect union with Him.

> *The Church is one Body, "For just as each of us has one body with many members, and these members do not all have the same function, so in Christ we, though many, form one body, and each member belongs to all the others." (Romans 12:4-5)*

Jesus should be first in our time, our attention, and our resources. So, when we step away from this union, when we sin, or when we put anything or anyone before our relationship with Christ, we are breaking this union. This is spiritual adultery. Think about that the next time you think following Jesus only happens for an hour on Sunday.

Notes

1: THE CREATION ERA

Week 3: Sin
Genesis 3:1-24

Key verse: *"And I will put enmity between you and the woman, and between your seed and her seed; He shall bruise you on the head, and you shall bruise him on the heel." (Genesis 3:15)*

LEADER'S NOTE

Begin this lesson with a review of Lessons 1 and 2. Remind the students of the key memory verses (Genesis 1:1, "In the beginning God, created the heavens and the earth," and 2:24, "For this reason a man shall leave his father and his mother, and be joined to his wife; and they shall become one flesh"). Remind them that we are seeing God's plan unfold, and it all began with His Creation.

The sin of Adam and Eve was not a surprise to God. He had a plan in motion. Philippians 2 and Galatians 4 reveal this to us. Help the students understand that God created us for a perfect relationship, and He made a way to stay in that relationship. When you finish this lesson, the students should be able to see Perfect Creation, Perfect Relationship, God's Perfect Plan—and how it was broken.

CONTEXT

The events in the opening chapters in Genesis take place more than 2,500 years before Jesus was born. They were not recorded until the time of Moses, approximately 1440 B.C. The Genesis account preserves the story of God's people that would be passed down to generations and provide a source of hope in God's perfect plan.

We do not know how long after the seventh day until the serpent entered the Garden. As we study, it is important to use Scripture to interpret Scripture. Anything apart from God's Word is unreliable. So be careful not to add to what is absent.

OPEN UP
- What is sin? What are some examples?
- Do you know anyone who sinned this week?
- What does the Bible say about sin? Read Romans 3:23.

THINK ABOUT

Why do we sin?

READ

Verse 1: The serpent enters the picture, and he begins the attack. Notice how he begins the attack: by questioning God's Word.

Verses 2-3: Notice the woman's response. Did she accurately quote God's command? "But from the tree of the knowledge of good and evil you shall not eat, for in the day that you eat from it you will surely die" (Genesis 2:17). By the way, this command was given to Adam before Eve was created. Verses 4-5: The serpent continues to sow the seed of doubt and question. So often people will ask us if the Bible talks about drugs or other issues of the day. We must be careful to search the Word before responding.

Verses 6-8: The little sin of doubt gave birth to the separation from the holy God.

> *Then when lust has conceived, it gives birth to sin; and when sin is accomplished, it brings forth death. (James 1:15)*

Verses 9-11: We learned in chapter 1 that we were created in the image of God. When sin entered the man and woman, that image was no longer pure. It was stained or naked. A better word is exposed.

Verses 12-13: The blame game begins. What if? What if they would have confessed their sin to the Lord?

Verses 14-19: The curses begin. However, in the midst of the curse is a promise. We cannot skim over verse 15. Read verses 20-24: The Lord covered them with the skins of animals. This is the first time we see something die to cover sin. This is the first picture of substitutionary atonement. So, the man and woman left the Garden and went to care for the earth.

FOCUS

> *And I will put enmity between you and the woman, and between your seed and her seed; He shall bruise you on the head, and you shall bruise him on the heel. (Genesis 3:15)*

Help the students to understand this verse. The Seed of the woman will bruise the head of the serpent. This seed would be Jesus.

All of the Old Testament is a picture of the people struggling with sin and looking forward to this coming Messiah. The New Testament points us back to the fulfillment of this promise.

> *Why the Law then? It was added because of transgressions, having been ordained through angels by the agency of a mediator, until the seed would come to whom the promise had been made. (Galatians 3:19 NASB)*

TALK

- What is this teaching me about God?
- What is this teaching me about people?
- Why is this important to me today?

CONNECT THE GOSPEL

This is the Gospel: "For what I received I passed on to you as of first importance: that Christ died for our sins according to the Scriptures, that he was buried, that he was raised on the third day according to the Scriptures" (1 Corinthians 15:3-4 NIV).

So, from the beginning of time God had a plan to save us from our sin that separates us from Him. We were created in His image, but our sin brought death, separation from the source of life. But God promised us in 3:15 that the thing that separates us from Him would be overcome. A bruise or a blow to the head is considered fatal compared to a bruise on the heel. The Gospel is the "good news" that God has fulfilled His promise in Genesis 3:15.

SO WHAT?

What does this mean to us today? It has been about 6,000 years since God said this to the serpent. Is it still relevant? The answer is yes! The promise of God is very relevant today because we continue to sin. If we do not have the promise of God then we will die in our sin. We will die separated from our Creator. This is the only hope we have of having peace with God. We can continue trying to cover our sin our way, or we can accept God's covering.

SERVE

We know the people around us are hurting because of our sin nature. We know that relationships are broken because of sin. What can we do about it? If we believe that Jesus died for us and rose again, let's share that with someone this week.

What does that look like in a broken relationship? It begins with asking someone about their family and friends. If they share a struggle with you, this will be your opening to share with them what you know from the Fall. Then you can tell them how God made a way for the relationship to be fixed. Adam and Eve had to accept what God had done for them in order to be right with Him.

DIG DEEPER

And I will put enmity between you and the woman, and between your seed and her seed; He shall bruise you on the head, and you shall bruise him on the heel. (Genesis 3:15)

This is the first promise of a Savior in the Bible. It is known as the "protoevangelium" in Greek. This verse is a promise from God that Satan will not live forever. The Seed of the woman, which is the Promised Messiah, will crush him.

The first two chapters of Genesis, and the last two chapters of Revelation are pictures of a perfect relationship between the Creator and Creation. From Genesis chapter 3, until Revelation chapter 20, we see the work of Satan, which is death, and his attempt to separate the people of God from God.

This Seed of the woman is seen in the prophecy of Isaiah 7:14, "Therefore the Lord himself will give you a sign: The virgin will conceive and give birth to a son, and will call him Immanuel." This promised Messiah would come from a woman, but not an earthly father.

Throughout Scripture, Satan used any method he could to draw the people of God away from God. The writings of Moses contain numerous examples of the people of God being tempted into sinful relationships with people from pagan religions.

Satan was constantly at the heel of the Seed of the woman. Satan met Jesus in the wilderness, and tried to tempt Jesus to sin. Matthew 4:1-11, gives us the account of Satan tempting Jesus to avoid the way of the Cross. When Peter tried to stop Jesus from going to the Cross, Jesus rebuked the work of Satan in Peter, "But when Jesus turned and looked at his disciples, he rebuked Peter. "Get behind me, Satan!" he said. "You do not have in mind the concerns of God, but merely human concerns." (Mark 8:33)

Then, on the night of Jesus' arrest, Satan entered Judas Iscariot to put an end to this Messiah. "As soon as Judas took the bread, Satan entered into him" (John 13:27a).

As Jesus prepared His disciples for His death, He also provided them with words of comfort.

Now is the time for judgment on this world; now the prince of this world will be driven out. (John 12:31)

When Jesus died on the cross and rose again three days later, He gave proof that Satan and death had no control over Him.

He will swallow up death forever; and the Lord God will wipe away tears from all faces, and the reproach of his people he will take away from all the earth, for the Lord has spoken." (Isaiah 25:8)

He has taken away our reproach, the sin that separates us from God.

LEADER'S GUIDE—SOJOURNER BIBLE STUDY

This word "enmity," means hostility. There will always be hostility between Satan and the Messiah until the end. Paul encouraged the Church at Rome, "The God of peace will soon crush Satan under your feet. The grace of our Lord Jesus Christ be with you" (Romans 16:20).

And, we have the promise of Revelation 12:9-10,

> *And the great dragon was thrown down, that ancient serpent, who is called the devil and Satan, the deceiver of the whole world—he was thrown down to the earth, and his angels were thrown down with him. And I heard a loud voice in heaven, saying, "Now the salvation and the power and the kingdom of our God and the authority of his Christ have come, for the accuser of our brothers has been thrown down, who accuses them day and night before our God."*

Jesus is the Seed of the woman, the Promised Messiah, and He has bruised the head of Satan. Death is defeated, and the debt of sin is paid!

Notes

1: THE CREATION ERA

Week 4: The Flood
Genesis 6:5-22; 7:21-24; 8:14-22

Key verse: *"Thus Noah did; according to all that God had commanded him, so he did." (Genesis 6:22)*

LEADER'S NOTE

We have studied Creation and the Fall of man. Now we begin to look at how God will fulfill His promise of the Messiah and how we are right with God through faith. Take a few moments to bring the students up to date. Use your discretion as to how much of these three chapters you want to read. Keep in mind some of these verses may open up conversation that will distract from the main focus.

Help the students understand that God created us for a perfect relationship, and He made a way to stay in that relationship. We will trace it back to the promise in Genesis 3:15. When you finish this lesson the students should be able to see how God is working to restore His Perfect Creation and bring people back into Perfect Relationship and God's Perfect Plan.

CONTEXT

Most major religions have a flood account. They recognize that there was a great disaster and attempt to explain how it happened. The most famous account comes from the Epic of Gilgamesh. However, none of these accounts contain the Rainbow Covenant.

> *In the Bible the rainbow is the first of the covenant signs and provides the key to understanding all of them, including those of baptism and the Lord's Supper in the new covenant. The rainbow in the clouds speaks to humankind from God. God allowed Noah to understand what the bow meant to him: a visible declaration that the Lord will never again destroy the earth by flood. (The Archaeological Study Bible)*

OPEN UP

How much water would it take to flood your house? How long would that take? What about flooding the earth over the highest mountains? Mount Everest is 29,029 feet tall.

THINK ABOUT

When God flooded the Earth, why didn't He kill everyone and start over? (God had seen the wickedness of the people He had created. It would have been easy to destroy everything, but He didn't. Why not? Was Noah "perfect"? Think about the promise God made in Genesis 3:15. If God destroys everything, how would the Seed of the woman crush Satan?)

READ

Chapter 6

Verses 5-8: Who is the center of these verses? What is the problem?

Verse 9: What does the Bible say about Noah? What does it mean to be "blameless"? Was Noah sinless? If Noah was without sin, then Romans 3:23 would be a lie. This verse tells us that Noah walked with God. What does that mean? (Read Hebrews 11:6-7.)

Verses 10-22: What is happening and what did Noah do?

Chapter 7

Verses 21-24: What does the flood tell us about God? (Discuss God's wrath and judgment and holiness.)

Chapter 8

Verses 14-22: Who is giving the orders? What does Noah do?

FOCUS

Thus Noah did; according to all that God had commanded him, so he did. (Genesis 6:22 NASB)

So often we hear about Noah building the Ark in the desert and how they had never experienced a flood. The story of Noah is so much more than that though. We need to understand that God is in control of all things. We have a choice to submit to His authority or not. Noah was not perfect, but he believed God. The Bible tells us that Noah "walked with God." How can anyone walk with God? What does that look like? We must be walking in faith. We must be made right through the forgiveness of sin. We will never walk in relationship with God if we are walking in disobedience. We see Noah's walk in his obedience to God. God commanded, and Noah responded in obedience.

TALK

- What is this teaching me about God?
- What is this teaching me about people?
- Why is this important to me today?

CONNECT THE GOSPEL

This is the Gospel: "For what I received I passed on to you as of first importance: that Christ died for our sins according to the Scriptures, that he was buried, that he was raised on the third day according to the Scriptures" (1 Corinthians 15:3-4 NIV).

We see God protecting His promise as He protects Noah's family. This ensures that the line of Adam will continue. But where is Jesus and the "good news"? We must look to the genealogy of Jesus found in Luke 3. Specifically, verse 36 tells us about Shem the son of Noah. "According to the Scriptures," as Paul said, is a reminder that Jesus came just like He was supposed to as the Old Testament told us.

SO WHAT?

What does this mean to you and I today? Does it influence the way I live or the way I interact with my friends? It should.

First, we have a picture of God's judgment. God will not tolerate wickedness forever. Second, we have a picture of God's plan of redemption. God is saving people to Himself. In the middle of God's judgment, He was rescuing His people. Not only was He rescuing His people, but He was keeping His promise. If God had destroyed everything then He would be a liar and a failure. We would be without hope. Noah's story shows us that the Judge of the world is also the Savior of the world.

SERVE

Everyone around us who is separated from God is destined for judgment. That should burden us. We should have a sense of urgency because we know that one day, God will pour out His wrath on the earth again. So, let's reach out to the people around us and encourage them to turn to God. Let us live our lives in a way that people notice something is happening.

DIG DEEPER

Thus Noah did; according to all that God had commanded him, so he did. (Genesis 6:22)

Children love the story of Noah and the big boat in the big storm with a lot of animals. However, that is not the point of the story.

The curse of Genesis 3 applied to all of Creation. The earth was cursed, and the people would have to toil. Genesis 5, closes with the birth of Noah, and his father named him Noah because, "Out of the ground that the Lord has cursed, this one shall bring us relief from our work, and from the painful toil of our hands."

The beginning of Genesis 6, tells us that the world was very wicked. In the midst of this wickedness there was a man named Noah.

But Noah found favor in the eyes of the Lord. (Genesis 6:8)

It does not say that Noah was perfect, but that the Lord favored him.

The flood story is a story of being obedient and being set apart in a fallen world. We live in a fallen world. Something that is falling will not stop falling until it is acted upon by an outside influence. That is physics.

Noah is a picture for us of obedience. Noah believed what God had said about destroying the earth.

So God said to Noah, "I am going to put an end to all people, for the earth is filled with violence because of them. I am surely going to destroy both them and the earth." (Genesis 6:22)

When God gives us warnings of His judgments, we would be wise to listen and obey. In Exodus 9:20-21, as God was bringing judgment on Pharoah and the people of Egypt, there were some who obeyed the word of God.

Those officials of Pharoah who feared the word of the Lord hurried to bring their slaves and their livestock inside. But those who ignored the word of the Lord left their slaves and livestock in the field.

When the Lord God brings judgment, we are wise to run to Him. In the twenty-first century we have experienced wars, natural disasters, famines, and plagues. The wise people run to God the Father.

The name of the Lord is a fortified tower; the righteous run to it and are safe. (Proverbs 18:10)

Noah entered into the refuge of God Most High. Noah was saved from a sinful world by being obedient to the call of God. Noah did "all that God had commanded." The ark is a picture of the means of salvation; only one ark with only one door. Just as Jesus is the way, the truth, and the life. No one can get to God the Father any other way but through Jesus (John 14:6). The obedience of Noah was a picture of his faith, and it was a stark contrast to the wickedness around him.

By faith Noah, being warned by God concerning events as yet unseen, in reverent fear constructed an ark for the saving of his household. By this he condemned the world and became an heir of the righteousness that comes by faith. (Hebrews 11:7)

Noah was saved by faith.

Notes

LEADER'S GUIDE—SOJOURNER BIBLE STUDY

Week 5: The Tower of Babel
Genesis 11:1-9

Key verse: *"So the LORD dispersed them from there over the face of all the earth, and they left off building the city." (Genesis 11:9)*

LEADER'S NOTE
The Tower of Babel is a turning point in the Creation story as we see people groups dispersed around the world. During this lesson, think about Acts 2 and the Pentecost account. As God used languages to separate the people, He also used languages to bring them to Himself again. We also know from the end of chapter 10 that there were seventy clans. We will connect this to Luke 10 when we connect the Gospel.

CONTEXT
According to missiologists at joshuaproject.net, there are 17,014 people groups in the world, and according to "Ethnologue," in 2009, there were 6,909 distinct languages.

OPEN UP
Ask the students how many languages are spoken in their schools. Ask them what it will take to get the Gospel to each of these people groups. How important is it to have a Bible in your main language?

THINK ABOUT
What was the sin that caused all of this? Why is that wrong?

READ
Verse 1: There was one language. We know from chapter 10 that there were seventy clans from Noah. Why is language important?

Verse 2: Where were they, and where were they going? Where is Shinar?

Verses 3-4: What were they doing and why? Ancient cities had towers, called Ziggurats, which were dedicated to their gods. Notice the people turning from God. They wanted to make a name for themselves.

Verses 5-7: What happens? Can you think of other times when God visits His people?

Verses 8-9: What did God do? Look again at verse 4. What were the people afraid would happen to them?

FOCUS
> *So the LORD dispersed them from there over the face of all the earth, and they left off building the city. (Genesis 11:9)*

The people who had descended from Noah after the flood were increasing in numbers and slowly moving from the area of the Ark. As this was happening, they were developing their own form of religion and turning away from the God who brought them through the flood.

1: THE CREATION ERA

The desire of the people was to make a name for themselves. What's wrong with wanting to make a name for yourself? This is not why we were created. We were created in the image of God, to make His name known. The punishment for this decision was to scatter the people and confuse their languages. They no longer had the ability to communicate with each other. Think about what this would mean for their work and their trading. How important is communication in our lives today?

Think about communication within your family and at school. Would you have problems if you didn't understand what you were being told? One of the greatest barriers in communicating the Gospel is language.

TALK
- What is this teaching me about God?
- What is this teaching me about people?
- Why is this important to me today?

CONNECT THE GOSPEL

This is the Gospel: "For what I received I passed on to you as of first importance: that Christ died for our sins according to the Scriptures, that he was buried, that he was raised on the third day according to the Scriptures" (1 Corinthians 15:3-4 NIV).

From Genesis chapter 1, we know that we have been created in the image of God. We were commanded to multiply that image. When Jesus told His disciples to take the Gospel to all the earth, did He know that there was a language problem (Matthew 28:16-20)? In Luke 10, Jesus sent out seventy disciples to the regions of the Jews. Remember that in Genesis 10, the seventy clans of Noah were beginning to fill the earth.

The language problem of Genesis 11 was answered in Acts 2. Read Acts 2:8-11. Then read verse 41, and see the result of the gift of languages. Three thousand people were saved.

The Gospel is God's answer to people being separated from Him. The "good news" is that Jesus has died for our sin. This message needs to be communicated to every people group.

SO WHAT?

Why does it matter to me if people speak a different language? We usually only speak to people who understand us. In our classes, sports, or other activities, we hang out with people who speak our language. What about the people around us? What about the people in our communities? Should we wait for them to hear the Gospel from someone like them?

SERVE

Do you know anyone who does not speak English, or they don't speak it well? Do you think it is difficult for them to be in our community?

Take some time this week to meet someone who speaks another language. Ask their name and where they are from. Ask them what the hardest part is about living in America. Ask them if they have a Bible in their own language. How can you develop a long-term relationship with this person?

DIG DEEPER

So the LORD dispersed them from there over the face of all the earth, and they left off building the city. (Genesis 11:8)

We have transitioned from the obedience of Noah to the disobedience of the people. Whereas Noah obeyed the Lord's commands throughout the flood, the descendants of the flood survivors chose to follow their own desires. In Genesis 9:1, God had told them to fill the earth, but here in chapter 11, they have said, "No," to God. Their, "No," response is seen in their disobedience.

In Genesis 10, we saw the tribes begin to spread out after the flood. It appears however, that they did not go too far away from each other. They were able to maintain a common language and engage in common activities. Genesis 11:2, tells us, "They found a plain in the land of Shinar and settled there."

Religion is an attempt by sinful people to reach their idea of a god, or to put themselves in the position of a god. Here in Genesis 11:4, the people wanted to make a name for themselves:

> *Then they said, "Come, let us build ourselves a city and a tower with its top in the heavens, and let us make a name for ourselves, lest we be dispersed over the face of the whole earth."*

In Genesis 11:8, God dispersed the people. What they feared would happen, happened. However, God also had a plan to bring them back. In the next chapter we will see God's plan for Global Redemption in Genesis 12.

In our Connect the Gospel section, we mentioned the Day of Pentecost. Let's dig deeper into that thought…

> *When the day of Pentecost arrived, they were all together in one place. And suddenly there came from heaven a sound like a mighty rushing wind, and it filled the entire house where they were sitting. And divided tongues as of fire appeared to them and rested on each one of them. And they were all filled with the Holy Spirit and began to speak in other tongues as the Spirit gave them utterance.*
>
> *Now there were dwelling in Jerusalem Jews, devout men from every nation under heaven. And at this sound the multitude came together, and they were bewildered, because each one was hearing them speak in his own language. And they were amazed and astonished, saying, "Are not all these who are speaking Galileans? And how is it that we hear, each of us in his own native language? Parthians and Medes and Elamites and residents of Mesopotamia, Judea and Cappadocia, Pontus and Asia, Phrygia and Pamphylia, Egypt and the parts of Libya belonging to Cyrene, and visitors from Rome, both Jews and proselytes, Cretans, and Arabians—we hear them telling in our own tongues the mighty works of God." (Acts 2:1-11)*

Throughout the Old Testament people were separated by languages and ethnicities. During the time of the Exile, the people of God, the Jews, were dispersed all over the known world. Now in the time of the Book of Acts, the people who had been scattered were being brought together. In Genesis 11, the people wanted to make a name for themselves. Here in Acts 2, the people began to "tell of the mighty works of God." Just as the Spirit of God dispersed the people, the Spirit of God would equip the people of God to once again be in fellowship with Him. In Acts 1:8, the Holy Spirit of God would disperse the people again, but for His glory. We know that this mission will be accomplished, and we know that language will not be a barrier any longer.

> *After this I looked, and behold, a great multitude that no one could number, from every nation, from all tribes and peoples and languages, standing before the throne and before the Lamb, clothed in white robes, with palm branches in their hands (Revelation 7:9)*

The day will come when people from all over the world will stand before the Throne not a tower. We will not work to make a name for ourselves, but we will worship the Name that is above every name: Jesus.

Notes

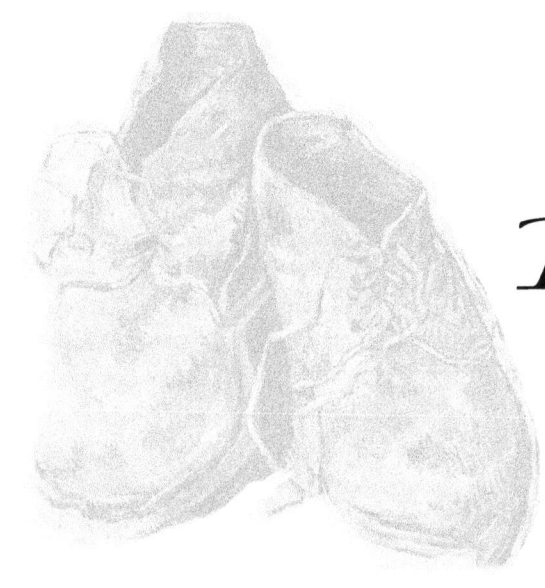

2: The Patriarch Era

LEADER'S GUIDE—SOJOURNER BIBLE STUDY

Week 6: The Abrahamic Covenant
Genesis 12:1-3

Key Verse: *"I will bless those who bless you, and the one who curses you I will curse. And in you all the families of the earth shall be blessed." (Genesis 12:3)*

LEADER'S NOTE

The Abrahamic Covenant is an unconditional covenant between God and Abram (Abraham). This means that God would do all the work to fulfill it. Emphasize to the students the five "I will" statements.

CONTEXT

The first eleven chapters of Genesis have shown us God and His Creation. We have seen the Fall of man through disobedience. We have seen God's judgment upon people through death and separation. In the midst of all the chaos from chapter 11 we see God at work to fulfill His promise from Genesis 3:15. We know that one day the Seed of the woman will crush the head of the serpent.

The time is approximately 2090 B.C. God has told Abraham that he will be the father of many nations. This is an indication that these scattered nations will one day have a common identity.

OPEN UP

Ask the students about the plan of God. Do they remember the Fall of man? After we left the Tower of Babel, where can we find hope for a Savior?

THINK ABOUT

How can a righteous God save an unrighteous people?

READ

Verse 1: Who is speaking?

Verses 2-3: What is the Covenant or Promise?

FOCUS

> *I will bless those who bless you, and the one who curses you I will curse. And in you all the families of the earth shall be blessed. (Genesis 12:3)*

Notice the command to Abram was to go. Notice also that the Lord God would do all the work. The promise to Abram was for his family and ALL the families of the earth. We are beneficiaries of this promise.

TALK

- What is this teaching me about God?
- What is this teaching me about people?
- Why is this important to me today?

CONNECT THE GOSPEL

This is the Gospel: "For what I received I passed on to you as of first importance: that Christ died for our sins according to the Scriptures, that he was buried, that he was raised on the third day according to the Scriptures" (1 Corinthians 15:3-4 NIV).

The plan of God from the beginning was to save His Creation. The story of Abram is a continuation of that plan. Through Abram all nations would be blessed because he would provide the line of Jesus, and in Jesus we all can be right with God.

When Simeon met the baby Jesus in the Temple, he said, "a light for revelation to the Gentiles, and for glory to your people Israel" (Luke 2:32). Paul and Barnabas said, "For so the Lord has commanded us, saying, 'I have made you a light for the Gentiles, that you may bring salvation to the ends of the earth'" (Acts 13:47).

SO WHAT?

What do I care if all the nations are blessed through this promise? What does it matter today?

When the Bible speaks of "nations" it is talking about people groups and ethnicities. When we know that the plan of God is for all people groups, we should not tolerate racism or prejudice, especially when we know that we are all created in the image of God.

SERVE

If you believe that the promise to Abram was truly for all peoples, will that influence how you treat other people? Do you think it is important for other people to know about this promise? How can you share this promise this week?

DIG DEEPER

> *I will bless those who bless you, and the one who curses you I will curse. And in you all the families of the earth shall be blessed. (Genesis 12:3)*

In the last lesson we saw how God dispersed the people because they tried to make a name for themselves. Today we read about how God is going to make the name of Abram (Abraham) great. What is the difference?

In Genesis 11, it was all about the work of the people. Now, in chapter 12, it is all about the work of God. Notice in these verses that it is God doing all the work.

> *I will make you into a great nation, and I will bless you; I will make your name great, and you will be a blessing. I will bless those who bless you, and whoever curses you I will curse; and all peoples on earth will be blessed through you. (Genesis 12:2-3)*

Notice that it is God doing all of the work. Abram was the recipient of the blessing and in turn, all the earth would receive the blessing. Just as everyone was dispersed in Genesis chapter 11, because of sin against God, everyone today is separated from God because of our sin. However, in Genesis 12, we see again the promise of hope in the blessing of God through Abram.

In order to understand the depth of God's promise, we need to look ahead to the New Testament, through the words of Stephen prior to his execution:

> *To this he replied: "Brothers and fathers, listen to me! The God of glory appeared to our father Abraham while he was still in Mesopotamia, before he lived in Harran. 'Leave your country and your people,' God*

said, 'and go to the land I will show you.' So, he left the land of the Chaldeans and settled in Harran. After the death of his father, God sent him to this land where you are now living." (Acts 7:2-4)

Stephen told them that, "The God of glory appeared." There can be no doubt about the authority of the message. God told Abraham to leave the place of comfort, his homeland, and his family. Abraham walked away from his place and people, and their name. Then God made his name great. However, Abraham did not see the fulfillment of this promise in his day.

The crown of Abraham's blessing is in the Messiah Jesus. The Gospel of Matthew opened with the fulfillment of the promise of Genesis 12:3, "This is the genealogy of Jesus the Messiah the son of David, the son of Abraham" (Matthew 1:1).

When Jesus told Zacchaeus that He was going to eat at his house, Jesus had a plan for the children of Abraham.

Jesus said to him, "Today salvation has come to this house, because this man, too, is a son of Abraham." (Luke 19:9)

Now, we need to know how all the families of the earth can be blessed. Salvation, the action of being made right with the Creator is only available through Jesus the Messiah, the descendant of Abraham. "Salvation is found in no one else, for there is no other name under heaven given to mankind by which we must be saved" (Acts 4:12). Everyone who believes in the redeeming work of God in Christ Jesus will be blessed.

Jesus told us about acceptance into His family. It is by obedience. Abraham was obedient.

For whoever does the will of my Father in heaven is my brother and sister and mother." (Matthew 12:50)

The hope for all of us is found in Galatians 3:6-9, "So also Abraham "believed God, and it was credited to him as righteousness." Understand, then, that those who have faith are children of Abraham. Scripture foresaw that God would justify the Gentiles by faith, and announced the Gospel in advance to Abraham: "All nations will be blessed through you." So, those who rely on faith are blessed along with Abraham, the man of faith."

Abraham saw Jesus's day, and he was glad (John 8:56). The line of Abram (Abraham) would provide the One who would bring restoration, and the blessing of fellowship with the Creator for all people.

We will talk about this more in the next lesson.

Notes

Week 7: Isaac
Genesis 22:1-18

Key verse: *"And in your seed all the nations of the earth shall be blessed, because you have obeyed my voice." (Genesis 22:18)*

LEADER'S NOTE

This is a very rich passage. You should spend a couple of minutes explaining that Abraham did not have a son from his wife Sarah until Isaac was born. When Isaac was born Abraham was 100 years old (Genesis 21:5). God was fulfilling His promise to Abraham which He had made in Genesis 12, and now Abraham was being asked to sacrifice this promised son. Hebrews 11:17-19 gives us more insight.

CONTEXT

As we read this passage, we need to remember the plan of God is to bring the Messiah, the Promised One. Ishmael could not be in the line of this promise because he was born according to Sarah's scheme, not God's plan. So, here we find Abraham being asked to give up his only son. It's the picture of what God would do for us in giving up His only Son. We see the faith of Abraham in his words in verse 8, that God would Himself provide the Lamb. We see his faith praised in verse 18.

How could Abraham do this? How could he sacrifice his only son? The writer of Hebrews gives us a little more information: "Abraham reasoned that God could even raise the dead, and so in a manner of speaking he did receive Isaac back from death" (Hebrews 11:19 NIV).

OPEN UP

What does God want from us?

THINK ABOUT

What would be the hardest thing for you to give up if God asked you to?

READ

Verse 1: After what things? (Remind the students that Abraham had waited a long time for a son.)

Verse 2: Who spoke? What did He say? What did God tell Abraham in Genesis 12:1? (Leave your father's house and go where I tell you.)

Verses 3-6: What happened?

Verse 7: What did Isaac ask?

Verse 8: What did Abraham say? (Some translations say, "God will provide Himself a Lamb." Don't be afraid to linger on this thought.)

Verse 12: What does it mean to fear God?

Verses 13-18: What happened?

LEADER'S GUIDE—SOJOURNER BIBLE STUDY

FOCUS

> *And in your seed all the nations of the earth shall be blessed, because you have obeyed my voice. (Genesis 22:18)*

When He says "seed," what does that mean? Who will receive the blessings and why? Remember that the word *nations* refers to ethnic groups.

TALK

- What is this teaching me about God?
- What is this teaching me about people?
- Why is this important to me today?

CONNECT THE GOSPEL

This is the Gospel: "For what I received I passed on to you as of first importance: that Christ died for our sins according to the Scriptures, that he was buried, that he was raised on the third day according to the Scriptures" (1 Corinthians 15:3-4 NIV).

This chapter is such a great picture of the Gospel. We see that God will provide the sacrifice, the Lamb. We also see that it was by faith that Abraham was obedient to God, and this led to our blessing.

SO WHAT?

Why is this important to me today? I will never be asked to sacrifice my child. That may be true, but you may be asked to give up something you love. Will you have the faith to be obedient?

SERVE

How can we serve our community because of this lesson? Are you willing to sacrifice your time, your talents, your things, so that other people will learn about Jesus?

DIG DEEPER

> *And in your seed all the nations of the earth shall be blessed, because you have obeyed my voice. (Genesis 22:18)*

In Genesis chapter 1, we got the idea of things being created with the ability to reproduce. Genesis 1:11, "And God said, "Let the earth sprout vegetation, plants yielding seed, and fruit trees bearing fruit in which is their seed, each according to its kind, on the earth. And it was so." This fact of reproducing something of the same kind, or species is vital to the truth of the humanity of Jesus. In Genesis chapter 3, it would be the "seed of the woman" who would crush Satan. In Genesis 22, it is the "seed" of Abraham who will bring the blessing for all the earth.

We are seeing the plan of God unfold. God Himself will bring the Savior through the line of the people He is going to save. When we read the genealogies found in Matthew 1, and Luke 3, we see Jesus, the Son of God, being born from a woman. He is the promised "seed of the woman," and the "seed" of Abraham.

After everything Abraham had been through, from leaving his family and his homeland, to waiting for a child, now the Lord God asked him to sacrifice this promised son. God called him to an act of faith. Some say that God tempted Abraham in the same way God tempted Job. They were not tempted to sin, but these godly temptations strengthened their faith.

In 1 Peter, as he was writing to encourage the exiles who were struggling in their faith in the days of the Roman Empire, he wrote,

> *In all this you greatly rejoice, though now for a little while you may have had to suffer grief in all kinds of trials. These have come so that the proven genuineness of your faith—of greater worth than gold, which perishes even though refined by fire—may result in praise, glory and honor when Jesus Christ is revealed. Though you have not seen him, you love him; and even though you do not see him now, you believe in him and are filled with an inexpressible and glorious joy, for you are receiving the end result of your faith, the salvation of your souls. (1 Peter 1:6-9)*

The end result of faith is salvation of our souls.

God had told Abraham to take his only son, Isaac, his laughter (Gen. 17:17-19), the son he loved, to the land of Moriah, and offer him as a burnt offering. When Abraham prepared to sacrifice his son, his only son, on the mountain of Moriah, we were given a picture of what God was going to do for us at Golgotha on Mount Moriah, for every ethnic group on His earth. Where Isaac carried the wood for the sacrifice in obedience to his father, Jesus carried His cross in obedience to His Father. Where they walked a three-day journey into the country in obedience to the command of God the Father, Jesus went into the earth for three days in obedience to the command of God the Father. Where Abraham said that God would provide Himself the lamb, Jesus was the Lamb that God provided. (The direct Hebrew translation reads, "And said Abraham God will provide himself a lamb for a burnt offering.")

Because Abraham obeyed the voice of God all the nations of the earth have been blessed. Last week in Genesis 12, we talked about this great blessing and how it was fulfilled in Jesus. Abraham's obedience to God the Father made him right with God. Jesus' obedience to God the Father made us right with God.

Notes

LEADER'S GUIDE—SOJOURNER BIBLE STUDY

Week 8: Jacob
Genesis 35:1-14

Key verse: *"And he built an altar there, and called the place El-bethel, because there, God had revealed Himself to him, when he fled from his brother." (Genesis 35:7)*

LEADER'S NOTE

Take time to review the life of Jacob before you meet with the students. How did he get here? From his birth in chapter 25, his history of deceitfulness, and his wrestling with God, the story of Jacob is the story of the patience of God. God had a plan for Jacob from the beginning, just as He has for your students.

CONTEXT

The story of Jacob is the story of the plan of God. From before Jacob was born, God had a plan for him just like it says in Psalm 139:16: "Your eyes saw my unformed body; all the days ordained for me were written in your book before one of them came to be" (NIV).

Jacob was a deceiver. He deceived his brother and his father and his father-in-law. In spite of his failures, God was going to use him in a great way. By the time we arrive in chapter 35, Jacob has wrestled with God. Jacob has reconciled with his brother, and he has moved away from his father-in-law. In the midst of his journey, God meets him and reestablishes the covenant, or promise, which He had made with Abraham and Isaac.

OPEN UP

What is the plan of God for you as a student?

THINK ABOUT

Do you believe that God has a plan for you? If you do, how can you know the plan of God for your life?

READ

Verse 1: What did God say? What did God tell Jacob's grandfather Abraham?

Verse 2: What did Jacob tell his family? What is the picture of putting away the foreign gods and changing their clothes?

Verse 3: What does Jacob say about God? "He answered me in the day of my distress, and he has been with me wherever I have gone."

Verse 7: Why did Jacob build an altar? What does this represent?

Verses 9-12: What did God say when He met Jacob this time? What does "Jacob" mean? What does "Israel" mean?

FOCUS

> And he built an altar there, and called the place El-bethel, because there, God had revealed Himself to him, when he fled from his brother. (Genesis 35:7)

If you are following Jesus, do you remember the place where He revealed Himself to you? Do you remember the situation? (Home, VBS, student camp?) Why is it important to remember how and where we met God? This is our testimony.

TALK

- What is this teaching me about God?
- What is this teaching me about people?
- Why is this important to me today?

CONNECT THE GOSPEL

This is the Gospel: "For what I received I passed on to you as of first importance: that Christ died for our sins according to the Scriptures, that he was buried, that he was raised on the third day according to the Scriptures" (1 Corinthians 15:3-4).

God met Jacob. Was Jacob perfect? No. Did God have a plan for Jacob? Yes. We were created in the image of God. We were told to multiply that image. Jacob was told to multiply the image of God as the Father of the nation of Israel. According to verse 11, other nations would come from him also. (Remember that the word *nations* represents ethnic groups or people groups.)

So, according to the Scripture, God is using a people to bring people to Himself. From this nation of Israel will come Jesus. The Gospel is the "good news" that the God of Creation changes lives. Christ came for us. He came for Jacob. Jacob trusted God and was made right. It's the same way we are made right with God.

SO WHAT?

How is the story of Jacob important to me today? Do you believe that God created you? Do you believe that He has a purpose for you? Ephesians 2:10 tells us that we are God's "handiwork" or "workmanship," created to do good work. "For we are God's handiwork, created in Christ Jesus to do good works, which God prepared in advance for us to do."

Jacob had to be changed before he could be used. Have you been changed? Are you ready to be used by God to make Him known?

SERVE

We live in a world that has many gods and idols. We have many distractions. The greatest way we can serve is to put away the things that distract us from following Jesus. After we do this, we will be able to focus on serving the people around us.

DIG DEEPER

And he built an altar there, and called the place El-bethel, because there, God had revealed Himself to him, when he fled from his brother. (Genesis 35:7)

God came to Jacob and revealed Himself to him. This is the good news of what God has done for us. God has come to us. This is so different from what we read in Genesis 11, about the Tower of Babel, and the attempt of the people to make a tower to heaven and a name for themselves.

The God of all Creation, God Almighty, revealed Himself to Jacob, so why is it so hard to believe that He would reveal Himself to us as well? We need to look back at Genesis 28, to see the first time God revealed Himself to Jacob when Jacob was fleeing from Esau:

When he reached a certain place, he stopped for the night because the sun had set. Taking one of the stones there, he put it under his head and lay down to sleep. He had a dream in which he saw a stairway resting on the earth, with its top reaching to heaven, and the angels of God were ascending and descending on it. There above it stood the Lord, and he said: "I am the Lord, the God of your father Abraham and the God of Isaac. I will give you and your descendants the land on which you are lying. Your descendants will be like the dust of the earth, and you will spread out to the west and to the east, to the north and to the south. All peoples on earth will be blessed through you and your offspring." (Genesis 28:11-14)

In the first revelation, God revealed Himself as the LORD God, in Hebrew this is Jehovah Elohim. In Genesis 35:11, God revealed Himself as the Lord God Almighty, in Hebrew this is Elohim El Shaddai. Jacob met the God of Creation the first time, here in chapter 35, God revealed His power as the Almighty. In the English translation it is easy to read past this. However, God revealed Himself as the Almighty before the Almighty God told Jacob, now Israel, that "A nation and a community of nations will come from you, and kings will be among your descendants. The land I gave to Abraham and Isaac I also give to you, and I will give this land to your descendants after you" (Genesis 35:11-12).

God revealed Himself to Jacob, and then He revealed His plan to Jacob. By knowing God in this way Jacob would be prepared for the long journey ahead of him. In Jacob's dying days he blessed the sons of Joseph in Genesis 48:15-16,

Then he blessed Joseph and said, "May the God before whom my fathers Abraham and Isaac walked faithfully, the God who has been my shepherd all my life to this day, the Angel who has delivered me from all harm -may he bless these boys. May they be called by my name and the names of my fathers Abraham and Isaac, and may they increase greatly on the earth."

Jacob saw His glory, and he worshiped God in that place. This same God of Jacob has also revealed Himself to us. Jesus is the revelation of God to us.

And the Word became flesh and dwelt among us, and we have seen his glory, glory as of the only Son from the Father, full of grace and truth. (John 1:14)

No one has ever seen God, but the one and only Son, who is himself God and is in closest relationship with the Father, has made him known." The Son has made the Father known to us. Jesus the Son, has revealed God to us. (John 1:18)

Notes

Week 9: Joseph
Genesis 50:1-26

Key verse: *"You intended to harm me, but God intended it for good to accomplish what is now being done, the saving of many lives." (Genesis 50:20)*

LEADER'S NOTE
We are skipping fourteen very rich chapters in Genesis. Feel free to use something different today to show the plan of God in the life of Joseph to preserve His people to fulfill the promise of Genesis 3:15.

CONTEXT
From chapter 37 to 50 in Genesis we read the story of Joseph—the story of how he was the favorite child of Jacob, he was sold into slavery by his brothers, he was put into prison in Egypt, and he interpreted dreams. At the end of his life, he reconciles with his brothers, and Joseph tells them that God had a bigger and better plan. Joseph was prime minister between 1885-1805 B.C.

OPEN UP
Has something bad ever happened to you that you don't understand why God would allow it to happen?

THINK ABOUT
If God is really God, if He is really in control, why does He allow bad things to happen to people who follow Him?

READ
Verses 1-14: What has happened? Where were they when Jacob died? Egypt. Where did they bury Jacob? Canaan. How far did they have to travel? Depending on the route they took, it was 175-200 miles.

Verse 15: What are the brothers worried about?

Verses 16-17: What is the message? Do you think it's true? Would you lie if you thought something bad was going to happen to you?

Verses 18-21: What happens? What do the brothers do? What did Joseph do?

Verse 24: Why is this important to remember?

FOCUS
> *You intended to harm me, but God intended it for good to accomplish what is now being done, the saving of many lives. (Genesis 50:20)*

How did Joseph know the plan of God? Did he have any examples in his life where he saw God working in his life? Do you remember times when God has been with you?

LEADER'S GUIDE—SOJOURNER BIBLE STUDY

TALK
- What is this teaching me about God?
- What is this teaching me about people?
- Why is this important to me today?

CONNECT THE GOSPEL

This is the Gospel: "For what I received I passed on to you as of first importance: that Christ died for our sins according to the Scriptures, that he was buried, that he was raised on the third day according to the Scriptures" (1 Corinthians 15:3-4 NIV).

Joseph is seen as a type of Christ, Messiah. Joseph was betrayed, but he was always faithful to God. God used Joseph to save many people. Specifically, God used Joseph to save the people of Israel, and this protected the promise of Genesis 3:15. Remember, as we walk through the Old Testament, we are looking forward to the One, the Seed of the woman who will crush the head of the serpent.

SO WHAT?

What does the story of Joseph mean to me today? It is so easy to think that God doesn't care, or maybe He doesn't remember me. But, as we read about Joseph, we are reminded that God does have a plan. Life won't always be easy, but God will always be with us.

This may be a good time to look at Romans 8:28: "And we know that in all things God works for the good of those who love him, who have been called according to his purpose."

SERVE

The greatest way to serve through this lesson is to find a way to forgive people who have hurt you. Pray about what God is showing you through the way these people are in your life. How can you help them to know Jesus?

DIG DEEPER

> *You intended to harm me, but God intended it for good to accomplish what is now being done, the saving of many lives. (Genesis 50:20)*

The book of Genesis began with light and life and ends with death and darkness. Just as God had pushed back the darkness in the beginning, He also pushes it back just enough for us, in chapter 50, to get a glimpse of hope. That hope comes in the form of Joseph's forgiveness and God's plan of salvation for the nation.

Here, at the end of Jacob's life, we see the fulfillment of Joseph's two dreams about the family (Gen. 37:5-11). The father, Jacob, and the mother, Rachel, had died. The sun and the moon in Joseph's life. Here in Genesis 50, once again, the eleven stars are bowing down to him. The first time they bowed to Joseph, they did not know who he was, and they were asking for food (Gen. 42:6). In Genesis 50, they are asking for forgiveness.

Joseph had compassion for them. Our heavenly Father has compassion for us when we come to Him for forgiveness. Read the parable of the Prodigal Son in Luke 15 and see the similarities. See the humility of Joseph's brothers in Genesis 50:18. See the humility of the Prodigal Son in Luke 15:21: "I am no longer worthy to be called your son." See the compassion of the father in Luke 15:20: "But while he was still a long way off, his father saw him and was filled with compassion for him; he ran to his son, threw his arms around him and kissed him."

In Genesis 50:19, Joseph reminded his brothers that it is God who is the Judge, and Joseph was not in the place of God. We need to be quick to ask for forgiveness, and we do not need to take revenge on anyone (Rom. 12:19). When we make peace with God, it should be easy to make peace with people.

Joseph did not ignore the sin of his brothers; instead, he acknowledged it. "You intended to harm me." The idea here is that the brothers intended to go against the plan of God because they were jealous of the dreams.

God had a plan to get Joseph to Egypt to preserve His people. We do not know if that was any different than the events in the Book of Genesis, and we should not read into the story for something that is not there. We know the end result: the nation of Israel was saved, and God was glorified.

Fast forward to the early first century and the Son of God. The Jewish leaders were jealous of Jesus, and they sought to put Him to death. Mark 15:10, "For he [Pontius Pilate] was aware that the chief priests had handed Him over because of envy." God had a plan from the beginning.

When Peter spoke to the people at Pentecost, he rebuked them for their sin of crucifying Jesus, and he told them that it was God's predetermined plan for His Son to die. "But God knew what would happen, and his prearranged plan was carried out when Jesus was betrayed. With the help of lawless Gentiles, you nailed him to a cross and killed him" (Acts 2:23).

God used Joseph to save his family, and in so doing, God was preserving the "seed of the woman." God used Joseph to save the people of God and give the Jewish people a picture of what the Messiah would do. The Messiah would also suffer at the hands of His own people.

Just as God sent Joseph to a foreign land to save His people, God also sent Jesus to our land to save us. Luke 19:10: "For the Son of Man came to seek and to save the lost."

From the beginning of time, God has had a plan to redeem His people to Himself. That plan could not be stopped. Throughout the Old Testament we can read about how God preserved His people so that He could fulfill His plan of saving us.

We do not always know the plan of God for us in these days. If we are faithful in our Christian walk, God will be glorified in our lives. We need to remain faithful just as Joseph was, and God was glorified.

Notes

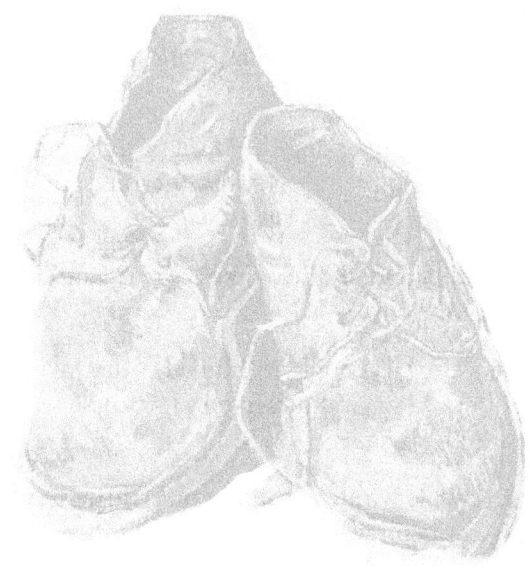

3:
The Exodus Era

3: THE EXODUS ERA

Week 10: Moses
Exodus 3

Key verse: *"So now, go. I am sending you to Pharaoh to bring my people the Israelites out of Egypt." (Exodus 3:10)*

LEADER'S NOTE

We want the students to understand that God had a plan for Moses, just as He had a plan for Pharaoh. Moses would be used to bring the people out of bondage. God would use Pharoah as an example so that the Egyptians would know the true God.

> *And the Egyptians will know that I am the Lord when I stretch out my hand against Egypt and bring the Israelites out of it. (Exodus 7:5)*

Help your students to see that Moses is a picture of how God will also rescue us from bondage, the bondage of sin, through His Son Jesus.

CONTEXT

When we meet Moses, around 1445 B.C., the nation of Israel has been in Egypt over 400 years. The situation changed a lot from the time Joseph was a leader. We need to remember that God moved His people to Egypt, during the time of Joseph, to save them from the famine. God allowed them to go into slavery. God will also bring them out of slavery in a mighty way to show His power.

In Moses we see a type of the Messiah. One who will rescue the people of God from the bondage of sin.

OPEN UP

Why is it important to get the people of Israel out of Egypt? Help the students understand that God keeps His promises, and the land of Canaan was the land that God had promised to Abraham, Isaac, and Joseph.

THINK ABOUT

How would you respond if God asked you to do something impossible?

READ

Verse 1: What was Moses doing?

Verses 2-3: What happened?

Verses 4-10: What did God say? What did Moses do in verse 6?

Verse 11: What did Moses say? "Who am I?"

Verse 12: What is the promise of God?

Verse 13: What is Moses' question? Who are you?

Verses 14-15: How does God introduce Himself? (Moses would have known the names of the Canaanite gods. When this God says "I AM," He is saying that He exists, He was not created. He does not have a before, during, or after. This God is present, and He doesn't change.)

Verses 16-22: What is God telling Moses?

FOCUS

So now, go. I am sending you to Pharaoh to bring my people the Israelites out of Egypt. (Exodus 3:10)

Why is this so important? Could God leave the people in Egypt and fulfill His promise to Abraham? What was Moses being told to do? He was going to confront the man who was keeping the people of God in slavery. Moses was also going to tell this man to free the children of God.

TALK

- What is this teaching me about God?
- What is this teaching me about people?
- Why is this important to me today?

CONNECT THE GOSPEL

This is the Gospel: "For what I received I passed on to you as of first importance: that Christ died for our sins according to the Scriptures, that he was buried, that he was raised on the third day according to the Scriptures" (1 Corinthians 15:3-4 NIV).

The "good news" of Jesus Christ is that He came to save us from the bondage of our sin. We are separated from God because of sin.

When God sent Moses to bring the people out of bondage, God was preparing them for the Messiah who would come and free us all from eternal bondage. People had to follow Moses out of Egypt. In the same way, we have to follow Jesus out of the slavery of sin to freedom.

SO WHAT?

What does this mean to me? If I am following Jesus, then I should recognize that I am not a slave to my sin. My sin should not control me. Jesus came to lead me and everyone who will follow Him out of slavery.

SERVE

If I am free, then I can help other people know how to be free. Moses had to go to the people. Jesus had to go to the people. We have to go to the people.

Ask the Lord to show you someone this week who you can help. Maybe it's yard work or homework, or helping your parents. As you are helping them, share this Bible story with them. Tell them how God sent a man to save the children of God.

DIG DEEPER

So now, go. I am sending you to Pharaoh to bring my people the Israelites out of Egypt. (Exodus 3:10)

Let's think deeper about what happened here and think about God's plan of salvation:

In the context of chapter 3, and in the context of all of Scripture, God is concerned for His people, and He is doing something about it. It had been more than four hundred years since the time of Jacob and Joseph. The patriarchs were gone, and it appeared that men with the vision of God were also gone.

Like Joseph, Moses was born to be Israel's deliverer. Then, in God's perfect timing, He raised up Moses and met him in a bush. A bush that was on fire and was not being burned up. That got Moses's attention, and God introduced Himself as the God of the fathers of the Hebrew people. "I am the God of your father—the God of Abraham, the God of Isaac, and the God of Jacob" (Ex. 3:6).

> *The Lord said, "I have indeed seen the misery of my people in Egypt. I have heard them crying out because of their slave drivers, and I am concerned about their suffering. So, I have come down to rescue them from the hand of the Egyptians and to bring them up out of that land into a good and spacious land, a land flowing with milk and honey—the home of the Canaanites, Hittites, Amorites, Perizzites, Hivites and Jebusites. And now the cry of the Israelites has reached me, and I have seen the way the Egyptians are oppressing them. So now, go. I am sending you to Pharaoh to bring my people the Israelites out of Egypt." (Exodus 3:7-10)*

We cannot overlook the fact that when God came to Moses, Moses was a shepherd. He was watching over his flock. In this work, he learned humility and contentment (Num. 12:3).

This God of all creation had seen the misery of His people. He heard their cries, and He came down to rescue them. We need to take note that God is aware of our cries, He is aware of our struggles, and He has come to help us.

In verse 8 of Exodus 3, the Bible says that He has come to "rescue" or "deliver" His people. "For the Son of Man came to seek and save those who are lost" (Luke 19:10). This idea of seeking and saving is the equivalent of rescuing from a bad situation.

In Exodus 3:10, after the promise of a rescue, we see the sending of the messenger of God. In Luke 2:30-32, Simeon saw the One who was sent for all people: "I have seen your salvation, which you have prepared for all people. He is a light to reveal God to the nations, and he is the glory of your people Israel!"

This is the Gospel. God Himself has come to rescue His people. Moses was His representative for this time. God moved His people from Egypt to Canaan to prepare a place for the Seed of the woman to be born. Then, when the time was right, God's perfect time, He came to us.

> *But when the set time had fully come, God sent his Son, born of a woman, born under the law, to redeem those under the law, that we might receive adoption to sonship. Because you are his sons, God sent the Spirit of his Son into our hearts, the Spirit who calls out, "Abba, Father." So you are no longer a slave, but God's child; and since you are his child, God has made you also an heir." (Galatians 4:4-7)*

The people of Israel were slaves in Egypt. We are slaves in our sin. God sent Moses to lead the captives from slavery to freedom. God sent Jesus to lead us, the captives, from slavery to freedom. In Christ, you are free indeed! (John 8:36).

Notes

LEADER'S GUIDE—SOJOURNER BIBLE STUDY

Week 11: The Passover
Exodus 12:1-33

Key verse: *"The blood will be a sign for you on the houses where you are, and when I see the blood, I will pass over you. No destructive plague will touch you when I strike Egypt." (Exodus 12:13)*

LEADER'S NOTE

There is a common thread which runs throughout Scripture, and it is the truth that the blood of the Innocent must be shed on behalf of the guilty. Hebrews 9:22 tells us, "In fact, the law requires that nearly everything be cleansed with blood, and without the shedding of blood there is no forgiveness." We saw this first in Genesis chapter 3, when God killed an animal to cover the sin of Adam and Eve. We want to help the students understand that by putting the blood on the door frame of the house the people were acting in faith and obedience to what God had commanded, and they were trusting Him for their salvation.

CONTEXT

The God of Creation is about to do a mighty work to bring His people out of bondage. All of the plagues have been signs for the people, including the Egyptians (approximately 1445 B.C.). Now God is going to bring the most destructive sign on the people. God had told Moses in his initial call that this would happen. "Then say to Pharaoh, 'This is what the Lord says: Israel is my firstborn son, and I told you, "Let my son go, so he may worship me." But you refused to let him go; so, I will kill your firstborn son'" (Exodus 4:22-23).

OPEN UP

What is significant about this plague?

THINK ABOUT

What do you think the people were thinking after they had seen all of the other plagues? Why would God require an innocent, spotless lamb?

READ

Verses 1-10: What are the requirements?

Verse 11: Why did they need to be prepared to go when they were eating?

Verse 12: Who or what was going to die? Who was being judged?

Verse 13: If the blood is a sign, what does it mean already happened?

Verses 14-20: What does it mean that this is a "memorial"?

Verse 28: Were the people obedient?

Verses 29-33: What happened?

FOCUS

> *The blood will be a sign for you on the houses where you are, and when I see the blood, I will pass over you. No destructive plague will touch you when I strike Egypt. (Exodus 12:13)*

We mentioned it already, but what does the blood show or represent? What has already happened? The spotless lamb has died, and the blood of the lamb covered the doorway. This act of obedience saved the first born of everyone who obeyed.

TALK

- What is this teaching me about God?
- What is this teaching me about people?
- Why is this important to me today?

CONNECT THE GOSPEL

This is the Gospel: "For what I received I passed on to you as of first importance: that Christ died for our sins according to the Scriptures, that he was buried, that he was raised on the third day according to the Scriptures" (1 Corinthians 15:3-4 NIV).

This passage is a picture of the Gospel message. Jesus is the Lamb of God. When the Hebrews were participating in the Passover they were pointing to a time when Jesus, the Sinless Man, would die and His blood would cover us. The Bible tells us that the cost of sin is death, and the gift of God is eternal life in Christ Jesus (Romans 3:23 and 6:23). Just as the people had to believe what God was telling them, so also we need to believe that Jesus has died for us. Just as the people had to be obedient to cover their doors, we also need to be obedient to accept what Jesus has done.

SO WHAT?

We don't need to kill a lamb and cover our doors with blood. The Lamb of God has done everything for us. All we need to do is accept what Jesus has done.

> *If you declare with your mouth, "Jesus is Lord," and believe in your heart that God raised him from the dead, you will be saved. For it is with your heart that you believe and are justified, and it is with your mouth that you profess your faith and are saved. As Scripture says, "Anyone who believes in him will never be put to shame." (Romans 10:9-11)*

SERVE

What does service look like when we consider the lesson of the Passover? You may know people who are trying really hard to be good. Many people think that if they are a good person then they will go to heaven. You can share with them that God has done all the work through His Son, Jesus.

DIG DEEPER

> *The blood will be a sign for you on the houses where you are, and when I see the blood, I will pass over you. No destructive plague will touch you when I strike Egypt. (Exodus 12:13)*

We know from last week's study of Exodus chapter 3 that God heard the cries of His people, and He came to visit them. God gave Moses the message of hope to take to the people. Here, in Exodus 12, the time has come for God Himself to bring the people out of the bondage of Egypt.

The night before the people would be freed from bondage, they were told to kill a spotless lamb. This sacrifice acknowledged God's goodness to them by delivering them from death. The blood of the sacrifice would be on the doorframes of the homes of the believers. Those who entered through the blood-stained doorframe found salvation and life. This sacrifice was followed by the Feast of Unleavened Bread. This feast represented the removal of sin. The Passover feasts were repeated annually.

The people who entered through the blood would be saved from God's wrath. In the same way, Noah and his family entered the ark through the door, and they were spared from God's wrath.

The people who were obedient to God's instructions through Moses were justified by the blood of the lamb. The Death Angel passed over them. Romans 5:9-10 tells us, "Since we have now been justified by his blood, how much more shall we be saved from God's wrath through him! For if, while we were God's enemies, we were reconciled to him through the death of his Son, how much more, having been reconciled, shall we be saved through his life!"

In Exodus 12:13, God told the people that "no destructive plague" would touch them. Death was the destructive plague that struck the Egyptians and anyone who failed to obey the Lord's command. Romans 8:1 tells us, "Therefore, there is now no condemnation for those who are in Christ Jesus."

This sacrifice of a spotless lamb, and the picture of the removal of sin to save people who were in bondage, was a picture of the Gospel. In this first Passover, it was very good news for those who obeyed.

The writer of the book of Hebrews connected the two events for us and showed us that the sacrifice has been paid, once for all. First, the writer told us that the law was a shadow of things to come. A shadow reveals to us the presence of something but not a clear understanding of it.

> *The law is only a shadow of the good things that are coming—not the realities themselves. For this reason, it can never, by the same sacrifices repeated endlessly year after year, make perfect those who draw near to worship. Otherwise, would they not have stopped being offered? For the worshipers would have been cleansed once for all, and would no longer have felt guilty for their sins. But those sacrifices are an annual reminder of sins. It is impossible for the blood of bulls and goats to take away sins. (Hebrews 10:1-4)*

The writer of Hebrews quoted Psalm 40 when the writer wrote,

> *First he said, "Sacrifices and offerings, burnt offerings and sin offerings you did not desire, nor were you pleased with them"—though they were offered in accordance with the law. Then he said, "Here I am, I have come to do your will." He sets aside the first to establish the second. And by that will, we have been made holy through the sacrifice of the body of Jesus Christ once for all.*

The first Passover set the people of Israel free from bondage. It was a shadow, or a pattern, of what God was preparing to do for every ethnic group in the world to set us free from our bondage. The gift of God is eternal life in Christ.

> *But now that you have been set free from sin and have become slaves of God, the benefit you reap leads to holiness, and the result is eternal life. For the wages of sin is death, but the gift of God is eternal life in Christ Jesus our Lord. (Romans 6:22-23)*

> *The blood will be a sign for you…*

Notes

Week 12: The Red Sea
Exodus 14:10-31

Key verse: "And when the Israelites saw the mighty hand of the Lord displayed against the Egyptians, the people feared the Lord and put their trust in him and in Moses his servant." (Exodus 14:31)

LEADER'S NOTE

Help the students understand that everything that God does has a purpose. That purpose is for us to know Him.

The people were sent to Egypt for a purpose, to save them from the famine. They were brought out of Egypt for His purposes: to show the nations that the God of Israel is the God over the earth, and to bring the people to the Promised Land.

CONTEXT

God has brought the people out of Egypt. He is leading them by a pillar of fire at night, and a cloud by day. However, the Egyptian army has decided to follow the Hebrews and bring them back. All of this has been orchestrated by God, for His glory.

OPEN UP

How has God displayed His power?

THINK ABOUT

The Hebrews have left Egypt, and they are walking to a land that they have never seen. They have only heard about it. How far could you walk in the wilderness before you began to question God's plan?

READ

Verses 10-12: What are the people saying?

Verses 13-14: What does Moses say?

Verses 15-15-18: What does God say?

Verses 19-22: What happened?

Verses 23-25: What happened?

Verses 26-30: What happened?

Verse 31: What happened to the people of Israel?

FOCUS

And when the Israelites saw the mighty hand of the Lord displayed against the Egyptians, the people feared the Lord and put their trust in him and in Moses his servant. (Exodus 14:31)

What did the Israelites see? Did they see the power of God in the plagues? Why is it important for the people to trust in God and in Moses? Can you follow someone you don't trust?

LEADER'S GUIDE—SOJOURNER BIBLE STUDY

TALK
- What is this teaching me about God?
- What is this teaching me about people?
- Why is this important to me today?

CONNECT THE GOSPEL

This is the Gospel: "For what I received I passed on to you as of first importance: that Christ died for our sins according to the Scriptures, that he was buried, that he was raised on the third day according to the Scriptures" (1 Corinthians 15:3-4 NIV).

The "good news" of Jesus Christ is the picture of God providing a way for people to be in a relationship with Him. Just as Jesus died to save us from the bondage of sin and bring us to new life, so also the journey through the Red Sea is a picture of God making a way for His people to see His power as He moves them from the old life to a new life.

SO WHAT?

Why do I care about the Hebrews walking across the sea? Did it really happen? Some people say that they must have crossed at a low point. If that is true, then the Egyptian army died in shallow water.

The journey from the bondage of sin to the place of freedom in Christ is not easy. You will have doubts, but if you will walk with God and follow Him in faith, you will see His power in your life. We need to do what the Israelites did and put our trust in this God.

SERVE

All around us there are people who are struggling with life. How can you take the lesson of God guiding the people through the sea and encourage someone to put their faith in this same God?

DIG DEEPER

> *And when the Israelites saw the mighty hand of the Lord displayed against the Egyptians, the people feared the Lord and put their trust in him and in Moses his servant. (Exodus 14:31)*

When did the Israelites see the mighty hand of God? In order to fully grasp what we are being told here; we need to look back at what God told Moses before the plagues began...

> *Therefore, say to the Israelites: "I am the Lord, and I will bring you out from under the yoke of the Egyptians. I will free you from being slaves to them, and I will redeem you with an outstretched arm and with mighty acts of judgment. I will take you as my own people, and I will be your God. Then you will know that I am the Lord your God, who brought you out from under the yoke of the Egyptians. And I will bring you to the land I swore with uplifted hand to give to Abraham, to Isaac and to Jacob. I will give it to you as a possession. I am the Lord." (Exodus 6:6-8)*

However, verse 9 tells us that the people did not listen to Moses.

It was also God's plan for the people of Egypt to know Him and His power. Exodus 7:5, "And the Egyptians will know that I am the Lord when I stretch out my hand against Egypt and bring the Israelites out of it." In the beginning, when Moses began meeting with Pharoah, the pharoah did not listen to Moses. Pharoah even admitted to no knowledge of Jehovah God (Ex. 5:2).

Then, after the exodus event, when the people were wandering in the wilderness, the Lord was glorified again. The Lord God allowed the armies of Pharoah to pursue the Israelites because the Lord God had a plan. "'And I will harden Pharaoh's heart, and he will pursue them. But I will gain glory for myself through Pharaoh and all his army, and the Egyptians will know that I am the Lord.' So, the Israelites did this" (Ex. 14:4). The end result was that the people saw the work of God, and they put their trust in Him.

How can we connect this public display of power for the glory of God to Jesus in the New Testament? Look at the miracles of Jesus and the response of the people.

When Jesus healed the paralyzed man, everyone was amazed, and they praised God (Mark 2:12). When Jesus healed the blind, the crippled, and the mute, the people were amazed, and they praised the God of Israel (Mat. 15:31). When Jesus healed a blind man, the man glorified God, and the people who saw it gave praise to God (Luke 18:43).

Every time God displayed His power, it got people's attention. In the Old Testament people feared the LORD, and they put their trust in the servant of the LORD. In the New Testament Gospels, the power of God was revealed through the person of God the Son with the same result. There was a lesson learned and a life changed. The Bible is full of stories of God displaying His power through His people in order to draw people to Himself and to display His wrath to the ungodly.

The book of Acts is also full of examples of how God worked miracles through the apostles and people came to faith. Just look at what happened in Acts chapter 2, when the Holy Spirit came, and lives were changed and people were saved.

> *"Therefore let all Israel be assured of this: God has made this Jesus, whom you crucified, both Lord and Messiah." When the people heard this, they were cut to the heart and said to Peter and the other apostles, "Brothers, what shall we do?"*
>
> *Peter replied, "Repent and be baptized, every one of you, in the name of Jesus Christ for the forgiveness of your sins. And you will receive the gift of the Holy Spirit. The promise is for you and your children and for all who are far off—for all whom the Lord our God will call."*
>
> *With many other words he warned them; and he pleaded with them, "Save yourselves from this corrupt generation." Those who accepted his message were baptized, and about three thousand were added to their number that day. (Acts 2:36-41)*

Many people saw the mighty hand of God, and they put their trust in Him and His Servant. Exodus 14:31, "And when the Israelites saw the mighty hand of the Lord displayed against the Egyptians, the people feared the Lord and put their trust in him and in Moses his servant."

Notes

LEADER'S GUIDE—SOJOURNER BIBLE STUDY

Week 13: The Ten Commandments
Exodus 20:1-17

Key verse: *"I am the Lord your God, who brought you out of Egypt, out of the land of slavery." (Exodus 20:2)*

LEADER'S NOTE

Feel free to spend time on each of the commandments if you desire. This lesson could be taught over two or more weeks. The key is that the students see that God has brought them out of bondage, and He has given them a way to know Him.

The Ten Commandments reveal to us the character of God. We see how to have a perfect relationship with Him and a perfect relationship with the people around us. We want the students to understand that only in Christ is it possible to keep these commandments. The Ten Commandments are sometimes referred to as the Law. Paul in his letter to the Galatians said that the Law was our tutor, or guardian. It was put in place until we would have faith in Jesus.

> *Therefore, the Law has become our tutor to lead us to Christ, so that we may be justified by faith. (Galatians 3:24 NASB)*

CONTEXT

From 1445 to 1405 B.C., Moses and the Israelites will wander in the wilderness. They are on their way to the Promised Land. The people, including us, need to understand who is this God, and how can we have a relationship with Him?

The Israelites are traveling through countries who worship many gods. They will enter a country with many gods. They need to know this God, YHWH.

OPEN UP

Do you like rules and laws? Do you like people telling you what to do?

THINK ABOUT

How do God's laws help us know Him?

READ

Verse 1: Who is speaking? Why is it important to know who is giving us these commands?

Verses 2-11: What is the focus of these commands?

Verses 12-17: What is the focus of these commands?

FOCUS

> *I am the Lord your God, who brought you out of Egypt, out of the land of slavery. (Exodus 20:2)*

What two things does God say about Himself in this verse? Why is it important to understand who this God is?

TALK
- What is this teaching me about God?
- What is this teaching me about people?
- Why is this important to me today?

CONNECT THE GOSPEL

This is the Gospel: "For what I received I passed on to you as of first importance: that Christ died for our sins according to the Scriptures, that he was buried, that he was raised on the third day according to the Scriptures" (1 Corinthians 15:3-4 NIV).

Without the Law of God, we would not know about sin. If our sin separates us from God, then we need a way to be restored to Him. The Gospel is the "good news" of God's plan to bring us out of the bondage of sin and into freedom in Christ.

The Ten Commandments reveal the character of God to us and our need for a Savior. Paul said in Romans 7:17, "In fact, it was the law that showed me my sin. I would never have known that coveting is wrong if the law had not said, 'You must not covet.'" Jesus said in Matthew 5:17, that He came to fulfill the Law. In order to have a right relationship with the God who created us, we need to understand what He requires of us. If Jesus is the fulfillment of the Law, then we need Jesus.

SO WHAT?

The Ten Commandments are a bunch of rules that are impossible to keep. If I am a good person, does it really matter if I know these commands?

If you are a good person, you don't need rules, laws, or commands. The problem is, you are not good. No one is good. We all have sin, and we all need a Savior (Romans 3:23). Remember that we can be slaves to sin, or we can have freedom in Christ. Let's remember the God who has made a way for us to be free.

Are you worried about memorizing these Ten? Remember two: love the Lord your God, and love your neighbor as yourself.

> *And one of the scribes came up and heard them disputing with one another, and seeing that he answered them well, asked him, "Which commandment is the most important of all?" Jesus answered, "The most important is, 'Hear, O Israel: The Lord our God, the Lord is one. And you shall love the Lord your God with all your heart and with all your soul and with all your mind and with all your strength.' The second is this: 'You shall love your neighbor as yourself.' There is no other commandment greater than these." (Mark 12:28-31)*

SERVE

Remember that the Ten Commandments reveal to us the character of God and our need for a Savior. If we are following Jesus then He has fulfilled these Laws. The only thing we need to do is to help people see Jesus. How can we do that? Love God and love people. Do you want what's best for the people around you, or do you want what is best for you?

DIG DEEPER

> *I am the Lord your God, who brought you out of Egypt, out of the land of slavery. (Exodus 20:2)*

In the last lesson, God revealed Himself to the Israelites and the Egyptians through the plagues and then the crossing of the sea. The Lord God had brought the people out of bondage with a powerful display of Himself.

In today's lesson, the Lord God has revealed Himself in His Law. These Commandments called the people to a holy relationship with God and with people. We need to understand this God and what He has done for all of us.

In Exodus 20:1, we are told that the LORD "spoke these words." In the beginning, when God spoke, He created the heavens and the earth. There is power and authority in the Word of God. In Exodus 20:2, God introduced Himself as Jehovah Elohim, the Existing God. In this title, God asserted His authority and the sole object of worship. The first four Commandments are all God-centered.

Also, in this introduction, we see God in three ways. He is the LORD God, He is the God of the Covenant, and He is the God who redeemed them from bondage. As the LORD God, He is self-existent and without equal. He is the One who gives life, and He has the authority to give us His Law. As the God of the Covenant, He would bless their faithfulness. In His covenant with Abraham, Isaac, and Jacob, all the families on the earth would be blessed through their faith.

The LORD God redeemed Israel from the bondage of Egypt. He moved them from bondage to freedom and from darkness to light. Because God redeemed them from bondage, they owed Him their obedience. To not obey was to deny His authority. In the same way, Christ Jesus has redeemed us, and we owe Him our obedience. "What shall I return to the Lord for all his goodness to me? I will lift up the cup of salvation and call on the name of the Lord" (Psalm 116:12-13).

We need to understand that the Law of God could not save anyone. It only pointed to the need for a Savior. Paul told the Galatians that the Law was our tutor, our guide, to help us understand Christ. "Therefore, the Law has become our tutor to lead us to Christ, so that we may be justified by faith" (Galatians 3:24).

The exodus from slavery is a picture of God providing a way to be free. The Law He gave to Moses did not have the power to save. The LORD God is revealed in His Law, but it did not have the power to save. The Law of God identified His perfection and our imperfection.

Paul puts it for us beautifully in Romans 8:1-4:

> *Therefore, there is now no condemnation for those who are in Christ Jesus, because through Christ Jesus the law of the Spirit who gives life has set you free from the law of sin and death. For what the law was powerless to do because it was weakened by the flesh, God did by sending his own Son in the likeness of sinful flesh to be a sin offering. And so, he condemned sin in the flesh, in order that the righteous requirement of the law might be fully met in us, who do not live according to the flesh but according to the Spirit.*

If Jesus came to fulfill the Law, then we need Jesus. For everyone who follows Jesus is free from the Law. Just as the LORD God did the work of bringing the Israelites out of slavery in Egypt, He has also done the work necessary to bring us out of the bondage of sin. He sent His Son to be a sin offering for our redemption "out of the land of slavery."

Notes

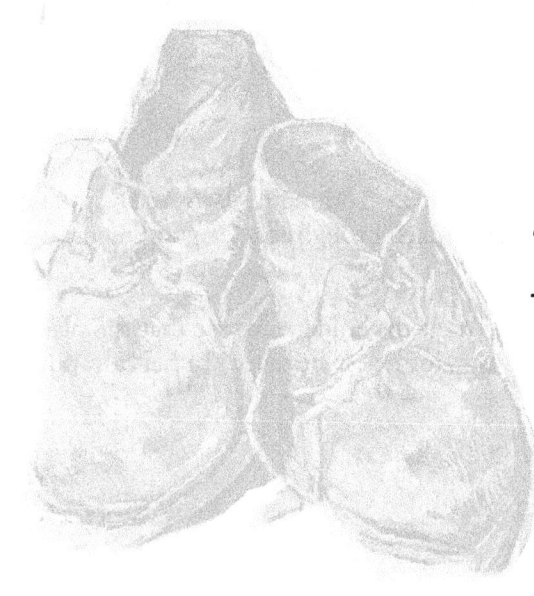

4:
The Conquest Era

LEADER'S GUIDE—SOJOURNER BIBLE STUDY

Week 14: Jericho and Rahab
Joshua 2:1-24

Key verse: "And as soon as we heard it, our hearts melted, and there was no spirit left in any man because of you, for the Lord your God, he is God in the heavens above and on the earth beneath." (Joshua 2:11)

LEADER'S NOTE

The language used to describe Rahab will depend on which translation you use. She may be called a harlot, or an inn keeper, or something else. Use your own discretion on how to approach this, but don't spend a lot of time on her profession. The focus needs to be on the reason for her salvation within the plan of God.

CONTEXT

The year is 1405 B.C., Moses has died, and the people are now under the command of Joshua. Joshua was one of the twelve spies that Moses sent to spy out the land. Joshua and Caleb brought back a good report, while the other ten were afraid to trust God.

As Joshua leads the people of God into the Promised Land, we want the students to see that the plan of God is for all nations. Rahab is not a Hebrew, but God is making a way for her to be saved. In her salvation we will see the continuation of the promise of God in Genesis 3:15.

OPEN UP

How do people learn about God?

THINK ABOUT

As you read this lesson, think about how Rahab learned about God. Does she know everything about this God?

READ

Verses 1-7: What happened?

Verses 8-11: What does Rahab know? How did she learn this?

Verses 12-13: What is the request of Rahab?

Verses 14-20: What are the instructions the men give to Rahab? What color is the cord they will use for a sign? What color is scarlet? Is it interesting that the color of blood at the window will save the people inside? What is another story of the blood protecting the people in the home?

Verses 21-24: What happened?

FOCUS

> And as soon as we heard it, our hearts melted, and there was no spirit left in any man because of you, for the Lord your God, he is God in the heavens above and on the earth beneath. (Joshua 2:11)

Rahab is not a Hebrew, but she has heard about everything that has happened as the people came out of Egypt. How do you think she learned all of this? Does Rahab make a profession of faith? Do you think she was saved by what she believed? Why or why not?

TALK

- What is this teaching me about God?
- What is this teaching me about people?
- Why is this important to me today?

CONNECT THE GOSPEL

This is the Gospel: "For what I received I passed on to you as of first importance: that Christ died for our sins according to the Scriptures, that he was buried, that he was raised on the third day according to the Scriptures" (1 Corinthians 15:3-4 NIV).

> *By faith Rahab the prostitute did not perish with those who were disobedient, because she had given a friendly welcome to the spies. (Hebrews 11:31)*

It is faith that saves us. It is faith in what God has done, and is doing, and will do. We can't always see it or understand it, but we know that God is working. Just as Rahab knew what God had done when He rescued the Israelites from Egypt, she also knew that this God is the Lord of the earth. Rahab was saved the same way you and I are saved. By faith.

The Gospel is the "good news" that God has made a way for us to be saved. How did God make a way for Rahab and her family to be saved?

SO WHAT?

What does it matter that a woman in a small town in Canaan put a scarlet cord in her window because she was afraid of being destroyed? Why should I care three thousand years later? Because, this woman was saved by faith. She believed, and she was obedient.

In Genesis 3:15, God promised that the Seed of the woman would crush the head of the serpent. Death will be defeated. Throughout the Old Testament we see God's plan in action. Here, He is saving Rahab because she is going to be a relative of Jesus.

> *...and Salmon the father of Boaz by Rahab, and Boaz the father of Obed by Ruth, and Obed the father of Jesse. (Matthew 1:5)*

SERVE

God has a plan for all of us. Can you find a way to help someone know Jesus through what you know about Him?

Rahab heard about how God saved His people. How did you hear about God's salvation? How will you help other people hear this "good news"?

DIG DEEPER

> *And as soon as we heard it, our hearts melted, and there was no spirit left in any man because of you, for the Lord your God, he is God in the heavens above and on the earth beneath. (Joshua 2:11)*

In our last lesson, we learned about how God revealed Himself in His Law. He has the authority to give us His commands, and He has the ability to rescue us when we fall. In our lesson today, we will look at Rahab, the spies, Rahab's confession of this God, and her salvation.

Rahab lived 1,400 years before Jesus. She had not heard the Gospel, but she had heard about this God of the Hebrews. She had heard about the great things this God had done to bring His people out of bondage. Rahab had not seen God, but she believed what she had heard.

This is even more amazing when we realize that when Rahab met the spies, it had been forty years since the Lord God had dried up the sea! "The Lord your God will lay the fear of you and the dread of you on all the land that you shall tread, as he promised you" (Deut. 11:25). Rahab's statement was confirmation of God's promise.

How did the two spies "happen" to find Rahab? We believe that God directed their steps to her place for the purpose of her salvation. God, through Moses, sent the spies into Jericho to bring back a report about the city.

The spies did not realize that the Lord God had prepared a family for them to meet. It was a Divine Appointment.

What was Rahab's confession? She believed in God's power. "He is God in the heavens above and on the earth beneath." Rahab also believed in God's promise. "I know that the Lord has given you the land" (Joshua 2:9).

Rahab was a woman with a bad reputation, and God sent His men to her. In the same way, God sent His Son to men and women who were not perfect. In Luke 7:36-50, we read about a "sinful woman" who washed Jesus' feet with her tears. She was saved by the same faith as Rahab and everyone else who believes in this God who can dry up the sea and remove kings (Joshua 2:10).

The writer of the book of Hebrews commended Rahab's faith, Hebrews 11:31, "By faith Rahab the prostitute did not perish with those who were disobedient, because she had given a friendly welcome to the spies."

James the Apostle also commended Rahab's faith when he explained that faith is active. "And in the same way was not also Rahab the prostitute justified by works when she received the messengers and sent them out by another way?" (James 2:25).

Rahab had enough faith, the faith of a mustard seed, to be saved. Rahab had the faith of a child. She didn't know everything about God. She had not grown up in Sunday School. She knew there was a God who could save His people, and she feared Him enough to put her faith in Him. She had not seen Him, but she believed in Him.

> *Jesus said to him, "Have you believed because you have seen me? Blessed are those who have not seen and yet have believed." (John 20:29)*

May we also have faith in the God of Rahab, the Lord God who removes kings, dries up seas, and rescues sinners.

Notes

5: The Sin Cycle/Judges Era

LEADER'S GUIDE—SOJOURNER BIBLE STUDY

Week 15: Failure to Keep the Law
Judges 2:10-19

Key verse: *"After that whole generation had been gathered to their ancestors, another generation grew up who knew neither the Lord nor what he had done for Israel." (Judges 2:10)*

LEADER'S NOTE

As you study this lesson, think about your students. Are they learning about the God of the Bible? If they never return to this class, will they know enough about this God to make a decision to follow Him? Do they know enough to tell someone else about Him?

It's nice if they can find a Scripture reference or quote a verse, but at the end of their lives will these things save them? Are we as teachers passing on the knowledge of God unto salvation?

CONTEXT

As the book of Judges opens, we learn that Joshua has died as well as the entire generation who saw the miracles of God. These would have been the children of the Hebrews who died in the wilderness wanderings.

The book of Judges is the story of our sin cycle. We sin and then suffer and then cry out to God, and He saves us, and then we get silent, and then we sin again, and the cycle continues. We want the students to understand that these Judges were temporary. They were a picture of the one Judge who would bring eternal redemption for all people.

The time frame of Joshua and Judges is 1405-1050 B.C.

OPEN UP

How did you learn about God?

THINK ABOUT

What can you do each day to remain strong in your walk with the Lord? Are you learning from people? Are you teaching others what you learn?

READ

Verse 10: What generation is the writer talking about? Look at verse 7.

Verses 11-13: What happened? Some translations say "forsook." What does that mean?

Verses 14-15: What was the punishment?

Verse 16: What happened?

Verses 17-19: What happened? Do you see the cycle?

FOCUS

> *After that whole generation had been gathered to their ancestors, another generation grew up who knew neither the Lord nor what he had done for Israel. (Judges 2:10)*

How do you think this could happen? How can we avoid it today? How can we help people know the Lord and what He has done?

TALK
- What is this teaching me about God?
- What is this teaching me about people?
- Why is this important to me today?

CONNECT THE GOSPEL

This is the Gospel: "For what I received I passed on to you as of first importance: that Christ died for our sins according to the Scriptures, that he was buried, that he was raised on the third day according to the Scriptures" (1 Corinthians 15:3-4).

The Gospel is the "good news" that God has made a way for us to know Him. However, it is only "good news" if someone hears it. You have heard the Gospel. What have you done with it?

Joshua's generation failed to pass on the knowledge of how God saved His people. What are you doing to help people know how to be saved?

What is a common theme in the lessons we have studied this year? Do you see God providing a way for people to be saved?

SO WHAT?

Why should I care about this lesson in Judges? It happened over 3,000 years ago. What does it mean to me today?

If I recognize the sin cycle in my life, then it is important for me to also recognize that God has made a way for me to be free from the cycle. I need to be active in sharing this knowledge with the people around me so that they can be free from the bondage of sin.

SERVE

Think about how you can break the cycle in your life. How can you help other people to understand that they can break free from this cycle too?

DIG DEEPER

After that whole generation had been gathered to their ancestors, another generation grew up who knew neither the Lord nor what he had done for Israel. (Judges 2:10)

These are chilling words in the twenty-first century. Every believer needs to ask ourselves if the next generation will know the Lord when we are gone.

How did this happen in such a short time? Joshua served the Lord and the elders who had seen the work of the Lord. Judges 2:6-8, "When Joshua dismissed the people, the people of Israel went each to his inheritance to take possession of the land. And the people served the Lord all the days of Joshua, and all the days of the elders who outlived Joshua, who had seen all the great work that the Lord had done for Israel." It is interesting to notice how we transition from our study of Rahab, a gentile, who knew about the Lord God, to a generation of Israelites who did not know anything about Him, or what He had done.

Israel had been given the Law from the Lord God Himself. The Word of God is enough for teaching, correcting, and instructions in righteousness (2 Timothy 3:16). The Lord God rebuked them when they broke their covenant, "But you have not obeyed my voice. What is this you have done?" (Judges 2:2).

Because they did not "know" the Lord, they did not have a relationship with Him. In this failure, they committed two sins. Israel turned away from the worship of God. When you turn away from the worship of God, you turn away from God Himself. Second, Israel turned to other gods. They had broken the first two commandments of God (Exodus 20:3-4).

It is so important to pass down what the Lord has taught us. Paul knew how important it was to pass down faithful teaching in the first-century church. This exhortation from Paul to Timothy applies to us, as well. We need to be strong in the grace of Christ, and we need to "entrust" what we have learned to others who will do the same.

> *You then, my son, be strong in the grace that is in Christ Jesus. And the things you have heard me say in the presence of many witnesses entrust to reliable people who will also be qualified to teach others. (2 Timothy 2:1-2)*

This word "entrust" is very strong. It does not mean just to pass on information. "Entrust" is the idea of giving something to someone to take care of and protect. A great example of entrusting people with the Word of God for the sake of passing it on is found in Acts chapter 18. In this chapter, we read about Paul, Silas, Timothy, Priscilla, Aquila, and Apollos, and how Paul had taught them and then he left them. These friends were entrusted to teach others.

This would be a good time to do a "self check." Is someone entrusting me with the Word of God? Am I entrusting someone in the next generation with the Word of God? And, finally, am I teaching them how to entrust the next generation with the Word of God?

May it never be said of us that a generation grew up who did not know the message of the Lord Jesus Christ.

Notes

5: THE SIN CYCLE/JUDGES ERA

Week 16: Ruth
Ruth 1:1-17, 2:8-13, 4:1-22

Key verse: *"'The Lord bless him!' Naomi said to her daughter-in-law. 'He has not stopped showing his kindness to the living and the dead.' She added, 'That man is our close relative; he is one of our kinsman-redeemers.'" (Ruth 2:20)*

LEADER'S NOTE

This is a long lesson. If you spend time preparing, you will be able to decide what to skip, or you may decide to teach it over two sessions.

The story of Ruth occurs during the time of the Judges. Her story is the story of a Redeemer. This four-chapter book is very rich, and it can also seem a little risqué. You may be asked some difficult questions, so prepare yourself ahead of time about how much you will read with your students.

You may want to take some time at the end of the lesson to take your students to the genealogy in Matthew 1:5-6.

CONTEXT

The story of Ruth ends by linking Ruth to David. The story of Ruth is an Old Testament picture of the Kinsman-Redeemer. In order to fully understand the concept of kinsman-redeemer, we need to understand his qualifications: He had to be related in some way. He had to be willing to redeem. He had to be able to redeem. He had to be able to pay the full price.

Boaz is the kinsman-redeemer who is related to the family, willing and able to redeem Ruth, a Moabite woman, and he was willing to pay the full price. This meant he was willing to bring her into the people of God and share the inheritance. Boaz wasn't first in line, but the man who was first was not willing to share the inheritance with the children of Ruth.

Something to think about: the shame on this first man was so great that his name is never mentioned in Scripture.

OPEN UP

What does it mean to redeem someone or something?

THINK ABOUT

Do we need to be redeemed? Why or why not?

READ

Chapter 1:

Verses 1-6: What happened? Where were they?

Verses 7-13: What did Naomi say?

Verses 14-17: What did Orpah do and what did Ruth do? Which girl is the example of faith?

Chapter 2:

Verses 8-13: Where is Ruth and what is she doing? What did Boaz say? What did Ruth say?

Chapter 4:

Verses 1-5: What did Boaz do and say?

Verses 6-8: What did Mr. No Name do and say?

Verses 9-13: What happened?

Verses 14-15: What did the women say?

Verses 16-22: Why is Ruth so important?

FOCUS

> "The Lord bless him!" Naomi said to her daughter-in-law. "He has not stopped showing his kindness to the living and the dead." She added, "That man is our close relative; he is one of our kinsman-redeemers." (Ruth 2:20)

What is Naomi saying? What has she realized has happened in her life? Take a moment to read Ruth 1:20-21. Has the Lord left us without a Kinsman-Redeemer? What do you think?

TALK

- What is this teaching me about God?
- What is this teaching me about people?
- Why is this important to me today?

CONNECT THE GOSPEL

This is the Gospel: "For what I received I passed on to you as of first importance: that Christ died for our sins according to the Scriptures, that he was buried, that he was raised on the third day according to the Scriptures" (1 Corinthians 15:3-4 NIV).

Is Jesus our Kinsman-Redeemer? If you say "Yes," how is that possible? How is He related to us? (Hebrews 2:17). Was He willing to redeem us? (Matthew 20:28). How was He able to redeem us? (1 Peter 1:19). Was He able to pay the full price? (Ephesians 1:17; 1 Peter 2:24). And what have we been redeemed from? (John 8:34).

This is the Gospel. We have been redeemed from the bondage of sin because of what Jesus has done for us.

SO WHAT?

Why do I care about a woman who worked in a field and married a rich man? Great question!

This is so important because it shows us that we are in a hopeless situation without someone to help us. It is impossible for us to help ourselves. We can take classes, we can exercise, we can work hard, but in the end, we haven't experienced what we need most. Our greatest need is to be restored, redeemed to a right relationship with our heavenly Father. We need Jesus, our Kinsman-Redeemer.

SERVE

Do you know someone who feels hopeless? Ask God to show you how you can share this story with them so that they will know that God has made a way for them to have a new relationship with Him.

DIG DEEPER

> *"The Lord bless him!" Naomi said to her daughter-in-law. "He has not stopped showing his kindness to the living and the dead." She added, "That man is our close relative; he is one of our kinsman-redeemers." (Ruth 2:20)*

In order to understand this verse deeper, we need to understand the characters in the story. Naomi, Ruth, and her sister Orpah, the two kinsman-redeemers, and the Lord God are all important in understanding our "Kinsman-redeemer."

Naomi was a poor widow. She and her family had traveled to the land of Moab because of a famine in their hometown of Bethlehem. While they were in Moab, the sons married Moabite women. Then, in time, all the men died. This left Naomi with two Moabite daughters-in-law. Naomi was poor, but she had a wealthy relative.

Boaz was the wealthy relative, and he had poor relatives. Boaz was a landowner from the tribe of Judah. Bible commentators believe that Boaz was the son of Salmon, who was the son of Nahshon, who was the son of Rahab. (Again, we see salvation is available to the Gentiles.) Boaz was qualified to be a kinsman-redeemer.

The other kinsman-redeemer was never named. This man did not want to share his wealth with anyone else (Ruth 4:6).

This is interesting: According to the Law of God in Deuteronomy 25:7-10, if a man would not carry on his brother's line, then the widow would remove his sandal and spit in his face. His family would be known as the Family of the Unsandaled. We do not have a different punishment listed for the one who refused to redeem a relative. (Leviticus chapter 25 contains several examples of redemption, but it does not indicate a different penalty.) So this man has remained nameless throughout history. This nameless kinsman-redeemer is an interesting contradiction to the faithfulness and love of Boaz.

The daughter-in-law, Orpah, is an interesting contradiction to the faithfulness and love of Ruth. We know that Orpah was a young widow and a Moabite. We know that Naomi gave Orpah and Ruth the same opportunity to return to their people. Naomi was releasing them from any obligation they would have to take care of their widowed mother-in-law. Orpah turned away from Naomi, her people, and her God.

Then there was Ruth. She was a Moabite and a widow. She was given the opportunity to return to her family and her home, but she refused. She preferred to be with her mother-in-law in a land she did not know, among a people who were not her own, and she wanted to follow the God of Naomi (Ruth 1:16). She was willing to go to work, and it was a low form of work. However, her attitude and her sacrifice did not go unnoticed (Ruth 2:11-12).

In our verse today, we read about the praise of Naomi. She called on the blessing of the Lord upon Boaz. Then she praised the Lord for His kindness in remembering her and her family. Naomi and her family had walked away from Bethlehem because they were hungry for food. The Lord brought Naomi and Ruth back to Bethlehem and to the one who would redeem them and save them.

In our study, we have seen the Lord prepare a people and a place for His Messiah. We have seen the Lord bring His people out of slavery and into freedom. We have seen the Lord save people because they had faith. Throughout the Old Testament, the people have been waiting for the Seed of the woman. They have been waiting for the promised Messiah.

> *I know that my redeemer lives, and that in the end he will stand on the earth. (Job 19:25)*

The Old Testament is the promise of God that He will redeem His people Himself. The New Testament is the promise that we have been redeemed. Yes, Brother Job, our Redeemer lives!

In Luke 1:68, Zechariah, the father of John the Baptist, knew that the work of God was complete. "Praise be to the Lord, the God of Israel, because he has come to his people and redeemed them." Zechariah affirmed that it was God Himself who came to His people.

> *For you know that it was not with perishable things such as silver or gold that you were redeemed from the empty way of life handed down to you from your ancestors, but with the precious blood of Christ, a lamb without blemish or defect. (1 Peter 1:18-19)*

Naomi saw that her family had not been forsaken or abandoned. She saw the love of God as He provided a redeemer. The book of Ruth helps us to understand that our Redeemer is like us, a person who is the Lord God Himself. The Lord God has not stopped showing His loving kindness to us, either.

Notes

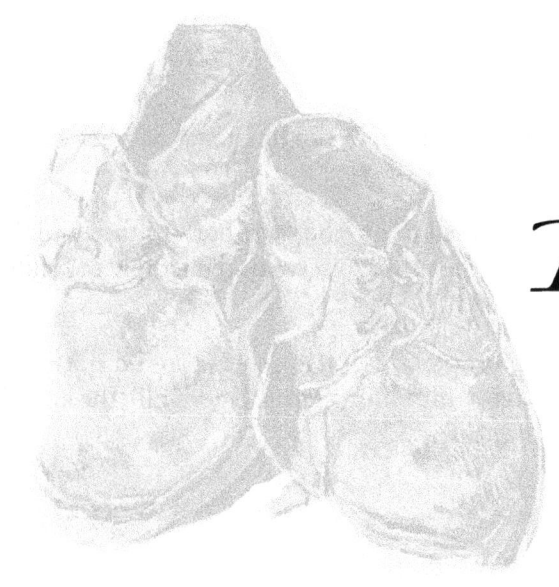

6: The Kingdom Era

LEADER'S GUIDE—SOJOURNER BIBLE STUDY

Week 17: Samuel
First Samuel 3:1-21

Key verse: *"The Lord was with Samuel as he grew up, and he let none of Samuel's words fall to the ground." (1 Samuel 3:19)*

LEADER'S NOTE

We won't cover everything about Samuel, but we want the students to understand that Samuel played an important role in the transition from the era of the Judges to the Kingdom Era.

CONTEXT

The time of Samuel begins around 1100 B.C. We are closing out the era of the Judges, as Samuel will be the last judge, and he will anoint the first and second kings of Israel.

Samuel's mother, Hannah, had prayed for a child. She had promised to give her first born to the Lord. When Samuel was weened, probably two years old, he was taken to Eli the priest to serve in the temple in fulfillment of her promise.

If we remember Judges chapter 2, we will remember that the people of Joshua's generation did not teach the following generations about God. Yet, here in 1 Samuel 3, we see Samuel ministering before Eli. The knowledge of God is being passed on, and Samuel will eventually take over Eli's role.

OPEN UP

How old do you have to be to help in the church?

THINK ABOUT

How would you feel if your mom brought you to the church office and left you with the pastor to live with him and work for him for the rest of your life?

READ

Verse 1: What does it say about the Word of the Lord? Why do you think this happened?

Verses 2-3: What do we learn about Eli?

Verses 4-9: What happened? Why couldn't Samuel recognize that the Lord was calling him?

Verses 10-14: What happened? What was God about to do? Why?

Verses 15-18: What happened? What did Eli say? Does he seem to be afraid?

Verses 19-21: What are some things that we learn about the relationship between Samuel and the Lord?

FOCUS

The Lord was with Samuel as he grew up, and he let none of Samuel's words fall to the ground. (1 Samuel 3:19)

What does it mean that the Lord was with Samuel as he grew? Has the Lord called you? How will you recognize His voice? What do you think is the key to knowing the Lord and recognizing His Voice?

If we are growing in the Lord and being obedient to His call in our life, then He will not let us fail when we talk about Him. Our words won't fall to the ground.

TALK
- What is this teaching me about God?
- What is this teaching me about people?
- Why is this important to me today?

CONNECT THE GOSPEL

This is the Gospel: "For what I received I passed on to you as of first importance: that Christ died for our sins according to the Scriptures, that he was buried, that he was raised on the third day according to the Scriptures" (1 Corinthians 15:3-4 NIV).

Paul wrote in 1 Corinthians 15, that he passed on what was important. What is so important about the Gospel? How was that passed to you?

We have seen in Judges and in 1 Samuel how people did not pass on what the Lord God was telling them, and so people could not recognize the Lord in their lives. What do you think about that?

SO WHAT?

Why do we care about a boy who was raised in the Temple? While you may not be growing up in church every day, you still have access to the Word of God. How are you handling it?

The Bible says that Samuel's words didn't fall to the ground. How can we live in a way that God's Word is protected?

SERVE

How do you access the Word of God? Do you know someone who does not have access to the Bible? Can you help them get a Bible? Ask your friends this week if they have a Bible, and then ask them how often they read it.

DIG DEEPER

The Lord was with Samuel as he grew up, and he let none of Samuel's words fall to the ground. (1 Samuel 3:19)

In week 15, we learned that a generation had grown up not knowing the Lord. Last week we learned about the faithfulness of God in providing a kinsman redeemer. The books of Samuel transition us from the time of the Judges (the books of Joshua, Judges and Ruth) to the Kingdom Era.

First Samuel 3:1, "The boy Samuel ministered before the Lord under Eli. In those days the word of the Lord was rare; there were not many visions." The word of the Lord was rare. Do you think it was rare because the preceding generations had not "entrusted" it to those who could pass it on?

Eli the priest had failed to be a spiritual leader to the people, and he failed as the leader of his family (1 Sam. 3:13). God used Samuel to carry on the work of getting the word of God to the people. All of Israel, from Dan to Beersheba, recognized that God was with Samuel. "And all Israel from Dan to Beersheba recognized that Samuel was attested as a prophet of the Lord" (1 Sam. 3:20).

How do people know that you follow Jesus? Is it your actions, or your words, or both? Your actions, if they are good, lead people to believe that you are a good person. Your actions do not tell people about Jesus.

Do your words tell people about Jesus? Think about the words you use every day. We will be judged by every word we have ever spoken.

Jesus said in Matthew 12:36-37, "But I tell you that everyone will have to give account on the day of judgment for every empty word they have spoken. For by your words you will be acquitted, and by your words you will be condemned."

Samuel had a reputation, even as a young man, for bringing the word of God. It seems that by our text today, Samuel did not waste his words.

There was a time in Samuel's young life when he did not recognize the voice of God in his life. "Now Samuel did not yet know the Lord: The word of the Lord had not yet been revealed to him" (1 Sam. 3:7). As Samuel grew to know the Word of God, he became a strong man of God. "The Lord continued to appear at Shiloh, and there he revealed himself to Samuel through his word" (1 Sam. 3:21). The Lord has also appeared to us through His Word.

The Lord did not allow Samuel's words to fall to the ground. Why? Because they were valuable for helping people know the God of Creation.

What are we doing with our words? Can we say the same things about our words? Are we gossiping or using bad language, or telling crude jokes, or cursing other people, or using words in any way that does not bring glory to the Lord? If you do not know what bad language is, it is any word or phrase that is not pleasing to God.

James said it best when he talked about taming the tongue:

> *With the tongue we praise our Lord and Father, and with it we curse human beings, who have been made in God's likeness. Out of the same mouth come praise and cursing. My brothers and sisters, this should not be. Can both fresh water and salt water flow from the same spring? My brothers and sisters, can a fig tree bear olives, or a grapevine bear figs? Neither can a salt spring produce fresh water. (James 3:9-12)*

If our words are pointing people to the Lord, He will not allow them to fail. He will not allow them to "fall to the ground." The Word of God has a purpose. Isaiah 55:10-11, "As the rain and the snow come down from heaven, and do not return to it without watering the earth and making it bud and flourish, so that it yields seed for the sower and bread for the eater, so is my word that goes out from my mouth: It will not return to me empty, but will accomplish what I desire and achieve the purpose for which I sent it."

Notes

6: THE KINGDOM ERA

Week 18: Saul
1 Samuel 15:1-29

Key verse: *"But Samuel replied: 'Does the Lord delight in burnt offerings and sacrifices as much as in obeying the Lord? To obey is better than sacrifice, and to heed is better than the fat of rams.'" (1 Samuel 15:22)*

LEADER'S NOTE

You are probably asking, why are we studying Saul? Good question. We will look at Saul in this lesson, and then we will look at David. Saul is the king that the people wanted. David is the king that God wanted. It's not always good when God gives us what we want.

It is important for the students to see that Saul's sin was his disobedience. This is the root of all of our sins.

CONTEXT

In 1 Samuel 8, the people came to Samuel and asked for a king. Partly because Samuel's sons were evil, but mainly because they wanted to be like the nations around them (1 Samuel 8:4-22).

After God, through Samuel, warned the people what a king would do, He gave them what they wanted. Saul was the answer to the worldly expectation of the king. He was just like the kings of the other nations.

OPEN UP

Do you like it when your parents or teachers tell you to do something?

THINK ABOUT

What happens when we are disobedient?

READ

Verses 1-3: What was the command from God? Why is God doing this?

Verses 4-9: What did Saul do? Was he obedient?

Verses 10-11: What happened? Why is Samuel sad?

Verses 12-16: What did Saul do in verse 12? This is an indication of his heart. What happened in these verses?

Verses 17-21: Describe the discussion between Samuel and Saul. Saul said that he was obedient.

Verses 22-23: What does the Lord require of us all?

Verses 24-29: What excuse does Saul give? Is he acting like a king? Read verse 29 again. How does this apply to us?

FOCUS

> *But Samuel replied: "Does the Lord delight in burnt offerings and sacrifices as much as in obeying the Lord? To obey is better than sacrifice, and to heed is better than the fat of rams." (1 Samuel 15:22)*

When was the first time someone sinned by being disobedient to God's command? What is the best thing we can do in our life? What are some examples of giving good things to God, but not obeying Him? We can come to church, give an offering, participate in church activities, and try to be nice to everyone, but if we disobey God, these things are meaningless.

LEADER'S GUIDE—SOJOURNER BIBLE STUDY

TALK
- What is this teaching me about God?
- What is this teaching me about people?
- Why is this important to me today?

CONNECT THE GOSPEL

This is the Gospel: "For what I received I passed on to you as of first importance: that Christ died for our sins according to the Scriptures, that he was buried, that he was raised on the third day according to the Scriptures" (1 Corinthians 15:3-4 NIV).

The truth of the Gospel is wrapped up in the obedience of Jesus the Messiah. "And being found in human form, he humbled himself by becoming obedient to the point of death, even death on a cross" (Philippians 2:8). Where the judges failed, and the kings failed, Jesus did not fail. He gave us an example of obedience.

What does He ask us to do? Love God and love people.

> *"Love the Lord your God with all your heart and with all your soul and with all your mind and with all your strength." The second is this: "Love your neighbor as yourself." There is no commandment greater than these. (Mark 12:30-31)*

SO WHAT?

What does this mean to us? We can say that we follow Jesus, or we can show that we follow Jesus by the way we live in obedience to Him.

SERVE

Begin by being obedient to the people whom God has placed over you.

DIG DEEPER

> *But Samuel replied: "Does the Lord delight in burnt offerings and sacrifices as much as in obeying the Lord? To obey is better than sacrifice, and to heed is better than the fat of rams." (1 Samuel 15:22)*

The people had begged for a king so that they could be like the nations around them. Their desire to be like the world was in complete contradiction to what the Lord God had called them to be: holy (Lev. 11:45). They were called to be holy, separate.

In order for us to understand Saul's sin and downfall, we need to understand the situation: Samuel was the one the Lord had sent to anoint Saul to be the king over Israel. This was a work of God. Now, God was giving Saul a work to do. Saul was told to totally destroy the Amalekites.

Four hundred years had passed from the time of the Exodus to the time of Saul. God's timeline is different from our calendar. He will bring judgment.

Saul was going to be used to bring the wrath of God on the Amalekites because of the evil that they had done to the Israelites when they came out of Egypt. Exodus chapter 17 tells us about how Moses sent Joshua to conquer the Amalekites. In Deuteronomy chapter 25, we find the reason for destroying the Amalekites and the command to not forget.

> *Remember what the Amalekites did to you along the way when you came out of Egypt. When you were weary and worn out, they met you on your journey and attacked all who were lagging behind; they had no fear of God. When the Lord your God gives you rest from all the enemies around you in the land he is giving you to possess as an inheritance, you shall blot out the name of Amalek from under heaven. Do not forget! (Deut. 25:17-19)*

Here, in 1 Samuel chapter 15, the judgment of God was delegated to Saul to carry out, "Now go, attack the Amalekites, and totally destroy all that belongs to them. Do not spare them; put to death men and women, children and infants, cattle and sheep, camels, and donkeys" (1 Sam. 15:3). God called for the total annihilation of everything that had life.

But Saul spared the king and the best of the animals (1 Sam. 15:9). We may wonder, what is the problem with saving the animals to make a sacrifice? First, it was against the command of God. Second, by using these animals for a sacrifice, Saul would use them for his purpose: essentially putting Saul's usage of the animals above the will of God. This idea is strengthened by what we read soon after in verse 12, that Saul had set up a monument for himself in his honor.

When Saul was confronted by Samuel, Saul said that he had carried out the command. "I went on the mission the Lord assigned me. I completely destroyed the Amalekites and brought back Agag their king. The soldiers took sheep and cattle from the plunder, the best of what was devoted to God, in order to sacrifice them to the Lord your God at Gilgal" (1 Sam. 15:20-21). This is similar to saying, "I did everything you told me, but…"

Jesus equated love for Him with obedience to Him. John 14:15, "If you love me, keep my commands."

The Apostle John, in his first epistle, explains very clearly that our obedience reveals our faith, "We know that we have come to know him if we keep his commands. Whoever says, 'I know him,' but does not do what he commands is a liar, and the truth is not in that person. But if anyone obeys his word, love for God is truly made complete in them. This is how we know we are in him: Whoever claims to live in him must live as Jesus did." (1 John 2:3-6)

John said that whoever claims to live in Christ must live as He did. How did Jesus live? He lived in complete obedience to God the Father, and He gave us an example of how to live.

In Genesis chapter 3, we read about the disobedience of the first man and woman. They were separated from God, and death entered the world. In Genesis chapter 6, God regretted making humans. Here, in 1 Samuel 15:11, the Lord God regretted making Saul king. It is still possible today to bring grief to the Spirit of God? (Ephesians 4:30)

Saul and his army believed that they were doing a good thing by making a sacrifice to God. However, God had not asked for a sacrifice; instead, He commanded them to totally destroy the Amalekites.

Are we doing good religious things while living in disobedience to God? If we love Him, we will keep His commandments.

Notes

LEADER'S GUIDE—SOJOURNER BIBLE STUDY

Week 19: David's Obedience to the Covenant
2 Samuel 7:1-29

Key verse: *"He shall build a house for My Name, and I will establish the throne of His Kingdom forever." (2 Samuel 7:13)*

LEADER'S NOTE

This week we are looking at David. His kingly success is described in chapter 8. His kingly sin and its effects are described over eleven chapters, chapters 10-20.

David's life demonstrates the need for another King who will come in purity and absolute loyalty to the Lord. In chapter 7 verse 13, we see the plan of God continue to unfold.

As the class leader, help your students see that David was a great king, but he wasn't the best king. There would be One King with an eternal kingdom.

CONTEXT

Samuel will anoint David to be the king after Saul in approximately the year 1010 B.C. David would reign until 970 B.C.

God allowed Saul to be a king to give the people a picture of the problem of their request. They didn't want God to rule over them. Now, God will use David to give the people a picture of a man after God's heart. First Samuel 13:14, Samuel speaks to Saul: "But now your kingdom will not endure; the Lord has sought out a man after his own heart and appointed him ruler of his people, because you have not kept the Lord's command."

This doesn't refer to David's moral character. He was a lying, murdering adulterer. However, he was committed to God's Law. When David sinned, he was broken over it. Whereas Saul was not.

OPEN UP

Do you ever stop to think that people know you by your name? So, when you do something, good or bad, it reflects on your name.

THINK ABOUT

What does it mean to call yourself a Christian?

READ

Verses 1-3: What does David want to do? Why?

Verses 4-16: What does God say to David through Nathan?

Verses 17-29: What does David say about God? (Leaders: spend time on these verses. Help the students understand how David feels about God.)

FOCUS

"He shall build a house for My Name, and I will establish the throne of His Kingdom forever." (2 Samuel 7:13)

We know that Solomon will follow David as king. In verse 14, God says that He will discipline David's son when he sins. So, we know that Solomon will not be the eternal king. So, what is God saying about an eternal kingdom? Read verse 16: "And your house and your kingdom shall endure before Me forever; your throne shall be established forever."

We need to remember Genesis 3:15, that the Seed of the woman will crush the head of the serpent. Now we are seeing the promise of an eternal kingdom, so there must be an eternal King coming one day.

TALK

- What is this teaching me about God?
- What is this teaching me about people?
- Why is this important to me today?

CONNECT THE GOSPEL

This is the Gospel: "For what I received I passed on to you as of first importance: that Christ died for our sins according to the Scriptures, that he was buried, that he was raised on the third day according to the Scriptures" (1 Corinthians 15:3-4 NIV).

The Gospel is the plan of God to restore people to Himself by paying the penalty for our sins.

The wages of sin is death, but the gift of God is eternal life in Christ Jesus. (Romans 6:23)

If God has promised an eternal kingdom, why would He raise Jesus from the dead? Is Jesus a descendant of David? See Matthew 1:1-17. Because Jesus overcame death and lives, He is worthy to be the eternal King.

SO WHAT?

What is the big deal about this promise to David? It shows the plan of God from the beginning. Just as Boaz was the picture of a kinsman-redeemer, now we see the promise of an eternal King.

SERVE

If God has promised an eternal King, and if that King is Jesus, should we submit to Him? If the answer is yes, should we help other people understand that God's plan is for them also? Find ways to talk about your King this week.

DIG DEEPER

He shall build a house for My Name, and I will establish the throne of His Kingdom forever. (2 Samuel 7:13)

David had the desire to build a house for God, but God was building an eternal house in His eternal kingdom, and He was doing it through David's line. The Gospel of Matthew is the first book of the New Testament, not because it was written first but because it connects Abraham, David, and the Messiah. Matthew 1:17 gives us the summary: "Thus there were fourteen generations in all from Abraham to David, fourteen from David to the exile to Babylon, and fourteen from the exile to the Messiah."

In this promise to David in 2 Samuel 7:13, God permitted the son of David to build the temple. The temple was a symbol of God dwelling among His people. This man-made temple was not eternal. The royal line after Solomon was not perfect, nor was it sinless. God was pointing ahead to a perfect King.

God was pointing ahead, through David, to a time of an eternal house and an eternal kingdom. When God told Isaiah that the virgin would have a son and name him Immanuel, God was pointing ahead to His presence among His people ("Immanuel, God with us," Isaiah 7:14). When the Gospel of John tells us that the Word became flesh and made His dwelling among us, John was telling us that the Lord God is not living in a man-made temple (John 1:14).

The Apostle John gave us the answer to 2 Samuel 7:13 in Revelation 21:3-5:

> *And I heard a loud voice from the throne saying, "Look! God's dwelling place is now among the people, and he will dwell with them. They will be his people, and God himself will be with them and be their God. He will wipe every tear from their eyes. There will be no more death or mourning or crying or pain, for the old order of things has passed away." He who was seated on the throne said, "I am making everything new!" Then he said, "Write this down, for these words are trustworthy and true."*

Blind Bartimaeus saw what many in his day could not see, and he begged for mercy, "Jesus, Son of David, have mercy on me!" (Luke 18:38). Jesus told Bartimaeus that his faith made him whole, healed.

Welcome to the eternal kingdom, Bartimaeus!

Notes

Week 20: David's Prophecies
Psalm 22:1-31

Key verse: "They will proclaim his righteousness, declaring to a people yet unborn: He has done it!" (Psalm 22:31)

LEADER'S NOTE

There are 150 psalms, and we obviously will not cover them all in this lesson. What we want to do is help the students see the Messiah in Psalm 22. This psalm is rich in Messianic prophecy. Help the students to understand that these prophecies were written a thousand years before Jesus was born.

CONTEXT

The book of Psalms is divided into five separate groupings or books. Each division concludes with a doxology that reflects Israel's history. They were written by David, Asaph, the sons of Korah, and others.

If you find yourself looking for something in the Bible to read, turn to the Psalms. A great place to begin is Psalm 119, because it speaks of the greatness of the Word of God.

OPEN UP

How is it possible to write about an event one thousand years before it happens?

THINK ABOUT

Verse 16 says his hands and feet were pierced. When was crucifixion used as punishment? (6th century B.C., 400-500 years after David wrote this!)

READ

Verse 1: What does it mean to be forsaken? (Matthew 27:46).

Verses 6-8: What are the people saying to this man? (Matthew 27:43).

Verses 12-18: What are the people doing? How is the man feeling? (Matthew 27:35; Mark 15:33-37; John 19:28).

Verses 27-31: What are the future promises? (Psalm 78:6).

FOCUS

They will proclaim his righteousness, declaring to a people yet unborn: He has done it! (Psalm 22:31).

Who will proclaim the righteousness of the Messiah? Who are the people who will hear? Are you one of them?

David wrote about the righteous Messiah. The righteousness of the Messiah was proclaimed through the prophets as they waited for His arrival.

LEADER'S GUIDE—SOJOURNER BIBLE STUDY

TALK
- What is this teaching me about God?
- What is this teaching me about people?
- Why is this important to me today?

CONNECT THE GOSPEL

This is the Gospel: "For what I received I passed on to you as of first importance: that Christ died for our sins according to the Scriptures, that he was buried, that he was raised on the third day according to the Scriptures" (1 Corinthians 15:3-4 NIV).

Jesus died for our sins according to the Scriptures? Which Scriptures? There are 332 prophecies in the Old Testament that Jesus fulfilled. These prophecies cover everything from His birth to His death.

Psalm 22 and Isaiah 53 are vivid pictures of His death. Here in Psalm 22, we read one of those places Paul was writing about when he wrote to the church at Corinth.

SO WHAT?

If the Bible is true, then what is so important about these Messianic prophecies, especially Psalm 22? Why is this important to us? If David wrote about the Messiah, if he wrote about crucifixion many years before these events, do you think that God has a plan?

If these Messianic prophecies are true, then shouldn't we be paying attention to the prophecies about His second coming which have not been fulfilled yet?

SERVE

The Bible says that the righteousness of the Messiah will be declared to coming generations. How can you tell people this week that God has a plan that has been in action since the beginning of time?

DIG DEEPER

They will proclaim his righteousness, declaring to a people yet unborn: He has done it! (Psalm 22:31)

God promised an eternal kingdom through the line of David. This eternal kingdom would have the Son of David on its throne. The Lord God revealed this Messiah to the prophets of which David was one, and David revealed Him to us in his Psalms.

Peter said this about the prophets and how they wrote looking forward to the coming Messiah:

> *Concerning this salvation, the prophets, who spoke of the grace that was to come to you, searched intently and with the greatest care, trying to find out the time and circumstances to which the Spirit of Christ in them was pointing when he predicted the sufferings of the Messiah and the glories that would follow. It was revealed to them that they were not serving themselves but you, when they spoke of the things that have now been told you by those who have preached the Gospel to you by the Holy Spirit sent from heaven. Even angels long to look into these things. (1 Peter 1:10-12)*

We should consider what the Lord showed David, and he recorded for us in Psalm 22: The Messiah would be forsaken by God (Mat. 27:46). The Patriarchs, Abraham, Moses, and David were all honored, but the Messiah was despised by men. Psalm 22:6, "But I am a worm and not a man, scorned by everyone, despised by the people."

David said that this One would be mocked and ridiculed, verses 7-8. Matthew wrote, "Those who passed by hurled insults at him, shaking their heads" (Mat. 27:39). Then He was crucified, pierced, and they cast lots for His clothing (Psalm 22:16-18). About Jesus, Matthew 27:35, "When they had crucified him, they divided up his clothes by casting lots."

A thousand years before the birth of Jesus, David, the prophet and king, gave us the picture of the Messiah. It was recorded for the future generations to know the righteousness of God.

Earlier in our studies, we learned how the generation after Joshua did not know the Lord God. We talked about "entrusting" the word of God to faithful people.

God told Abraham that the nations would be blessed through him. David wrote, "All the ends of the earth will remember and turn to the Lord, and all the families of the nations will bow down before him, for dominion belongs to the Lord and he rules over the nations" (Psalm 22:27-28).

Isaiah also talked about this Messiah and how many would hear about Him: "Just as there were many who were appalled at him—his appearance was so disfigured beyond that of any human being and his form marred beyond human likeness—so he will sprinkle many nations, and kings will shut their mouths because of him. For what they were not told, they will see, and what they have not heard, they will understand" (Isa. 52:14).

Jesus prayed for those who would hear about this message in the future: "My prayer is not for them alone. I pray also for those who will believe in me through their message, that all of them may be one, Father, just as you are in me and I am in you. May they also be in us so that the world may believe that you have sent me" (John 17:20-21).

Matthew 28:19, Jesus sent His disciples to proclaim His righteousness around the world: "Therefore go and make disciples of all nations, baptizing them in the name of the Father and of the Son and of the Holy Spirit." We also have this command to proclaim the righteousness of God that is the person of Jesus the Messiah.

Notes

LEADER'S GUIDE—SOJOURNER BIBLE STUDY

Week 21: Solomon
1 Kings 3:4-14 and 1 Kings 11:1-13

Key verse: *"Yet I will not tear the whole kingdom from him, but will give him one tribe for the sake of David my servant and for the sake of Jerusalem, which I have chosen." (1 Kings 11:13)*

LEADER'S NOTE

There is so much to study under the heading of Solomon. You may decide to just look at some of the Proverbs and focus on "the fear of the Lord is the beginning of wisdom."

Help the students see that Solomon had a relationship with God, but after God blessed him, he turned away from God and began to follow his desire for women, money, and power. His desire for women was what turned his heart away from God.

CONTEXT

The time of Solomon is 970-931 B.C. He was the son of David and Bathsheba. He is known as the wisest man to ever live. He was also far from perfect.

Why would we study Solomon? He wrote most of the Proverbs. He wrote Ecclesiastes and the Song of Solomon (or Song of Songs).

He was also the last king to rule Israel as a united kingdom. His failures, spiritually and morally, led to the downfall and division of Israel.

OPEN UP

How would you feel if God gave you everything you wanted?

THINK ABOUT

If you are content in your life, would you want to follow God?

READ

1 Kings 3:

Verse 4: What do we learn about Solomon?

Verse 5: What did God say?

Verses 6-9: What does Solomon say?

Verses 10-13: What is God's response to Solomon?

Verse 14: What is the "if", "then"?

1 Kings 11:

Verses 1-6: What happened?

Verses 7-8: What did he do? This was mentioned in chapter 3, but it seemed small then.

Verses 9-10: How many times did the Lord appear to Solomon and warn him?

Verses 11-12: What is the punishment?

Verse 13: What is the promise?

FOCUS

> *Yet I will not tear the whole kingdom from him, but will give him one tribe for the sake of David my servant and for the sake of Jerusalem which I have chosen. (1 Kings 11:13)*

A question we need to ask today is this: does God keep His promises? Do you remember the promise that was made in Genesis 3:15? The Seed of the woman will crush the head of the serpent. Throughout Scripture we see God protecting a line of people for Himself because God will not break His promise.

Look at Numbers 23:19: "God is not a man, so he does not lie. He is not human, so he does not change his mind. Has he ever spoken and failed to act? Has he ever promised and not carried it through?" God made an agreement, or covenant, with Solomon, but Solomon broke it. So, God began to take the kingdom away. However, because God does not break His promises, He preserves a line to fulfill the Promise of Genesis 3:15. That Seed will come from the line of David, so God will not destroy the tribe of Judah.

TALK

- What is this teaching me about God?
- What is this teaching me about people?
- Why is this important to me today?

CONNECT THE GOSPEL

This is the Gospel: "For what I received I passed on to you as of first importance: that Christ died for our sins according to the Scriptures, that he was buried, that he was raised on the third day according to the Scriptures" (1 Corinthians 15:3-4 NIV).

Solomon was a great king. He was very wise, and people from all over the world visited him and brought him gifts, but Solomon wasn't perfect. He had an opportunity to point people to the God of Creation, but he focused on pleasing himself.

Jesus in Matthew chapter 12 talked about how people came to listen to Solomon, but verse 42 says, "The Queen of the South will rise at the judgment with this generation and condemn it; for she came from the ends of the earth to listen to Solomon's wisdom, and now something greater than Solomon is here."

When God promised Solomon that He would save a tribe for the sake of David, He was preparing the way for His Son Jesus. The greatest people, wealthiest people, and smartest people will get a lot of attention, but they can't save us. We need Someone greater. We need Jesus.

Wealth and fame attract a lot of attention. People from every nation went to visit Solomon. We may not be as famous as Solomon, but we also have opportunities every day to tell people about Jesus.

SO WHAT?

So what? A smart, rich man had a lot of girlfriends and temples, and he lost his kingdom. What does that mean to me today?

We need to see that everything the world craves can't satisfy us. We need Jesus. He may give us everything or nothing, and that's ok. Jesus is actually all we need. Here is what Solomon wrote in his last days from Ecclesiastes 12:13-14: "Now all has been heard; here is the conclusion of the matter: Fear God and keep his commandments, for this is the duty of all mankind. For God will bring every deed into judgment, including every hidden thing, whether it is good or evil."

SERVE

Do you have friends who want to have a lot of money, or things, or girlfriends or boyfriends? Think about how you can help them see that Jesus is what they need more than anything.

DIG DEEPER

> *Yet I will not tear the whole kingdom from him, but will give him one tribe for the sake of David my servant and for the sake of Jerusalem, which I have chosen. (1 Kings 11:13)*

God had promised that the Seed of the woman would crush the head of the serpent in Genesis 3:15. Because of this promise, God protected a line.

In Genesis chapter 4, after Cain killed Abel, God gave Eve a son whom she named Seth. Genesis 4:26, "Seth also had a son, and he named him Enosh. At that time people began to call on the name of the Lord." It would be the line of Seth that would separate from the others and give us the Messiah.

This godly line would produce Noah, whom the Lord would save while everyone else was destroyed. This line produced Abraham and separated him from an ungodly nation to prepare a place and a people for the Messiah and a blessing for the nations. This line would produce Judah and his brothers, whom God delivered from bondage. This line produced David, whom God used to establish His Kingdom and prepare us for the King of Kings. (The genealogy of Jesus from Adam is found in Luke 3.)

To understand this royal line, we need to look at the genealogy of Jesus, and we will begin with David, then Solomon and his descendants. In Matthew 1:6-16, we see that Joseph, the husband of Mary, was descended from Solomon. According to Luke 3:31, Mary was also a descendant of David through David's son Nathan.

God's promise of an eternal Throne from the line of David was passed down through the prophets. Jeremiah 33:14-17,

> *"The days are coming," declares the Lord, "when I will fulfill the good promise I made to the people of Israel and Judah. In those days and at that time I will make a righteous Branch sprout from David's line; he will do what is just and right in the land. In those days Judah will be saved and Jerusalem will live in safety. This is the name by which it will be called: The Lord Our Righteous Savior." For this is what the Lord says: 'David will never fail to have a man to sit on the throne of Israel.*

Isaiah saw the glory of this promise, Isa. 9:6-7,

> *For to us a child is born, to us a son is given, and the government will be on his shoulders. And he will be called Wonderful Counselor, Mighty God, Everlasting Father, Prince of Peace. Of the greatness of his government and peace there will be no end. He will reign on David's throne and over his kingdom, establishing and upholding it with justice and righteousness from that time on and forever. The zeal of the Lord Almighty will accomplish this.*

The promise to David and the nation of Israel, and by adoption the promise is ours too, was fulfilled in the birth of Jesus the Messiah. Luke 1:31-33, "You will conceive and give birth to a son, and you are to call him Jesus. He will be great and will be called the Son of the Most High. The Lord God will give him the throne of his father David, and he will reign over Jacob's descendants forever; his kingdom will never end."

That brings us to the failure of Solomon. It is obvious that Solomon was not the eternal king. God did not fail, but Solomon did. The plan of God is not dependent upon people.

The plan of God is dependent on God. Therefore, the promise of 2 Samuel 7:16, "Your house and your kingdom will endure forever before me; your throne will be established forever," is confirmed here in today's verse. We can trust the plan, purpose, and promise of God.

This verse, 1 Kings 11:13, "Yet I will not tear the whole kingdom from him, but will give him one tribe for the sake of David my servant and for the sake of Jerusalem, which I have chosen," has been fulfilled in Jesus.

In Christ, we are the "one tribe." "There is neither Jew nor Gentile, neither slave nor free, nor is there male and female, for you are all one in Christ Jesus" (Gal. 3:28).

Notes

LEADER'S GUIDE—SOJOURNER BIBLE STUDY

Week 22: Proverbs (or Christmas)
Proverbs 1:1-7; 8:22-31

Key verse: *"The fear of the Lord is the beginning of knowledge, but fools despise wisdom and instruction." (Proverbs 1:7)*

LEADER'S NOTE

Solomon wrote most of the Proverbs. There are two major themes found in the Proverbs: Attain wisdom and reject folly; walk in righteousness and avoid evil.

You can remind the students that the Proverbs are good advice, but they don't cover every situation. The key in every situation is to think about how a question, a choice, or a decision will affect our walk with the Lord.

Help the students to understand what it means to fear the Lord. This involves respect for the One in authority, and it involves the fear of His wrath.

Here is a quote from David Platt from his Secret Church lesson on the Proverbs: "The goal of wisdom literature is to apply the Word to practical living."

CONTEXT

The time of the Proverbs is 970-930 B.C. Solomon is the new king, and the Lord had granted him wisdom.

In chapter 1, we see the key to knowing the Lord, and we see the value of knowledge. In chapter 8, we see that Jesus is ultimately the wisdom of God.

Many times, you will see the pronoun "she" used to talk about wisdom. This is because the Hebrew word for wisdom receives the feminine gender assignment, similar to the way Spanish says that a ball is a pelota, with a feminine assignment although the ball is not a girl.

OPEN UP

What's the difference between wisdom and knowledge?

THINK ABOUT

Have you ever seen a smart person do something dumb?

READ

Chapter 1:

Verses 1-4: What are the purposes of the Proverbs?

Verses 5-6: What do we learn about wise people?

Verse 7: Can a foolish person know the Lord?

Chapter 8:

Verses 22-29: How would you compare these verses to Genesis chapter 1?

Verses 30-31: What is He telling us?

6: THE KINGDOM ERA

FOCUS

The fear of the Lord is the beginning of knowledge, but fools despise wisdom and instruction. (Proverbs 1:7)

Should we fear the Lord? If you say yes, why? If you say no, why not? Should we respect the One Who created us? Should we fear the One Who has the ability to destroy the earth with a flood because people were wicked?

TALK

- What is this teaching me about God?
- What is this teaching me about people?
- Why is this important to me today?

CONNECT THE GOSPEL

This is the Gospel: "For what I received I passed on to you as of first importance: that Christ died for our sins according to the Scriptures, that he was buried, that he was raised on the third day according to the Scriptures" (1 Corinthians 15:3-4 NIV).

How can we know that the Gospel is true? How can we know anything about God?

In the Old Testament, God revealed Himself to the people through His prophets. In the New Testament, God revealed Himself in Jesus. Colossians 1:15 tells us that, "The Son is the image of the invisible God, the firstborn over all creation." If Jesus is the revelation of God, if He is the Wisdom of God, and if we want to know if this is true, then we need to ask Him to help us understand Him.

If any of you lacks wisdom, you should ask God, who gives generously to all without finding fault, and it will be given to you. (James 1:5)

The "good news" of the Gospel is that it is true. God has revealed Himself to us in Christ, and He has made a way for us to know Him.

SO WHAT?

Many people want to be smart, go to college, and be someone famous or special. How does that happen? They need to learn a lot. Who do they go to for learning? They need a teacher.

Think of all of your teachers. Do they know everything? Are they perfect? They can teach you a lot, but they can't teach you everything, especially if they don't know everything. Would it make sense then to begin seeking wisdom from the God of the universe first? If you or your friends are struggling in school, check your relationship with Jesus. Are you right with Him? Are you spending time with Him?

SERVE

You are surrounded by a lot of smart people, and you are surrounded by a lot of people who make bad choices. How do you choose who to spend time with?

Do you have friends who need help making good choices? Why don't you share some of the Proverbs with them? Help them find wisdom by knowing Jesus first.

DIG DEEPER

The fear of the Lord is the beginning of knowledge, but fools despise wisdom and instruction. (Proverbs 1:7)

Most people don't want to talk about the fear of the Lord, and those who do will say it is a "respectful" fear. We live in a time when we think of God in the same way we think of imaginary characters such as Santa Claus and the Easter Bunny. We believe in the god we have created in our minds, and not the God who created our mind. As we dig deeper today, we are going to see that the Lord God is someone to fear for those who do not know Him or follow Him.

In Genesis 7, God destroyed the earth with water. This was a symbol of the wrath of God being poured out on His creation.

In the exodus from Egypt, God brought ten plagues on everyone who did not fear Him. In the last plague, God killed the firstborn of every person and every animal. Moses warned the people, "be careful that you do not forget the Lord who brought you out of the land of Egypt, out of the house of slavery. You shall fear only the Lord your God; and you shall worship Him and swear by His name" (Deut. 6:12-13).

When Joshua brought the Hebrew people across the Red Sea, he had them place twelve stones as a memorial. He wanted them to remember what God had done for them. Joshua 4:23-24, "For the Lord your God dried up the waters of the Jordan before you until you had crossed, just as the Lord your God had done to the Red Sea, which He dried up before us until we had crossed; so that all the peoples of the earth may know that the hand of the Lord is mighty, so that you may fear the Lord your God forever."

The King of Assyria attempted to take the land of Judah during the reign of Hezekiah, but God destroyed his army in one night! "Then it happened that night that the angel of the Lord went out and struck 185,000 in the camp of the Assyrians; and when the rest got up early in the morning, behold, all of the 185,000 were dead" (2 Kings 19:35).

When Jesus warned His followers of the persecution they would face, He also warned them about Who they really needed to fear: Matthew 10:28, "And do not be afraid of those who kill the body but are unable to kill the soul; but rather fear Him who is able to destroy both soul and body in hell."

> *By this, love is perfected with us, so that we may have confidence in the day of judgment; because as He is, we also are in this world. There is no fear in love, but perfect love drives out fear, because fear involves punishment, and the one who fears is not perfected in love. (1 John 4:17-18)*

Proverbs 1:7, "The fear of the Lord is the beginning of knowledge, but fools despise wisdom and instruction." When we understand Who God is, we can begin to know Him.

This knowledge is the knowledge that will lead us to salvation. Contrast the knowledge of the Lord with the fool who resists Him: "The fool has said in his heart there is no God" (Psalm 14:1).

Notes

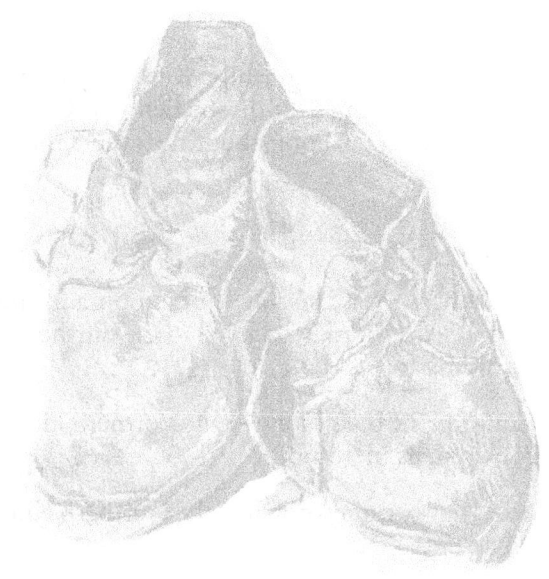

7: The Divided Kingdom Era

LEADER'S GUIDE—SOJOURNER BIBLE STUDY

Week 23: The Kingdom Splits
1 Kings 12:1-33

Key verse: *"Thus says the LORD, 'You must not go up and fight against your relatives the sons of Israel; return every man to his house, for this thing has come from Me.'" (1 Kings 12:24)*

LEADER'S NOTE

Now then, if you will indeed obey My voice and keep My covenant, then you shall be My own possession among all the peoples, for all the earth is Mine. (Exodus 19:5)

God had made it clear to the people that they had a responsibility in this relationship. We want the students to understand that when we go against God and His plan, it creates division. Our disobedience to God affects our relationships with our family and our friends. Try to spend some time talking about the events that led to this division. Use it as a review.

CONTEXT

The division came after the death of Solomon in 931 B.C. Rehoboam was the son of Solomon and the new king. However, Rehoboam had some bad advisors, which led to bad decisions, which led to the northern tribes under Jeroboam rebelling. And all of this came from God, according to verse 24.

God would allow the Northern Kingdom to fall to the Assyrians in 722 B.C. None of the northern kings were good. The south had a few good kings, but they fell to the Babylonians in 586 B.C.

God separated the nation of Israel because of their disobedience. They became known as the Northern Kingdom (known as Israel or Samaria) and the Southern Kingdom (Judah).

OPEN UP

Have you ever had a problem in a relationship? Are you willing to talk about what caused the problem?

THINK ABOUT

Has disobedience ever created a problem in your relationships?

READ

Verse 1: What happened? It's interesting that they met at Shechem, which was the capitol of the north, and also came to be identified with the sin of the north.

Verses 2-14: What happened? Who did the king listen to?

Verse 15: Why did this happen? Will God do what He says He is going to do?

Verse 16: What is happening here? The house of David is also known as the Tribe of Judah, which became the Southern Kingdom and was referred to as Judah.

Verses 17-20: What happened?

Verses 21-24: What happened? It's interesting that in this incident the people listened to the Word of the LORD.

Verses 25-33: What happened? What are some of the sins committed by Jeroboam and the people?

7: THE DIVIDED KINGDOM ERA

FOCUS

> *Thus says the LORD, "You must not go up and fight against your relatives the sons of Israel; return every man to his house, for this thing has come from Me." (Kings 12:24)*

How did the nation of Israel fall into this situation? Think about our lessons, and can you see places where the people were disobedient to God? What would have happened to the Jewish people if the Lord had not stopped them from fighting each other?

TALK

- What is this teaching me about God?
- What is this teaching me about people?
- Why is this important to me today?

CONNECT THE GOSPEL

This is the Gospel: "For what I received I passed on to you as of first importance: that Christ died for our sins according to the Scriptures, that he was buried, that he was raised on the third day according to the Scriptures" (1 Corinthians 15:3-4 NIV).

What is the message of the Gospel in broken relationships, especially when the split is the direct result of sin? A relationship needs someone to bring reconciliation. God had a plan to bring Israel and Judah together again.

Look at what Ezekiel said in Ezekiel 37:22-28: "I will make them one nation in the land, on the mountains of Israel. There will be one king over all of them and they will never again be two nations or be divided into two kingdoms. They will no longer defile themselves with their idols and vile images or with any of their offenses, for I will save them from all their sinful backsliding, and I will cleanse them. They will be my people, and I will be their God."

See the Gospel: when God allowed the nation to be divided, He also had a plan to bring healing and restoration. Only through Jesus can we have a restored relationship with God our Father and with other people.

SO WHAT?

So what? Why should we care about something that happened three thousand years ago?

If you want to disobey God, He will allow you to be separated from Him. If you are separated from Him now, He has made a way to be restored to Him. Sin caused the division of Israel. Sin causes us to be separated from family and friends and God. Only in faith in Jesus can our relationships be healed.

In Isaiah 49:6, God said through the prophet Isaiah that He wasn't just going to save Israel through the Messiah, but all nations: "He says, 'You will do more than restore the people of Israel to me. I will make you a light to the Gentiles, and you will bring my salvation to the ends of the earth.'"

SERVE

Do you know of any broken relationships? What can you do to help bring healing?

DIG DEEPER

> *Thus says the LORD, You must not go up and fight against your relatives the sons of Israel; return every man to his house, for this thing has come from Me. (1 Kings 12:24)*

In our lesson today, God sent a prophet to Rehoboam and told him not to go to war. Rehoboam was obedient to this warning. If Rehoboam had continued on this path, he would have been fighting against his relatives. He would also have been in opposition to God.

Rehoboam and his army had a good chance of victory with one hundred eighty thousand soldiers, but the victory would have been at a great loss to all of the Jewish people. They "hearkened" to the Word of God (they listened and obeyed).

It was not the plan of God for His people to be divided; however, God will not tolerate sin and disobedience. "To obey is better than sacrifice."

We know that God made a promise to David to establish an eternal kingdom, and we know that Solomon broke the covenant with God. In today's lesson, we see the result of God's punishment against His people.

The divided kingdom also created divided worship. Jeroboam set up golden calves in Dan and Bethel. He told the people of the northern kingdom that they did not need to go all the way to Jerusalem to worship (1 Kings 12:29).

The northern government was established on idolatry, and they had turned from the Lord God. Judah maintained the worship of God in Jerusalem. However, Judah was weakened by the loss of people to the north.

We read this earlier in our lesson today, Ezekiel 37:22-28,

> *I will make them one nation in the land, on the mountains of Israel. There will be one king over all of them and they will never again be two nations or be divided into two kingdoms. They will no longer defile themselves with their idols and vile images or with any of their offenses, for I will save them from all their sinful backsliding, and I will cleanse them. They will be my people, and I will be their God.*

The Lord God allowed the kingdom to be divided, and He will provide a way for it to be restored and reconciled. Jeremiah 31:31 tells us of a day when the kingdoms will be united under one King, "'The days are coming,' declares the Lord, 'when I will make a new covenant with the people of Israel and with the people of Judah.'"

As of today, the nation of Israel consists primarily of people from the tribe of Judah. They are not united under one King. Many commentators believe the unity of Israel, and all nations, will occur when Christ returns to establish His eternal kingdom.

When Jesus met the woman at the well, we saw the beginning of God's plan for national reconciliation. John 4:19-21, "The woman said to Him, 'Sir, I perceive that You are a prophet. Our fathers worshiped on this mountain, and yet you Jews say that in Jerusalem is the place where one must worship.' Jesus said to her, 'Believe Me, woman, that a time is coming when you will worship the Father neither on this mountain nor in Jerusalem.'"

We do not always understand divisions and broken relationships in our lives. Some may be from God for a reason. We do know that in Christ, He can bring reconciliation.

Notes

7: THE DIVIDED KINGDOM ERA

Week 24: The Fall of Israel and the Promised Redemption
Isaiah 2:1-4; 9:1-7; 56:8

Key verse: *"The Lord God, who gathers the dispersed of Israel, declares, 'Yet others I will gather to them, to those already gathered.'" (Isaiah 56:8)*

LEADER'S NOTE

We closed last week's session of "So What" with Isaiah 49:6, and the picture of the salvation of God going out to the ends of the earth.

We want the students to see that while the people of God had failed, and they were going through the promised judgment of God, it was not the end. The promise given in Genesis 3:15 will be fulfilled. Isaiah gives us several prophecies of the coming Messiah, Messianic Prophecies.

As you prepare for the lesson, we encourage you to preview these verses or find others that show the hope of the Promised Messiah in the middle of what appears to be a hopeless situation, and show the plan of God for all peoples.

CONTEXT

The name Isaiah is from the Hebrew *Yesha'yahu*, which means "God saves." The book of Isaiah gives us the picture of judgment and salvation for the people of God.

Israel had failed to follow God, and their judgment was coming, as the Lord had promised. He also gave them the hope of salvation.

The Northern Kingdom fell to the Assyrians in 722-721 B.C. Isaiah saw the fall of the north to Assyria, and he saw the fall of the south to the Babylonians. The book of Isaiah is a miniature Bible. The first 39 chapters, like the Old Testament, show the effects of sin and God's judgment. The last 27 chapters, like the New Testament, tell us about the comfort of God.

OPEN UP

Have you ever felt like God was far away from you?

THINK ABOUT

Have you ever been in a situation that seemed hopeless? Maybe it was at school, or at home. Maybe you are in it now.

READ

Isaiah 2:1-4: What do we see in these verses? What is going to happen? What will the people be seeking? Is that happening today?

Isaiah 9:1-7: (Zebulun and Naphtali were two of the northern tribes. They were destroyed by the Assyrians.) What do we learn in verse 1? What do we learn in verses 2-3? What happens in verses 4-7?

Isaiah 56:8: Who are the two groups being gathered? What is an "exile"?

LEADER'S GUIDE—SOJOURNER BIBLE STUDY

FOCUS

> *The Lord God, who gathers the dispersed of Israel, declares, "Yet others I will gather to them, to those already gathered." (Isaiah 56:8)*

During the days of King Solomon, God had determined that the Kingdom would be divided because of the sins of Solomon and the people. In this verse, look at Who is performing all of the action. Who dispersed the people? Who will gather the people? Why would God do this?

TALK

- What is this teaching me about God?
- What is this teaching me about people?
- Why is this important to me today?

CONNECT THE GOSPEL

This is the Gospel: "For what I received I passed on to you as of first importance: that Christ died for our sins according to the Scriptures, that he was buried, that he was raised on the third day according to the Scriptures" (1 Corinthians 15:3-4 NIV).

The Gospel, the "good news" of Jesus' death, burial, and resurrection to take the punishment for our sin and give us life is the picture of restoration. This Gospel is "good news" for all peoples, not just Israel.

How do you see God working to bring people to Himself in the verses that we read today?

SO WHAT?

What's the big deal about a promise that was made 2,700 years ago? How does it affect me now? That's a good question.

You and I have also sinned against God. We have been separated from God just like the nation of Israel was separated from Him. God allowed them to suffer in their situation, and He allows us to suffer in our situation. However, He also makes a way for us to be right with Him again.

It's a big deal, because we are part of that group of "others" He was talking about.

SERVE

How can you get this message to someone who is separated from God? How can you tell someone this week that God has brought light into a dark world?

When was the last time you told someone about how you were separated from God because of your sin, but God made a way for you to be restored to Himself?

DIG DEEPER

> *The Lord God, who gathers the dispersed of Israel, declares, "Yet others I will gather to them, to those already gathered." (Isaiah 56:8)*

The nation of Israel was divided after the death of Solomon because Solomon had broken his covenant with God. Solomon did not remain faithful to the God of Israel; instead, he went after the gods of all his wives. Our God will not share His glory with another (Isa. 42:8).

Deuteronomy 7:6-8 tells us that the Lord chose Israel because He loved them, not because they were righteous. In that love, God made a covenant with His people beginning with Abraham, that all the nations, *ethne*, would be blessed through him.

Isaiah prophesied during a dark time in the history of the Hebrew people. Their kingdom had been divided, and they had suffered greatly under ungodly leaders. Now the Assyrians were about to take the northern kingdom into captivity. Isaiah's message for the people of Israel was a message of hope. Even though God was disciplining them, He would also restore them.

> *He says, "It is too small a thing that You should be My Servant to raise up the tribes of Jacob and to restore the protected ones of Israel; I will also make You a light of the nations, so that My salvation may reach to the end of the earth." (Isaiah 49:6)*

This would be the work of the Messiah, the Anointed One. In Isaiah 56:8, it is the Lord God who is doing all the work, and He would also be the One to restore Israel and others to Himself.

When Mary and Joseph brought Jesus to the temple to fulfill the custom of the Jews, they met Simeon. Simeon had been promised by God that he would not die until he saw the Lord's Messiah. Luke 2:30-32, "For my eyes have seen Your salvation, which You have prepared in the presence of all the peoples: A light for revelation for the Gentiles, and the glory of Your people Israel."

The prince of this world, Satan, has been creating division and causing destruction in the lives of people since Genesis chapter 3. God promised that Satan would be crushed. In John 12:31-32, Jesus said, "Now is the time for judgment on this world; now the prince of this world will be driven out. And I, when I am lifted up from the earth, will draw all people to myself."

The promise to Israel was also a promise for us. In John 17:20-21, Jesus prayed for the people who would hear the message that we would be united, one: "I am not asking on behalf of these alone, but also for those who believe in Me through their word, that they may all be one; just as You, Father, are in Me and I in You, that they also may be in Us, so that the world may believe that You sent Me."

In Acts 1:8, Jesus told His followers that they would receive power from the Holy Spirit to go and tell the world about Him. The Power of God works in people to accomplish the Promise of God to His people to reconcile us to Himself.

> *For I am not ashamed of the Gospel, for it is the power of God for salvation to everyone who believes, to the Jew first and also to the Greek. (Romans 1:16)*

Notes

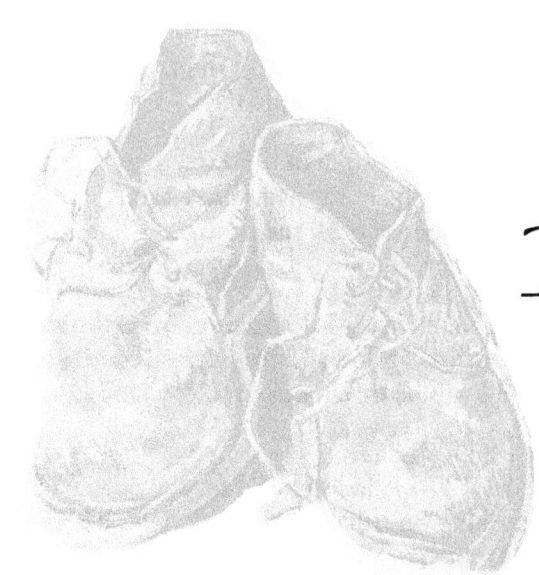

8:
The Captivity Era

Week 25: The Fall of Judah
2 Chronicles 36:15-23

Key verse: *"The Lord, the God of their ancestors, sent word to them through his messengers again and again, because he had pity on his people and on his dwelling place." (2 Chronicles 36:15)*

LEADER'S NOTE

We will begin our study in the last chapter of 2 Chronicles. We want the students to see that the fall of Judah had a reason: the people had disregarded the messengers of God too long. God had sent messengers according to verse 15, "again and again."

Help the students to understand that God is patient, but He won't be patient forever. He will bring judgment. The Bible is God's Messenger to us, and we need to listen.

The people of God were going into captivity. God was also preparing a way for them to return. Every person is a captive to sin, but God has made a way for us to return to Him.

More details of the prophesied destruction come from Huldah the priestess in chapter 34 verses 22-28.

CONTEXT

Chronicles was originally written as one long book, and it was divided because the scrolls could not contain all of it. The same is true of 1 and 2 Samuel and 1 and 2 Kings. It covers the history of Israel from Adam to the fall of the southern kingdom, Judah. It was written by Ezra after the exile, about 400 B.C., and it is the last book of the Hebrew Bible.

The focus of Chronicles is on the positive aspects of the Kingdom of Judah and the Temple. We see a lot about the few good kings in Judah.

Ezra writes with the perspective of restoring the nation. Remember they have come out of seventy years of exile and are facing a time of great uncertainty. They have experienced God's judgment through invading armies.

OPEN UP

What does it mean to be patient? How do you know if someone is patient?

THINK ABOUT

Have you ever been warned that you would be punished if you did or did not do something? If your parents or your teachers gave you a command, how many chances will they give you before you get punished?

READ

Verse 15: Why did God send messengers?

Verse 16: What does it mean that "there was no remedy"?

Verses 17-20: What happened? Who would you say was responsible for all of this? Why do you say that?

Verse 21: Why did this happen? Who said it was going to happen?

Verses 22-23: What did God do with Cyrus and why?

LEADER'S GUIDE—SOJOURNER BIBLE STUDY

FOCUS

The Lord, the God of their ancestors, sent word to them through his messengers again and again, because he had pity on his people and on his dwelling place. (2 Chronicles 36:15)

What was the first catastrophic event in the Bible that affected a lot of people? Did God give the people time to repent in the days of Noah? (2 Peter 2:5).

Who are some of the messengers God has used in the Old Testament? Have there been any messengers in your life encouraging you to follow Jesus and not people who cause you to sin? Are you willing to talk about it?

TALK

- What is this teaching me about God?
- What is this teaching me about people?
- Why is this important to me today?

CONNECT THE GOSPEL

This is the Gospel: "For what I received I passed on to you as of first importance: that Christ died for our sins according to the Scriptures, that he was buried, that he was raised on the third day according to the Scriptures" (1 Corinthians 15:3-4 NIV).

The Gospel is not "good news" if we don't believe that we have sin in our lives. From the time of Genesis 3, we all have struggled with sin, and we all have been separated from God because of our sin.

God spoke face to face with Adam and Eve. He did not need to send messengers to them because they had a perfect relationship. After they sinned, that relationship was broken. People could no longer get that close to God unless you made a way for it to happen.

Because God has pity on His people and His dwelling place, He has sent messengers. The message has been the same. Turn from our sin and turn to Him. We are captives in our sin, but God has had pity on us and sent us a Messenger, Jesus. How will you respond to His message to you?

SO WHAT?

Why should I care about this? Great question!

The answer is: because it represents you and I on a bigger scale. God judged an entire nation because they had turned away from Him. In Genesis chapter 3, He judged three creatures because they turned away from Him. However, just like He did for Judah, He also has done for us. God has provided a way for us to be restored to Him.

SERVE

Do you know anyone who is angry at God because something bad has happened in their lives? Can you take time this week to help them understand that God has made a way to bring healing into their life?

DIG DEEPER

The Lord, the God of their ancestors, sent word to them through his messengers again and again, because he had pity on his people and on his dwelling place. (2 Chronicles 36:15)

Our verse tells us that God had "pity on His people, and on His dwelling place." The King James Bible uses the word "compassion." In the Hebrew text, it is the word *hamal*.

When we think of the word "pity," we think, "oh, how sad." However, in the context of the Hebrew, it means "to spare." In the context of 2 Chronicles, the Lord God had compassion on His people, and He spared them from ruin.

The Hebrew Bible ends with the book of Chronicles. These chilling words seem hopeless, "but they continually mocked the messengers of God, despised His words, and scoffed at His prophets, until the wrath of the Lord rose against His people, until there was no remedy."

The book closed with the fulfillment of the prophecy of Jeremiah about the return from exile under King Cyrus, and then the prophets were silent. When the people stopped listening, the Lord stopped speaking.

The Gospel of Luke told the people that the silence had been broken, and the Lord had sent His messenger, the birth of John the Baptist. "And he will turn many of the sons of Israel back to the Lord their God. And it is he who will go as a forerunner before Him in the spirit and power of Elijah, to turn the hearts of fathers back to their children, and the disobedient to the attitude of the righteous, to make ready a people prepared for the Lord" (Luke 1:16-17).

Jesus rebuked the Jewish people for their mistreatment of the messengers of God, Luke 13:34, "Jerusalem, Jerusalem, the city that kills the prophets and stones those who have been sent to her! How often I wanted to gather your children together, just as a hen gathers her young under her wings, and you were unwilling!"

> *God, after He spoke long ago to the fathers in the prophets in many portions and in many ways, in these last days has spoken to us in His Son, whom He appointed heir of all things, through whom He also made the world. (Hebrews 1:1-2)*

Matthew 9:36, "Seeing the crowds, He felt compassion for them, because they were distressed and downcast, like sheep without a shepherd." In 2 Chronicles 36:15, the Lord had pity on His people, and here we see it again: the Lord had compassion for them.

John chapter 1:11, "He came to His own, and His own people did not accept Him." Jesus came to the Jewish people, He had been sent from God with the message of redemption, but His people did not accept Him. John 1:12-13, "But as many as received Him, to them He gave the right to become children of God, to those who believe in His name, who were born, not of blood, nor of the will of the flesh, nor of the will of a man, but of God."

We talked about God's "pity" or how He "spared" His people. What about His "pity" on His dwelling place?

History tells us that the temple was destroyed by Nebuchadnezzar in 587/586 B.C. The temple was rebuilt after the exile, and it was destroyed again in A.D. 70. Does this mean that God did not have compassion on His dwelling place?

Not at all. The God of all Creation does not dwell in temples made by hands (Acts 7:48). The dwelling place of God is among His people. The Gospel of John tells us that the Word became flesh and made His dwelling among us. In the days of Moses, the glory of the Lord filled the tabernacle. In the days of Solomon, the glory of the Lord filled the Temple. When the Word became flesh, John said, "we beheld His glory" (John 1:14).

How did the Lord God spare His dwelling place? He has come to us. He has made it possible through the Holy Spirit for us to now be the dwelling place of God for everyone who believes (1 Cor. 6:19).

God sent His Word through His messengers to the people because He had pity on them. Finally, in the fullness of time (Gal. 4:4), God sent His Son. Jesus is the Word of God for whoever will receive Him.

The book of the Revelation gives us the best news, that the day will come again when God will dwell among His people. He had pity on them in the days of the Old Testament, and He has had pity on us, and He spared us.

> *And I heard a loud voice from the throne saying, "Look! God's dwelling place is now among the people, and he will dwell with them. They will be his people, and God himself will be with them and be their God." (Rev. 21:3)*

Notes

Week 26: Jeremiah
Jeremiah 18:1-12

Key verse: *"And if that nation I warned repents of its evil, then I will relent and not inflict on it the disaster I had planned." (Jeremiah 18:8)*

LEADER'S NOTE

Last week we talked about the messengers who God sent to warn the people. Today we look at the prophet Jeremiah. He was given the task of telling people to turn from their sin and turn back to God.

His mission was not going to be easy. Our mission is not easy. No one wants to hear that he is a sinner facing the judgment of God unless they repent. Help the students to see that God's desire is for us to turn to Him.

Jeremiah wasn't allowed to marry, his friends abandoned him, and others tried to kill him. It is believed that he died in 570 B.C., after being taken into Egypt after the fall of Judah.

David Platt said about Jeremiah, "God's heart for His people is revealed through the heart of His prophet."

Teachers you may want to review these questions before asking your students. You should be familiar enough with their families to know if one of your students has a strained family relationship.

CONTEXT

As a prophet, Jeremiah suffered much. God used him in a great way. In chapter 1, God had told Jeremiah in verse 10, "See, today I appoint you over nations and kingdoms to uproot and tear down, to destroy and overthrow, to build and to plant."

Jeremiah was a prophet during the last forty years of Judah, from 626-586 B.C. He prophesied during the reign of five kings. Jeremiah is known as the Weeping Prophet. He also gave us the book of Lamentations.

David Platt said about Jeremiah, "God's heart for His people is revealed through the heart of His prophet."

OPEN UP

Do you think that your parents want to punish you when you do something bad? Why do you think that?

THINK ABOUT

What would your parents say to you if you said to them, "I'm not going to listen to you. I'm going to live my way?" How would they feel seeing the child they love turn against them?

READ

Verses 1-2: Where did Jeremiah go? What does a potter do?

Verses 3-4: What happened?

Verses 5-6: What are we like in the hand of God? What does that mean?

Verses 7-10: What would cause God to change His mind about our punishment? (The students should say something about their own actions.)

Verse 11: What does God desire of us?

Verse 12: What do the people desire?

LEADER'S GUIDE—SOJOURNER BIBLE STUDY

FOCUS

> *And if that nation I warned repents of its evil, then I will relent and not inflict on it the disaster I had planned. (Jeremiah 18:8)*

Look again at verse 8. If we know that we have sinned and fallen away from God, what do we need to do? What will God do when the people repent? What does it mean to repent, and when do you think it is too late to repent?

A great example of people hearing the warning from God and repenting is found in the action of the Ninevites in Jonah 3:10: "When God saw what they did and how they turned from their evil ways, he relented and did not bring on them the destruction he had threatened."

TALK

- What is this teaching me about God?
- What is this teaching me about people?
- Why is this important to me today?

CONNECT THE GOSPEL

This is the Gospel: "For what I received I passed on to you as of first importance: that Christ died for our sins according to the Scriptures, that he was buried, that he was raised on the third day according to the Scriptures" (1 Corinthians 15:3-4 NIV).

How can we connect Jeremiah 18 to the Gospel? This is a good time to bring Romans 6:23 into the picture: "For the wages of sin is death, but the gift of God is eternal life in Christ Jesus our Lord."

If we will turn from our sins, and turn toward what God has given us, His free gift of salvation in Christ Jesus, we will have eternal life and not judgment.

SO WHAT?

How does this apply today? It's just as important to us as it was to the people of Judah 2,600 years ago. The One Who created you is also the One Who can save you or judge you.

Have you been told about sin against God? Has anyone told you or shown you that your sin separates you from Him? If you have read this lesson, then you have been warned. How will you respond?

SERVE

Let's apply this to ourselves this week. Spend this week thinking about the ways you are not following God, and then ask Him to help you turn back to Him.

DIG DEEPER

> *...and if that nation I warned repents of its evil, then I will relent and not inflict on it the disaster I had planned. (Jeremiah 18:8)*

The King James Bible says, "If that nation, against whom I have pronounced, turn from their evil, I will repent of the evil that I thought to do unto them." In the King James version, we see the idea of two changes, or reorientations. First, the people needed to "turn from their evil."

The second turn, or reorientation, comes from God Himself. If the people will turn, then He will repent. He will reorient Himself from bringing disaster. We follow a God who wants people to follow Him completely.

The Lord God spoke through the prophet Ezekiel, "For I take no pleasure in the death of anyone, declares the Sovereign Lord. Repent and live!" (Ezek. 18:32). God does not want to destroy anyone; we are His creation. However, He will not overlook sin.

Our study last week in 2 Chronicles told us about the messengers whom God had sent with His message for the people. The message was rejected. First Timothy 2:4 tells us that the Lord wants "all people to be saved and to come to a knowledge of the truth."

The hope of salvation is the grace of God. He gives people and nations multiple opportunities to turn to Him. Repentance means turning away from our way and turning to God and His way. You could say "reorienting ourselves under His authority."

Nineveh repented, and God withheld His judgment. Their change only lasted a hundred years, and then they turned again, and God destroyed them (the book of Nahum).

Jeremiah spoke of national repentance. How can an entire nation change if the people in that nation do not change first?

When John the Baptist preached, he preached a message of repentance. He warned the people to turn from their ways because the Messiah had arrived.

After John the Baptist was put in prison, Jesus preached repentance. Matthew 4:17, "From that time on Jesus began to preach, 'Repent, for the kingdom of heaven has come near.'"

> *After John was put in prison, Jesus went into Galilee, proclaiming the good news of God. "The time has come," he said. "The kingdom of God has come near. Repent and believe the good news!" (Mark 1:14-15)*

The message of Jeremiah is the same today; if we want to be saved from God's judgment, we need to repent. We need to turn away from living our way, and we need to orient ourselves to live in a way that pleases our God.

In Acts 2, after Peter had preached his sermon at Pentecost, the people were "cut to the heart," and they wanted to know how to be saved. Verses 37-39, "When the people heard this, they were cut to the heart and said to Peter and the other apostles, 'Brothers, what shall we do?' Peter replied, 'Repent and be baptized, every one of you, in the name of Jesus Christ for the forgiveness of your sins. And you will receive the gift of the Holy Spirit. The promise is for you and your children and for all who are far off—for all whom the Lord our God will call.'" The gift of salvation is for us, our children, and those who are far off.

> *...and if that nation I warned repents of its evil, then I will relent and not inflict on it the disaster I had planned. (Jeremiah 18:8)*

> *The Lord is not slack concerning his promise, as some men count slackness; but is longsuffering to us-ward, not willing that any should perish, but that all should come to repentance. (2 Peter 3:9)*

Praise God for His patience, and we should praise Him for our salvation.

Notes

Week 27: Ezekiel
Ezekiel 10:15-19; 36:22-28; 43:1-7

Key verse: *"I will give you a new heart and put a new spirit in you; I will remove from you your heart of stone and give you a heart of flesh." (Ezekiel 36:26)*

LEADER'S NOTE

The book of Ezekiel emphasizes the glory of God. From the beginning when Ezekiel sees the glory of God, to the departure of God from the temple, and then the return of God to the temple, it's all about the glory of God. We serve a God-centered God. When the Lord God judges a nation or restores a nation, the purpose is His glory.

This week, we want the students to see that in the midst of God's judgment there is also the picture of healing. The departure of the glory of God from the temple and the return of His glory are the bookends in our lesson with the focus being on the promise of a new heart.

CONTEXT

Ezekiel prophesied from 592-570 B.C. The people had been taken into captivity by the Babylonians.

Ezekiel means "God strengthens." We see this in his book. We see Ezekiel promote repentance and faith. We also see him stimulate hope and trust. The beginning of the book is judgment against Judah and the nations, and then the last chapters bring the prophecy of restoration.

It's interesting to note that Ezekiel has a vision of the glory of God leaving the temple, and he has a vision of the glory of God returning to the temple.

OPEN UP

Have you ever had a good friend or a family member go away for a long time and then return? How did you feel when they left? Did you know they were coming back? How did you feel when they came back?

THINK ABOUT

What would it be like if God left you? (Hebrews 13:5 reminds us that the Lord will never leave us.)

READ

Ezekiel 10:15-19: When God told Moses to build the tabernacle, He told him to put the Ark of the Covenant in the Holy Room. The Ark held the Ten Commandments. Above the Ark were cherubim. So, what is happening here in Ezekiel's vision.

> *There, above the cover between the two cherubim that are over the ark of the covenant law, I will meet with you and give you all my commands for the Israelites. (Exodus 25:22)*

Ezekiel 36:22-23: Why was God taking action?

Ezekiel 36:24-28: What will God do? In verse 27, Who will help us follow God's laws?

Ezekiel 43:1-5: What did Ezekiel see?

Ezekiel 43:7: What did God say?

FOCUS

> *I will give you a new heart and put a new spirit in you; I will remove from you your heart of stone and give you a heart of flesh. (Ezekiel 36:26)*

Think about this verse. Why do we need a new heart and a new spirit? What do we need to do to get a new spirit? Look at John 3:3. In our focus verse, who is doing all of the work? Do you think this is a message of hope?

TALK

- What is this teaching me about God?
- What is this teaching me about people?
- Why is this important to me today?

CONNECT THE GOSPEL

This is the Gospel: "For what I received I passed on to you as of first importance: that Christ died for our sins according to the Scriptures, that he was buried, that he was raised on the third day according to the Scriptures" (1 Corinthians 15:3-4 NIV).

What happens when we decide to follow Jesus? Read John 3:16, 2 Corinthians 5:17, and Ephesians 2:8-9.

This promise in Ezekiel 36:26 is what happens when we turn to the Lord. In the Gospel, Jesus has done all of the work. He removes our heart of stone, and He gives us a new heart.

Second Corinthians 5:17 tells us that in Christ we are new creations.

SO WHAT?

We live in a fallen, broken world. We have laws, rules, codes and restrictions everywhere, but they don't make people better. Only a changed heart can change a person.

Jeremiah 17:9 tells us that the heart is deceitful above all things. The "so what" to this lesson is that we all need help. We can't change ourselves, no matter how hard we try. The only way to have new life is by accepting what Jesus has done for us.

SERVE

How can you apply this lesson this week? Everywhere we go we see or hear about something bad that has happened. When you are aware of something bad happening in your community, pray for changed hearts. Use current events to talk to people around you about the promise of a new heart from God.

Try to find ways to help someone. Use this interaction to share how God changes hearts.

DIG DEEPER

> *I will give you a new heart and put a new spirit in you; I will remove from you your heart of stone and give you a heart of flesh. (Ezekiel 36:26)*

From Genesis chapter 1 to today's study, we see God doing all the work. The process, or act, of salvation is not something anyone can work for or earn. It is a gift from God.

God created the earth and everything in it. God covered Adam and Eve after they sinned. God closed the door of the ark after Noah and his family entered. God called Abram. God provided a ram in the place of Isaac for a sacrifice. God met Moses in the wilderness. God led the Hebrews through the wilderness. God sent His messengers to bring His people back.

Today, again, we see a messenger of God, Ezekiel, with a message from God. The message is that God will do the work of changing us from the inside.

God told the people that this act was not for them, but it was for the glory of His name. "Therefore, say to the house of Israel, 'This is what the Lord God says: It is not for your sake, house of Israel, that I am about to act, but for My holy name, which you have profaned among the nations where you went'" (Ezek. 36:22).

This same truth, that God saves us for the glory of His name, is also found in 1 John 2:12, "I am writing to you, little children, because your sins have been forgiven you on account of His name." Every good thing that the Lord God does for us is not because we are worthy, but every gift reveals His greatness.

"Then the nations will know that I am the Lord," declares the Lord God, "when I show Myself holy among you in their sight." (Ezek. 36:23)

We do not have the ability to live for God. We saw that in our study of the Ten Commandments. The only way for us to live for God is for Him to cleanse us. Sin defiles us; it makes us dirty. It is only by the cleansing power of the water and Spirit of God that we can be made clean. We do not have the ability to sanctify the Lord God unless He sanctifies us first. How can something that is unclean bring glory to the Holy God?

When Jesus met with Nicodemus, He explained to him how this would work. John 3:3-6:

Jesus replied, "Very truly I tell you, no one can see the kingdom of God unless they are born again." "How can someone be born when they are old?" Nicodemus asked. "Surely they cannot enter a second time into their mother's womb to be born!" Jesus answered, "Very truly I tell you, no one can enter the kingdom of God unless they are born of water and the Spirit. Flesh gives birth to flesh, but the Spirit gives birth to spirit."

This "born again" and being "born of water and the Spirit" both refer to one new birth. Jesus is not talking about a natural birth in the amniotic fluid and then a spiritual birth when you are saved. He is talking about one new birth by being cleansed from our sin and filled with the Spirit of the Living God.

John 3:3 is the statement, "Except a man be born again, he cannot see the kingdom of God." Verse four is the question: "How can a man be born when he is old? can he enter the second time into his mother's womb, and be born?" And then John 3:5 is the explanation of the statement in verse three: "Except a man be born of water and of the Spirit, he cannot enter into the kingdom of God."

Since Nicodemus was a teacher of Israel (John 3:10), he should have known what Ezekiel wrote. Today's verse is the result of the promise of God in verse 25. Ezekiel 36:25-27,

I will sprinkle clean water on you, and you will be clean; I will cleanse you from all your impurities and from all your idols. I will give you a new heart and put a new spirit in you; I will remove from you your heart of stone and give you a heart of flesh. And I will put my Spirit in you and move you to follow my decrees and be careful to keep my laws.

The One who created your heart is the only One who can change your heart. If you will accept what He has done, you will be born again.

Notes

Week 28: Daniel's Prayer
Daniel 2:1-28

Key verse: *"He changes times and seasons; he deposes kings and raises up others. He gives wisdom to the wise and knowledge to the discerning." (Daniel 2:21)*

LEADER'S NOTE

There is so much in Daniel that can be discussed. We want the students to see that God is in control of all things. He puts people in positions of authority for a reason, and He removes them for a reason, and we don't need to know why. We only need to stay near Him and trust Him.

CONTEXT

The book of Daniel begins in 604 B.C. and ends two years after the exile in 532 B.C. Daniel had been taken into Babylon when Judah was a young teenager. He served under three kingdoms: Babylon, Media, and Persia.

Throughout the book we see that God is sovereign over all kings and all of history.

OPEN UP

Have you ever been in a situation where you couldn't understand why it was happening?

THINK ABOUT

Are you afraid or hesitant to tell people about the power of God?

READ

Verse 1: What happened?

Verses 2-9: What did the king say, and what did his servants say?

Verses 10-11: Based on what you know about God and the Bible, how would you respond if someone said this to you?

Verses 12-13: What is the king's decision?

Verses 14-16: How did Daniel reply to the captain of the bodyguard? What did Daniel ask of the king?

Verses 17-18: What did Daniel do with his friends? What was their prayer request?

Verses 19-23: What happened and what was Daniel's response?

Verses 24-28: What did the king ask in verse 26? What did Daniel reply in verse 28?

FOCUS

> *He changes times and seasons; he deposes kings and raises up others. He gives wisdom to the wise and knowledge to the discerning. (Daniel 2:21)*

How was Daniel able to approach the king with such boldness? What did God reveal about Himself to Daniel through his vision? To whom did Daniel give credit in verse 28?

The king had a vision and it troubled him. Daniel had a vision and it gave him confidence. What was the difference between the two men? How can we have this wisdom?

TALK

- What is this teaching me about God?
- What is this teaching me about people?
- Why is this important to me today?

CONNECT THE GOSPEL

This is the Gospel: "For what I received I passed on to you as of first importance: that Christ died for our sins according to the Scriptures, that he was buried, that he was raised on the third day according to the Scriptures" (1 Corinthians 15:3-4 NIV).

Jesus stepped into a world of pagan kings and armies. He came to a world that looked for hope in wealth and prosperity. Daniel lived in that type of world.

When the wise men said in verse 11 that the gods don't dwell among men, they didn't know the One True God. Daniel was given an opportunity to introduce the king to the King of kings.

The God Daniel worshiped is the God who became a man and made His dwelling among us (John 1:14).

SO WHAT?

All around us there are people who are looking for answers to the situations and problems in their lives. Maybe you are in a situation that you don't understand and you need answers. The God of the Bible is in control of kings and times. Do you think He can help in your situation?

SERVE

When you hear people talking about the situation in the world, you can help them understand that God is in control. Think about someone you can tell this lesson to this week.

DIG DEEPER

He changes times and seasons; he deposes kings and raises up others. He gives wisdom to the wise and knowledge to the discerning. (Daniel 2:21)

In Daniel 2:11, the wise men said that the gods do not dwell among men. This idea continues today in many religions, that the god, or object of worship, is far away, and we must work to get to him or achieve enlightenment. The God of the Bible can be known, and Daniel knew Him.

The Bible has many examples of how God controls kings and leaders. God spoke to Pharoah through Moses during the time of the plagues in Exodus 9:16, "But I have raised you up for this very purpose, that I might show you my power and that my name might be proclaimed in all the earth."

In the midst of Job's suffering, Job told Zophar, "He makes nations great, and destroys them; he enlarges nations, and disperses them" (Job 12:23).

In Psalm 47:7-9, a Psalm from the Sons of Korah, they describe the King of kings, "For God is the King of all the earth; sing to him a psalm of praise. God reigns over the nations; God is seated on his holy throne. The nobles of the nations assemble as the people of the God of Abraham, for the kings of the earth belong to God; he is greatly exalted."

The Lord God had sent messengers to His people. He had raised up judges to guide His people. The Lord God gave them kings to rule His people. The people did not listen to the messengers. The judges failed. The kings failed. However, Daniel knew the one true God. "It is He who reveals the profound and hidden things; He knows what is in the darkness, And the light dwells with Him" (Dan. 2:22). Our God is in control, and Daniel knew Him.

After Jesus was arrested and prior to His crucifixion, Jesus told Pilate, "Jesus answered, "You would have no power over me if it were not given to you from above" (John 19:11a). Pilate did not understand who was in control.

When Jesus gave His disciples the authority to go into all the world with the Gospel, He was giving them the ability to do what Daniel had done: tell the people that there is a God who has revealed Himself to us, and we can know Him. Matthew 28:18, "Then Jesus came to them and said, 'All authority in heaven and on earth has been given to me.'"

In Acts 17, Paul was speaking to Greek philosophers in Athens, and he was sharing the Gospel with them in their cultural context. They worshiped many gods, but Paul told them about the one true God.

From one man he made all the nations, that they should inhabit the whole earth; and he marked out their appointed times in history and the boundaries of their lands. God did this so that they would seek him and perhaps reach out for him and find him, though he is not far from any one of us. (Acts 17:26)

In our world today, in every nation, there appears to be political chaos and turmoil. We need to have the faith that Daniel had to tell people about the God who is in control.

Before Daniel spoke to the king, he spoke to God. In Daniel 2:17-18, Daniel urged his friends to plead with God for mercy in interpreting the dream of the king. How often do we plead with God for wisdom to speak with people? If this is true, "He gives wisdom to the wise and knowledge to the discerning," then we should be in communion with this God as Daniel was.

Notes

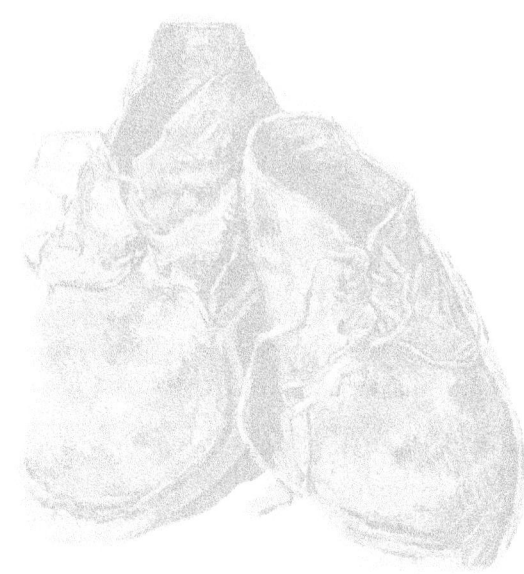

9: The Return Era

Week 29: Ezra
Ezra 7:11-28

Key verse: *"For Ezra had set his heart to study the Law of the LORD, to practice it, and to teach its statutes and ordinances in Israel." (Ezra 7:10)*

LEADER'S NOTE

Ezra shows us how God sovereignly works to preserve His people for His glory. In Ezra and Nehemiah, we see three key leaders and their purposes. Ezra (457 B.C.) restored worship, Nehemiah (444 B.C.) rebuilt the walls, they both followed after Zerubbabel (536 B.C.) who rebuilt the temple.

In this lesson we want the students to see how God uses us when we are truly devoted to Him. Help your students to see that they can play a part in spiritual transformation if they too will set their hearts on the Word of God.

CONTEXT

The book of Ezra begins where 2 Chronicles ended, with the decree of Cyrus to send people to Jerusalem. In the Hebrew Bible, Ezra and Nehemiah are treated as one book. They tell the story of the return of the exiles to Jerusalem. In some passages these exiles are known as the Remnant. Ezra chapters 1-6 show a time of national restoration. Chapters 7-10 show a time of spiritual revival.

The time period is 480-440 B.C. Ezra was sent to Jerusalem to help teach the people the Laws of the God of Israel, approximately 457 B.C. Jewish tradition credits Ezra with beginning the process of bringing together the Hebrew Bible known as the Torah.

OPEN UP

Would you like to see your community, your family, your school, and your nation changed to follow God?

THINK ABOUT

What would you need to do to play a part in changing the world around you for God's glory?

READ

Verses 11-12: What do we learn about Ezra? Who wrote the letter?

Verses 13-14: What is Ezra supposed to do?

Verses 15-20: What were they to take and where did it come from? (Daniel 1:2, some of the articles which were taken by Nebuchadnezzer.)

Verses 21-24: Why was the king being so generous?

Verses 25-26: What was Ezra authorized to do? What type of person was he looking for?

Verses 27-28: What did Ezra do? Who got the glory?

LEADER'S GUIDE—SOJOURNER BIBLE STUDY

FOCUS

> *For Ezra had set his heart to study the Law of the LORD, to practice it, and to teach its statutes and ordinances in Israel. (Ezra 7:10)*

What does it mean to set your heart on something? Think about Ezra and Daniel. They were two men whom God used to do great things. Compare Ezra 7:10 and Daniel 1:8: "But Daniel resolved not to defile himself with the royal food and wine, and he asked the chief official for permission not to defile himself this way."

What do the two men have in common? When was the last time you set your heart to do something or resolved to do it?

TALK

- What is this teaching me about God?
- What is this teaching me about people?
- Why is this important to me today?

CONNECT THE GOSPEL

This is the Gospel: "For what I received I passed on to you as of first importance: that Christ died for our sins according to the Scriptures, that he was buried, that he was raised on the third day according to the Scriptures" (1 Corinthians 15:3-4 NIV).

The Gospel of Jesus Christ is all about how God has made a way for us to be in a right relationship with Him. In the book of Ezra, we see God moving in the heart of a pagan king to bring the people of God back into the city of God, and with this return the people have a chance at new life.

God used men like Ezra to guide the people back to the Word of God. In the Gospel, God sent Jesus, the Word of God, to the people to reveal Himself to us and make a way for us to return to Him.

SO WHAT?

Why is this important? Under Ezra and Nehemiah there was a period of spiritual and social reform. However, the revival wasn't complete. There was still the need for a heart transformation.

When Jerusalem was rebuilt, it prepared the people for the Messiah who was to come. Only through Jesus would the people of God experience complete restoration.

Acts 7:48 tells us that God does not live in temples made by human hands. John 1:14 tells us that "the Word became flesh and made His dwelling among us." Paul wrote in 1 Corinthians 3:16, "Don't you know that you yourselves are God's temple and that God's Spirit dwells in your midst?"

We don't need a place, we need a Person, and that is Jesus. The temple would only stand until 70 A.D. when it was destroyed by the Romans. But, the Word of God lives forever.

SERVE

How devoted are you to the Word of God? Spend time this week thinking about how Ezra set his heart to study the Word of God. His study of the Word equipped him to do the work that he was asked to do.

Try to share this lesson with someone this week. You can do this by studying the Bible together, or just tell them what you are learning in your Bible study.

DIG DEEPER

For Ezra had set his heart to study the Law of the LORD, to practice it, and to teach its statutes and ordinances in Israel. (Ezra 7:10)

In the beginning of Ezra 7, the Bible tells us about the man Ezra. Ezra 7:1-5 gives us his pedigree. Ezra, "this Ezra," was from the priestly line of Aaron, the brother of Moses. Therefore, Ezra had credibility among the Jewish people, and he had the authority to bring the word of God because he descended from Aaron.

What do we know about "this Ezra"? We know that he descended from Aaron. We know that he was a teacher, and in the New Testament, he would have been considered a scribe, an expert in the Law. The writer makes us aware that "He was a teacher well versed in the Law of Moses, which the Lord, the God of Israel, had given" (Ezra 7:6a).

Ezra was not a prophet. Ezra lived during the same time as Malachi, and Malachi is considered the last prophet of the Old Testament. God spoke through Malachi, "Remember the law of my servant Moses, the decrees and laws I gave him at Horeb for all Israel" (Mal. 4:4). Ezra showed himself faithful to do this.

Ezra remembered the Law of Moses. Jesus had this to say about faithful scribes, "He said to them, 'Therefore every teacher of the law who has become a disciple in the kingdom of heaven is like the owner of a house who brings out of his storeroom new treasures as well as old'" (Mat. 13:52).

Remember that Ezra was born and raised during a time when his people were in exile in foreign lands. "He came up from Babylon," the Bible tells us. The Babylonians, the Medes, and the Persians were all people who had a strong regard for education. Ezra could have followed the teaching of his captors, but "he set his heart to study the Law of the LORD." Just as Daniel set himself apart from his captors, Ezra did the same.

We mentioned Daniel earlier in the lesson. Daniel 1:8, "'But Daniel resolved not to defile himself with the royal food and wine, and he asked the chief official for permission not to defile himself this way." Daniel had set his heart not to do something, and when the temptation came, he was ready.

As for Ezra, "The king had granted him everything he asked, for the hand of the Lord his God was on him" (Ezra 7:6b). In verse 25 of chapter 7, the king acknowledged that Ezra possessed the wisdom of his God. It was this knowledge that gave Ezra the position with the king, and God used Ezra in a great way.

We know that Jeremiah had prophesied that the nation of Israel would be in exile seventy years. Now, under the king who the Lord God had raised up, the nation of Israel was returning to their land. Ezra was prepared when the time came because he knew the word of God.

In Job 11, Zophar was talking about knowing God Almighty. Zophar did not always say the right thing, but this is true, "Yet if you devote your heart to him and stretch out your hands to him, if you put away the sin that is in your hand and allow no evil to dwell in your tent, then, free of fault, you will lift up your face; you will stand firm and without fear" (Job 11:13-15).

Jeremiah, Daniel, and Ezra were focused on the Kingdom of God and His glory. They did not focus on, or "set their hearts on," the kingdoms of the world. They did not set their hearts on building their own kingdoms, either. The Lord blessed their faithfulness.

Jesus also spoke about what our hearts should be "set on." Matthew 6:33, "But seek first his kingdom and his righteousness, and all these things will be given to you as well." Ezra did not seek his own comfort or glory, but he was set on the Word of God and the ability to teach it.

Paul wrote to the Church at Colossae, "Since, then, you have been raised with Christ, set your hearts on things above, where Christ is, seated at the right hand of God. Set your minds on things above, not on earthly things. For you died, and your life is now hidden with Christ in God. When Christ, who is your life, appears, then you also will appear with him in glory" (Colossians 3:1-4).

Ezra 7:10, "For Ezra had set his heart to study the Law of the LORD, to practice it, and to teach its statutes and ordinances in Israel." May we be faithful students of the Word of God.

Notes

Week 30: Nehemiah
Nehemiah 1:1-11 and 2:1-4

Key verse: "*And it came to pass, when I heard these words, that I sat down and wept, and mourned certain days, and fasted, and prayed before the God of heaven.*" *(Nehemiah 1:4)*

LEADER'S NOTE

Nehemiah was not a priest like Ezra. He was a regular guy who just happened to work in the palace for the king of Persia. We want the students to see that God will use us where we are to accomplish His purposes. Help the students to understand that when the time came for Nehemiah to speak to the king, he was spiritually prepared for the task.

CONTEXT

Let's remember that Nehemiah and Ezra were originally written together, around 440 B.C. Zerubbabel had returned first in 536 B.C., and he rebuilt the temple. Ezra restored worship, and Nehemiah came to repair the walls.

Chapters 1-6 show us the physical repair of the walls, and then chapters 7-13 show us the spiritual repair of the people.

The book of Nehemiah is the last historical book of the Bible. The book of Esther comes after Nehemiah in the Bible today, but the events of Esther actually took place before the time of Nehemiah.

OPEN UP

Have you ever been upset about something in your family, your school, or your community?

THINK ABOUT

How do you usually react when you receive bad news about something in your world?

READ

Chapter 1

Verses 1-3: What happened?

Verse 4: What all did Nehemiah do?

Verses 5-11: How would you describe Nehemiah's prayer? What does he say about God, and who does he say sinned?

Chapter 2

Verse 1: How long has it been since Nehemiah got the bad news? You have to look at chapter 1, verse 1, and chapter 2, verse 1. It's approximately five months.

Verses 2-4: What were the questions, and what did Nehemiah do?

LEADER'S GUIDE—SOJOURNER BIBLE STUDY

FOCUS

And it came to pass, when I heard these words, that I sat down and wept, and mourned certain days, and fasted, and prayed before the God of heaven. (Nehemiah 1:4)

By the time we read verse 4 in chapter 2, we are tempted to think that Nehemiah has just thrown up a quick prayer. But, if you consider the time frame of when he began praying until the king questioned him, it's almost five months. Nehemiah was spiritually prepared to respond.

How much time do we usually spend praying about a situation that concerns us? At what point in our prayers do we forget or give up hope?

TALK

- What is this teaching me about God?
- What is this teaching me about people?
- Why is this important to me today?

CONNECT THE GOSPEL

This is the Gospel: "For what I received I passed on to you as of first importance: that Christ died for our sins according to the Scriptures, that he was buried, that he was raised on the third day according to the Scriptures" (1 Corinthians 15:3-4 NIV).

Nehemiah was broken because his people were suffering and the walls of the city were in ruins. This may seem unimportant to us, but it was very important in the time of Nehemiah. The walls represented security.

We live in a fallen, hurting, and suffering world. All around us are people who need repairs. This is why Jesus came, to repair our broken relationships. Our relationship with God the Father is our greatest need, and Jesus has made a way for us to be restored.

SO WHAT?

Why do we care about a guy who was the cupbearer?

> God uses all manner of people in all manner of places doing all manner of work. Do you feel you must be "in ministry" in order to serve God? Be encouraged; He is not limited by your vocation. In fact, God has placed you where you are for a purpose. Have this attitude about your work: "Whatever you do in word or deed, do all in the name of the Lord Jesus, giving thanks through Him to God the Father" Colossians 3:17. (Chuck Swindoll)

You may think this lesson doesn't apply to you. However, God can use you if you are willing to be used by Him.

In verse 11 of chapter 1, Nehemiah told us that he was the cupbearer. Nothing special. However, Nehemiah had a heart for the people of God, and God used Nehemiah to rebuild the walls and to help restore the faith of the people.

SERVE

Are you ready to make a difference where you are? This week, spend time praying about how you can make a difference in someone's life, and then do it.

DIG DEEPER

And it came to pass, when I heard these words, that I sat down and wept, and mourned certain days, and fasted, and prayed before the God of heaven. (Nehemiah 1:4)

You may be wondering why we are reading this passage in the middle of our study, and why is the focus verse about a man who was crying. We need to understand the significance of Jerusalem and the significance of the wall. To a non-Jew, this may not seem important. The Book of Nehemiah is a picture of the physical state of Israel and its spiritual state.

During the time of the kings, Solomon built the Temple in Jerusalem. The Temple was a representation of the presence of God with His people. The city represented the covenant that God had made with David of an eternal king. Solomon said in 2 Chronicles 6:4-6,

> *Praise be to the Lord, the God of Israel, who with his hands has fulfilled what he promised with his mouth to my father David. For he said, "Since the day I brought my people out of Egypt, I have not chosen a city in any tribe of Israel to have a temple built so that my Name might be there, nor have I chosen anyone to be ruler over my people Israel. But now I have chosen Jerusalem for my Name to be there, and I have chosen David to rule my people Israel."*

We have talked about the failure of Solomon and the fall of the divided kingdom. When the southern kingdom fell to the Babylonians, the Temple was destroyed. The Temple was a representation of the presence of God, and there was a feeling that the presence of God was no longer with His people.

Nehemiah may have been in a foreign land, but his heart was concerned for his homeland and his people. Judging by how he felt after hearing the report about the city walls, it is safe to say that he was concerned for the city of his God. Psalm 137:5-6, "If I forget you, Jerusalem, may my right hand forget its skill. May my tongue cling to the roof of my mouth if I do not remember you, if I do not consider Jerusalem my highest joy."

It is important to see that Nehemiah was broken because the city of God was broken. It is also important to see what Nehemiah did. He prayed. In his prayer, he began by confessing his sin and the sins of the people. He recognized the greatness of God in His plan. Nehemiah 1:6-7, "I confess the sins we Israelites, including myself and my father's family, have committed against you. We have acted very wickedly toward you. We have not obeyed the commands, decrees, and laws you gave your servant Moses."

Nehemiah wept over the place of God and the people of God. The Lord heard his prayer. Jesus said in Matthew 5:4, "Blessed are those who mourn, for they will be comforted." In the context of the Sermon on the Mount in Matthew chapter 5, this mourning is because of sin and the brokenness it causes.

Now, because of faith in the Son of God, the Spirit of God is with His people. Are we brokenhearted about the brokenness of our spiritual walls? First Corinthians 3:16, "Don't you know that you yourselves are God's temple and that God's Spirit dwells in your midst?"

How do you feel when the place of God or the people of God are in ruins?

Notes

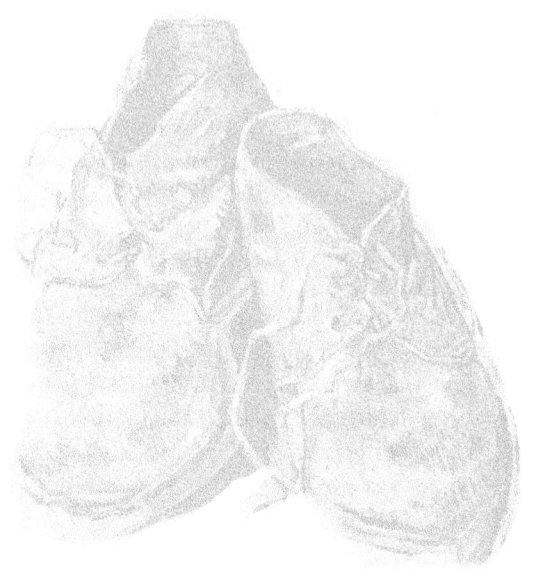

10:
The Silent Era

Week 31: Malachi
Malachi 3:1-18

Key verse: *"'I will send my messenger, who will prepare the way before me. Then suddenly the Lord you are seeking will come to his temple; the messenger of the covenant, whom you desire, will come,' says the Lord Almighty." (Malachi 3:1)*

LEADER'S NOTE

We have studied Ezra and Nehemiah, and we have seen the Lord restoring His relationship with His people. However, there is still a problem. The people have been unfaithful, and in the book of Malachi, He confronts them.

We want the students to see that the Lord is faithful, and He requires faithfulness in every aspect of our lives. God is always working, even in the silent times. Feel free to spend time telling the students about how God worked in the days between Malachi and the New Testament, also known as the intertestamental period. For example: the Greeks developed a common language throughout their empire. This allowed for greater communication between peoples.

The Romans developed a road system across the empire that allowed for easier travel. The time of the Roman Empire was also a time of peace, known as the Pax Romana. This peace allowed for safe travel across the empire.

Help the students understand that this final Old Testament prophet is being used by God to warn the people and to tell them that He is sending the one who will prepare the way (John the Baptist), and He is sending His Messiah.

CONTEXT

The book of Malachi was written during the time of Nehemiah's return, approximately 444 B.C. It is the last book of prophecy, and it is the last book of our Old Testament.

The book of Malachi leads us into what is known as the Silent Era. That period of time between the Old Testament and the New Testament.

The book of Malachi consists of six disputes between the Lord and His people regarding their disloyalty. The Lord confronts, then the people question, then the Lord responds.

OPEN UP

Have you ever been told about a future event? Did it have a date and time or was it open? For example: the championship game will be Saturday night at 7 pm. Or: The school superintendent will visit the school one day.

THINK ABOUT

If someone famous is going to visit you, would you want a warning or a sign so that you can prepare? What if Jesus came to your house today, would you recognize Him?

READ

Verse 1: Is Malachi talking about one person or two? Who are they?

Verses 2-4: What will the Lord do?

Verses 5-6: What do these verses mean? Is this "good news" or bad?

Verses 7-12: What is the charge against the people?

Verses 13-15: Is it a waste of time to serve God? Do you see bad people living good lives?

Verses 16-18: What is the "good news"?

FOCUS

> *"I will send my messenger, who will prepare the way before me. Then suddenly the Lord you are seeking will come to his temple; the messenger of the covenant, whom you desire, will come," says the Lord Almighty. (Malachi 3:1)*

If Malachi is a prophet, a messenger of God, and if the temple has been restored by Ezra and Nehemiah, why does God need to send another prophet to prepare for the Lord to enter?

What do you think was missing from the spiritual lives of the people? Who would be the messenger of the covenant?

Read what Jesus said in the Lord's Supper: "This cup is the new covenant in my blood, which is poured out for you" (Luke 22:20).

It was over 400 years between the prophecy of Malachi and the time Jesus entered the temple. That's a long time to wait. How long do you think the people waited for these signs?

When John the Baptist arrived, do you think the people recognized him as the fulfillment of this prophecy? Mark quotes Isaiah and Malachi: "Behold, I send My messenger before Your face, who will prepare Your way before You" (Mark 1:2).

Do you think the people understood what was happening when Jesus entered the temple and cleansed it?

> *And making a whip of cords, he drove them all out of the temple, with the sheep and oxen. And he poured out the coins of the money-changers and overturned their tables. (John 2:15)*

TALK

- What is this teaching me about God?
- What is this teaching me about people?
- Why is this important to me today?

CONNECT THE GOSPEL

This is the Gospel: "For what I received I passed on to you as of first importance: that Christ died for our sins according to the Scriptures, that he was buried, that he was raised on the third day according to the Scriptures" (1 Corinthians 15:3-4 NIV).

The "good news" of the Gospel is that God was making a way for us to be restored to Him by taking away our sin debt. Here in Malachi, we see the promise of the Lord coming to His temple.

In Malachi 3:1, he says that the messenger of the covenant is the one we desire. Why do we desire one to come as a messenger of the covenant? Do you think that the Lord is saying through Malachi that the covenant is not complete?

SO WHAT?

What is the big deal about this prophecy from 2,400 years ago?

Let's think about what this proves in the New Testament era. We have seen God restore His people to their place in Israel. We know that the people have not been completely restored. Just because they have the temple doesn't mean they have experienced new life.

How many times have you gone to church, but nothing has changed? Why? What is missing? In the days of Malachi, without a Savior, the people were unchanged in their hearts. We have churches everywhere, but many people are unchanged. We all need a Savior to change us.

SERVE

Can you be a messenger of "good news" this week? Do you know someone who is wondering if God is working in their life? Help them to know that He is working.

DIG DEEPER

> *"I will send my messenger, who will prepare the way before me. Then suddenly the Lord you are seeking will come to his temple; the messenger of the covenant, whom you desire, will come," says the Lord Almighty. (Malachi 3:1)*

In our study, we have learned that God sent His messengers to the people, but the people did not listen. From the time when the kingdom was divided to the time when the northern and southern kingdoms were taken into captivity, until the time of the return from exile, messengers (prophets) had been telling the people that the Messiah was coming.

If we were living in the days of Malachi, how would we respond to one more prophet telling us that the Messiah is coming? Would we be impatient and begin to live and worship our own way?

Malachi 3 is a picture of religious people who turned their back on the God of their religion, and they were not afraid of Him (Mal. 3:5).

Malachi told the people what to look for in the future. First would be the one to come and prepare the way for the Lord. God was speaking through Malachi, and God said, "prepare the way before me." God Himself was about to come to His people, and Malachi had the message.

Malachi was reminding them of what Isaiah had said 300 years earlier: "A voice of one calling: 'In the wilderness prepare the way for the Lord; make straight in the desert a highway for our God'" (Isa. 40:3).

So when John the Baptist arrived, the people should have connected the signs. The angel told Zechariah about his son John: "And he will go on before the Lord, in the spirit and power of Elijah, to turn the hearts of the parents to their children and the disobedient to the wisdom of the righteous—to make ready a people prepared for the Lord" (Luke 1:17).

Then in John 1:23, John the Baptist said of himself, "John replied in the words of Isaiah the prophet, 'I am the voice of one calling in the wilderness, "Make straight the way for the Lord."'" John was quoting what Isaiah had prophesied seven hundred years earlier about him.

With these signs, the people should have been looking for the "messenger of the covenant." They should not have been surprised when Jesus entered the temple and cleansed the courts. "So, he made a whip out of cords, and drove all from the temple courts, both sheep and cattle; he scattered the coins of the money changers and overturned their tables" (John 2:15).

Many teachers believe this "messenger of the covenant" refers to the New Covenant which Jesus spoke of, and which Jeremiah told them about, "'The days are coming,' declares the Lord, 'when I will make a new covenant with the people of Israel and with the people of Judah'" (Jer. 31:31).

It was not until the Last Supper that Jesus identified the New Covenant. His life was spent showing the people, and us, who He is, God with us. Then, when Jesus shared the wine and broke the bread, He showed us the New Covenant. "In the same way, after the supper he took the cup, saying, 'This cup is the new covenant in my blood, which is poured out for you'" (Luke 22:20).

Malachi confronted the people in their sin. He also pointed them to their Savior, and he told them how they would know that He had come. Malachi did not preach the prosperity Gospel, but he did give the people hope, "'On the day when I act,' says the Lord Almighty, 'they will be my treasured possession. I will spare them, just as a father has compassion and spares his son who serves him'" (Mal. 3:17).

Notes

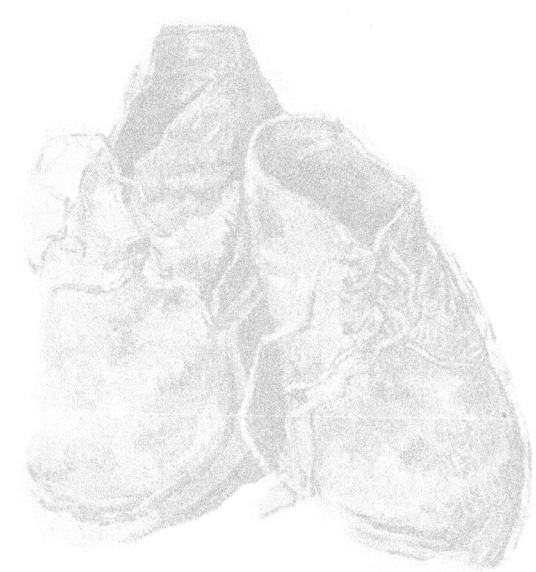

11:
The Gospel Era

LEADER'S GUIDE—SOJOURNER BIBLE STUDY

Week 32: Jesus' Birth Announced
Luke 1:1-17; 1:26-38

Key verse: *"The angel answered, 'The Holy Spirit will come on you, and the power of the Most High will overshadow you. So, the holy one to be born will be called the Son of God.'" (Luke 1:35)*

LEADER'S NOTE

This could be a tricky lesson to cover with your students depending on the level of their maturity. Try not to allow the discussion to drift into the virginity side of the story, or the conception between the Holy Spirit and a teenage girl.

In this lesson we want to connect the Old Testament with the New. We are connecting last week's lesson from Malachi; the promise of a "messenger" and the promise of the Lord's arrival, to its fulfillment in the New Testament.

CONTEXT

The Gospel of Luke was written by Luke, a Gentile physician. It was written to an audience of Gentiles and Jews with the purpose of showing that Jesus is the Son of Man who brings salvation to Jews and Gentiles. It was written between 70-80 A.D.

In the opening of chapter 1, Luke tells us that he is writing to give an accurate account of everything that Theophilus has heard concerning Jesus.

> ...so that you may know the certainty of the things you have been taught. (Luke 1:4)

OPEN UP

How much of the Bible do you think is true?

THINK ABOUT

Is there anything that God can't do? (Yes, He can't sin. It's against His nature.)

READ

Verses 1-4: Why was this written?

Verses 5-7: What do we learn about Zechariah and Elizabeth? They are descendants of Aaron the priest, and priests were messengers of God for the people.

Verses 8-12: What happened?

Verses 13-17: What does the angel tell Zechariah?

Verses 26-27: What do we learn about Mary? Mary is a descendant of David, so she is in the royal line.

Verses 28-33: What does the angel say about the Baby?

Verses 34-38: How did Mary respond?

11: THE GOSPEL ERA

FOCUS

The angel answered, "The Holy Spirit will come on you, and the power of the Most High will overshadow you. So, the holy one to be born will be called the Son of God." (Luke 1:35)

How long have the people been waiting for the Messiah? Do you remember last week's lesson about Malachi's prophecy? What does the Bible say about the one to be born? What is special about Mary?

Read verse 35. Who is doing all of the work? What did Mary have to do? Can you see Mary's faith in verse 38?

TALK

- What is this teaching me about God?
- What is this teaching me about people?
- Why is this important to me today?

CONNECT THE GOSPEL

This is the Gospel: "For what I received I passed on to you as of first importance: that Christ died for our sins according to the Scriptures, that he was buried, that he was raised on the third day according to the Scriptures" (1 Corinthians 15:3-4 NIV).

When the Holy Spirit came to fill Mary, He was preparing her to be the vessel for the Word of God. This is in fulfillment of what the prophet Isaiah said in 7:14: "Therefore the Lord himself will give you a sign: The virgin will conceive and give birth to a son, and will call him Immanuel."

Remember that Isaiah 9:6 told us that a Son was coming: "For to us a child is born, to us a son is given, and the government will be on his shoulders. And he will be called Wonderful Counselor, Mighty God, Everlasting Father, Prince of Peace."

When the angel announced to Mary that she would be carrying the Son of God, she was carrying the "good news." In Acts 1:8, also written by Luke, we have a similar message given to us from Jesus. The power of the Most High will come upon us, and we will be His messengers to the world. The Word became flesh and dwelt among us for a time. Now the Word dwells within us in the power of the Holy Spirit. Now we carry the message.

SO WHAT?

We have spent thirty-one weeks studying the Old Testament and looking forward to the promised Messiah. Now we have seen the fulfillment of prophecy as the angel of the Lord announced the birth of John and the birth of the Son of the Most High.

What does all of this have to do with us today? Everything. When the angel of the Lord appeared to Mary, God was connecting the promises He made to His people in the Old Testament with the promise of His presence in the New Testament. The announcement of the coming Messiah shows us that God has a plan for us. The God of creation came to us so that we could be right with Him.

SERVE

Think about the people in your life every week. How can you help them hear about Jesus?

Think about a way that you can serve someone this week. As you are helping them, ask them if they know that God has a plan for them to know Him.

DIG DEEPER

The angel answered, "The Holy Spirit will come on you, and the power of the Most High will overshadow you. So, the holy one to be born will be called the Son of God." (Luke 1:35)

It seems like a long time ago when we read Genesis 3. "And I will put enmity between you and the woman, and between your seed and her Seed; He shall bruise your head, and you shall bruise His heel" (Gen. 3:15). Now, Luke is telling us that the Seed of the woman has come.

We have seen through our study how God has protected the godly line. We saw the promise to David that he would have an eternal kingdom. In Luke 3:31, Luke will show the reader the link to David.

We have talked about the prophecy of Isaiah, that the Lord would give the sign through a virgin birth. If God is a Spirit, how could that be possible?

Now let's look at the work of the Holy Spirit. Jewish readers would have recognized the wording here, "the power of the Most High will overshadow you." In the Old Testament, God arrived in a cloud or the shadow of a cloud.

Exodus 40:34, "Then the cloud covered the tabernacle of meeting, and the glory of the Lord filled the tabernacle." The cloud covered the tabernacle or "overshadowed" it. The visible sign of the presence of God in the place where you could meet God.

Second Chronicles 5:14, "so that the priests could not continue ministering because of the cloud; for the glory of the Lord filled the house of God." The visible sign of the presence of God in the place where you could meet God.

Second Chronicles 7:1, "Now when Solomon had finished praying, fire came down from heaven and consumed the burnt offering and the sacrifices, and the glory of the Lord filled the house." The visible sign of the presence of God in the place where you could meet God.

Exodus 19:16-17, "Then it came to pass on the third day, in the morning, that there were thunderings and lightnings, and a thick cloud on the mountain; and the sound of the trumpet was very loud, so that all the people who were in the camp trembled. And Moses brought the people out of the camp to meet with God, and they stood at the foot of the mountain." The visible sign of the presence of God in the place where you could meet God. Here, on the mountain, in the cloud, Moses met God and received the Word of God.

John the Apostle told us that the Word became flesh and made His dwelling among us (John 1:14). How? The power of the Most High God overshadowed a young woman, and the Word became flesh. Now, Mary was carrying the visible sign that the presence of God was coming to His people.

Paul puts it in words that Jews and non-Jews would understand when he wrote about Jesus, "made Himself of no reputation, taking the form of a bondservant, and coming in the likeness of men. And being found in appearance as a man, He humbled Himself and became obedient to the point of death, even the death of the cross" (Phil. 2:7-8).

The Holy One would be called the Son of God.

Notes

11: THE GOSPEL ERA

Week 33: John the Baptist
Luke 3:3-18

Key verse: *"John answered them all, 'I baptize you with water. But one who is more powerful than I will come, the straps of whose sandals I am not worthy to untie. He will baptize you with the Holy Spirit and fire.'" (Luke 3:16)*

LEADER'S NOTE

You may want to review the Malachi lesson as you prepare for our study of John the Baptist. John the Baptist is vital to the New Testament because he prepares the people to hear the Messiah.

Help the students to understand that when John began to minister, he was fulfilling Old Testament prophecy and pointing people to the Messiah. We want the students to understand that the Old Testament prophets pointed to the coming Messiah, and John announced His arrival, He is here.

John preached repentance. Jesus brought the way to new life.

CONTEXT

The birth of John the Baptist was announced by an angelic messenger. His ministry ended four hundred years of prophetic silence. The birth of John was very similar to the birth of Isaac to aged parents, Abraham and Sarah.

John the Baptist is the transitional figure between the Old and New Testaments. He marks the culmination of the Law and the prophets, and he proclaims the arrival of the kingdom of God.

> *The Law and the Prophets were proclaimed until John. Since that time, the "good news" of the kingdom of God is being preached, and everyone is forcing their way into it. (Luke 16:16)*

OPEN UP

If the Old Testament points to Jesus, do we need to study it if we already follow Jesus?

THINK ABOUT

Is it possible to learn from people who are older than us? Give some examples.

READ

Verse 3: What did John preach?

Verses 4-6: What is John doing?

Verse 7: What does John call the people? Is this a good way to encourage people to join your church or group?

Verses 8-14: What is repentance? How do you know if someone has repented or changed their life? Do you believe their words or their actions?

Verses 15-18: Who does John talk about? What will this next Person do?

FOCUS

> *John answered them all, "I baptize you with water. But one who is more powerful than I will come, the straps of whose sandals I am not worthy to untie. He will baptize you with the Holy Spirit and fire." (Luke 3:16)*

What was John's mission? Do you think he understood his role in the plan of God? Was he trying to get people to follow himself? How was John preparing people to meet Jesus? Here's a hard question: Can baptism save you?

TALK

- What is this teaching me about God?
- What is this teaching me about people?
- Why is this important to me today?

CONNECT THE GOSPEL

This is the Gospel: "For what I received I passed on to you as of first importance: that Christ died for our sins according to the Scriptures, that he was buried, that he was raised on the third day according to the Scriptures" (1 Corinthians 15:3-4 NIV).

Verse 18 tells us that John preached the Gospel to the people. How could he do that if Jesus hasn't been crucified yet? What would be the "good news" that John would proclaim?

John preached the "good news" that Jesus was coming, and Jesus would bring new life. The people have been waiting for God to move for over four hundred years. Very similar to the time the Hebrews were slaves in Egypt. Now John is announcing that the Messiah they have been waiting for is coming.

The Gospel is "good news" for people who have been waiting to know the truth about God. Now, God is coming to the people, and John is preparing their hearts for Him.

SO WHAT?

Just as John announced the coming of Jesus to the people two thousand years ago, someone told us about Jesus in our time. The message hasn't changed. We are not worthy to untie the shoes of Jesus, but He has come to us so that we can enter His presence. And we have been given the opportunity to announce His presence.

SERVE

What did you learn from this lesson?

Do you know anyone who does not go to church? If you do, how can you talk to them this week about how God has sent messengers to us so that we can know Him? Ask God to help you connect with people so that you can announce the "good news" in their lives.

DIG DEEPER

> *John answered them all, "I baptize you with water. But one who is more powerful than I will come, the straps of whose sandals I am not worthy to untie. He will baptize you with the Holy Spirit and fire." (Luke 3:16)*

Baptism was a Jewish tradition that had been passed down from generation to generation. If this was a Jewish tradition, then John was not doing anything unusual or against the Jewish people. John the Baptist had a reputation for being like the prophets of the Old Testament. When someone described Elijah the prophet, "They replied, 'He had a garment of hair and had a leather belt around his waist'" (2 Kings 1:8). The same was said about John.

Mark 1:4-6 gives us a picture of John the Baptist:

> *And so John the Baptist appeared in the wilderness, preaching a baptism of repentance for the forgiveness of sins. The whole Judean countryside and all the people of Jerusalem went out to him. Confessing their*

sins, they were baptized by him in the Jordan River. John wore clothing made of camel's hair, with a leather belt around his waist, and he ate locusts and wild honey.

John's actions caused the people to wonder if he was the Messiah. When people asked John the Baptist to explain himself, he always referred them to the Word of God. Isaiah 40:3, "John replied in the words of Isaiah the prophet, 'I am the voice of one calling in the wilderness, "Make straight the way for the Lord."'"

We need to understand that John was doing great work. He was not preaching about peace and prosperity, but instead he told the leaders that they were a bunch of snakes! People were listening to his message, and they were even asking what their group should do (Luke 3:10). It would have been easy for John to build his own following, but he did not.

A true prophet of God knows his or her role, and the prophet always points people to God. In 1Kings 18:37, when Elijah called down fire on his sacrifice, he prayed, "Answer me, Lord, answer me, so these people will know that you, Lord, are God, and that you are turning their hearts back again."

John pointed to the One greater, the One who existed before him (John 1:30). John's baptism did not change the heart or transform a life, but it did prepare the hearts of the people to hear the message. John's message pointed them to the One who would save.

This Savior would baptize with the Holy Spirit and fire. These are two baptisms for two different groups of people. In the context of today's reading, John had already told them that the axe is at the tree, and if you do not produce good fruit, you will be thrown into the fire (Luke 3:9). In 3:17, John told us about how the chaff would be destroyed by fire.

The baptism of the Holy Spirit is the work of the Spirit of God in the believer. This is the promised Spirit from Joel 2:28. The Holy Spirit in us produces the fruit of the Spirit, "But the fruit of the Spirit is love, joy, peace, forbearance, kindness, goodness, faithfulness, gentleness and self-control" (Gal. 5:22-23b).

God has created us to do good work in Christ Jesus, which He prepared beforehand (Eph. 2:10). Just as God prepared John to be a messenger, He has also prepared us to be messengers of His Gospel.

If you have been baptized by the Holy Spirit, you have the power to do the work God has called you to do. Acts 1:8, "But you will receive power when the Holy Spirit comes on you; and you will be my witnesses in Jerusalem, and in all Judea and Samaria, and to the ends of the earth."

Notes

LEADER'S GUIDE—SOJOURNER BIBLE STUDY

Week 34: Love Your Enemies
Matthew 5:43-48

Key verse: *"But I say to you, love your enemies, and pray for those who persecute you." (Matthew 5:44)*

LEADER'S NOTE

As we study the Gospel Era, we are looking at some of the events that occurred during Jesus' ministry as well as some of His teachings. Feel free to take this section to teach from other accounts in the Gospels. We will begin the Church Era in Week 47, with a look at Acts 2.

This week we want the students to begin to think differently about "enemies." This is a vastly different worldview from the culture around us. We live in a self-centered culture that loves revenge and "pay-backs."

CONTEXT

The Gospel of Matthew focuses on the kingdom of God. The book is written as "a battle for the heart and soul of the Jews," according to David Platt.

The theme of Matthew is that Jesus is the King of the Jews. In chapter 1, Matthew connects the birth of Jesus to the line of David and Abraham. The teaching of Jesus goes beyond head knowledge to the heart. Simply put, love God and love people.

OPEN UP

Do you have any enemies? Why?

THINK ABOUT

According to a lot of movies and television series today, how should we treat our enemies?

READ

Verse 43: What did Jesus say? Are these two things in the Old Testament? (Leviticus 19:18).

Verses 44-48: What does Jesus say? Is this different from the way many people think?

FOCUS

> *But I say to you, love your enemies, and pray for those who persecute you. (Matthew 5:44)*

Think about movies and television shows that you enjoy. If someone is the enemy, how are they usually treated? What would your friends think if you began being nice to people who are mean to you? What would happen in your school or in your neighborhood if Christians began to love their enemies?

TALK

- What is this teaching me about God?
- What is this teaching me about people?
- Why is this important to me today?

CONNECT THE GOSPEL

This is the Gospel: "For what I received I passed on to you as of first importance: that Christ died for our sins according to the Scriptures, that he was buried, that he was raised on the third day according to the Scriptures" (1 Corinthians 15:3-4 NIV).

The Gospel is the message of hope. The Gospel is the message of love for enemies. Do you know that you were an enemy of God until you turned to Him in faith?

Look at what Paul wrote in Colossians 1:21-23: "Once you were alienated from God and were enemies in your minds because of your evil behavior. But now he has reconciled you by Christ's physical body through death to present you holy in his sight, without blemish and free from accusation—if you continue in your faith, established and firm, and do not move from the hope held out in the Gospel."

Think about this: what if God loved you the same way that you love your enemies?

SO WHAT?

So what? We live in a hurting world. All around us there are people who hurt other people, and there are people who have been hurt by other people. Chances are you have been hurt by someone, or you have hurt someone.

Every day, you have a choice. You can help, or you can hurt. We can only truly help someone when we learn to love like Jesus. That means loving people who are hard to love. Are you easy to love?

SERVE

Let's spend this week praying for our enemies. Pray that God will bring healing in their lives. Pray that God will give you the ability to show them the love of Jesus.

DIG DEEPER

> *But I say to you, love your enemies, and pray for those who persecute you. (Matthew 5:44)*

The message of Jesus is countercultural. When God brought His people out of bondage from Egypt, and they traveled in the wilderness for forty years, He gave them laws for how to be in relationships with each other. He also gave them laws to guide them in their relationship with Him.

> *If you come across your enemy's ox or donkey wandering off, be sure to return it. If you see the donkey of someone who hates you fallen down under its load, do not leave it there; be sure you help them with it. (Exodus 23:4-5)*

> *Do not seek revenge or bear a grudge against anyone among your people, but love your neighbor as yourself. I am the Lord. (Leviticus 19:18)*

Solomon wrote in Proverbs 20:22, "Do not say, 'I'll pay you back for this wrong!' Wait for the Lord, and he will avenge you."

Dr. Martin Luther King, Jr, in a sermon on November 17, 1957; Dexter Avenue Baptist Church, Montgomery, Alabama; said this about our text today: "The first reason that we should love our enemies, and I think this was at the very center of Jesus' thinking, is this: that hate for hate only intensifies the existence of hate and evil in the universe. If I hit you and you hit me and I hit you back and you hit me back and go on, you see, that goes on ad infinitum."

The teaching of Jesus transforms individuals and cultures. Other religions talk about revenge and inner peace. Jesus taught us to love our enemies, so "that you may be children of your Father in heaven" (Mat. 5:45a). Our love for our enemies, and our love for the unlovable, is a reflection of Whose we are. In Christ, we are children of the Living God, and we bear His image.

> *If you love those who love you, what credit is that to you? Even sinners love those who love them. And if you do good to those who are good to you, what credit is that to you? Even sinners do that. And if you lend to those from whom you expect repayment, what credit is that to you? Even sinners lend to sinners, expecting to be repaid in full. But love your enemies, do good to them, and lend to them without expecting to get anything back. Then your reward will be great, and you will be children of the Most High, because he is kind to the ungrateful and wicked. Be merciful, just as your Father is merciful. (Luke 6:32-36)*

By loving our enemies, we are showing the love of Christ. By praying for our enemies, we are showing our desire for their salvation. Many times, when we pray for our enemies, we will see the Lord change us.

The two greatest commandments are summed up like this: love God and love people.

Notes

11: THE GOSPEL ERA

Week 35: Fishers of Men
Luke 5:1-11

Key verse: *And when they had brought their boats to land, they left everything and followed Him. (Luke 5:11)*

LEADER'S NOTE

This passage is so rich, and you may decide to approach this differently. That's fine because you know your students better than we do.

It's our desire that the students see the results of the miracle. These men left everything to follow Jesus. What have we left to follow Jesus?

CONTEXT

The Gospel of Luke was written by Luke, a Gentile. He was not an apostle. His desire was to provide an accurate, historical account of Jesus.

In the opening chapters we saw the birth story, then the temptation, then the beginning of His ministry. Now we are seeing Him calling His disciples.

OPEN UP

What did you leave behind when you decided to follow Jesus?

THINK ABOUT

Is there anything in your life now that you need to leave behind so that you can follow Jesus more closely? (Hobbies, activities, friends, etc.).

READ

Verses 1-3: What was happening? Why were the multitudes trying to be near Him? You may want to read Luke 4:40-44.

Verses 4-5: What happened? How was Simon feeling?

Verses 6-7: What happened?

Verse 8: What did Simon Peter say? Why would he feel this way?

Verses 9-11: What did Jesus say? What does that mean? Did the disciples believe Him? How do you know?

FOCUS

And when they had brought their boats to land, they left everything and followed Him. (Luke 5:11)

The disciples left everything to follow Jesus. That was a sign of their faith.

Do you know people who have decided to follow Jesus? How do you know if they have been truly saved? What changed in their life? If you are following Jesus now, what is different about your life?

TALK

- What is this teaching me about God?
- What is this teaching me about people?
- Why is this important to me today?

CONNECT THE GOSPEL

This is the Gospel: "For what I received I passed on to you as of first importance: that Christ died for our sins according to the Scriptures, that he was buried, that he was raised on the third day according to the Scriptures" (1 Corinthians 15:3-4 NIV).

The Gospel is the "good news" of how Jesus has saved us and changed us. If we are truly saved then we won't be the same as we were before we met Jesus.

In this passage we see Jesus call these men away from their jobs for a reason. He was giving them a new mission. What was it? If they are fishing for men, what are they doing? They are telling people about Jesus. They are bringing the "good news" to them.

SO WHAT?

What's the big deal about some fishermen who stopped fishing and followed Jesus? The big deal is that they were changed. These men would be used in a great way after Jesus ascended to heaven. These men would be leaders in the early church. The big deal is that their lives were changed so much that they spent the rest of their lives telling people about Jesus.

SERVE

If you are going to fish for people, what do you need to focus on? This week, spend time thinking about the things you do each day that take up your time. Is there something you can change in your daily routine that will give you time to tell people about Jesus?

Are you too busy doing what you want to do that you don't see opportunities to help people know about Jesus?

DIG DEEPER

> *And when they had brought their boats to land, they left everything and followed Him. (Luke 5:11)*

In Luke 4:38-39, Jesus had been in Simon's home, and He had healed Simon's mother-in-law. After that miracle, we do not really see any response from Simon, but the mother-in-law responded immediately by serving Jesus. This event is reported in each of the synoptic Gospels. There is something in this miracle that opened Simon's eyes. A point of conjecture: could it be that Jesus the Teacher did something that Simon the fisherman was not able to do in his own area of expertise?

Every miracle in the Bible points to the work of God. In these miracles, we see lives changed and lessons learned. The miracle of the catch revealed to these fishermen that they were in the presence of God.

Jesus had been teaching near the lake, and the people were crowding around Him. There were so many people that He got into a boat to separate Himself from the press of the crowd. Jesus was no ordinary itinerant teacher. Matthew 7:29 tells us, "He taught as one who had authority, and not as their teachers of the law."

The people recognized there was something different in Jesus. When Jesus had finished teaching and He spoke to Simon, Simon called Him "master." This word in the Greek, *epistatata*, has the idea of a commander, a leader, or a boss. Simon recognized the authority of Jesus in His teaching.

Simon could have made any excuse to avoid the request of Jesus, but he did not. His response was the same response that we should have when the Lord calls us to action. "Nevertheless, at Your word I will let down the net." Immediate obedience to the call of the Lord is a picture of our faith in Him.

At Your word, I will obey. From the beginning of time, we have seen God speak, and all of creation obeyed Him except the people. The people seem to be the only part of God's creation who seem to struggle with obedience.

Genesis 1:3, "Then God said, 'Let there be light,' and there was light." Throughout Genesis chapter 1, we see God speak, and it happened. Did Simon recognize the Word of God in the boat?

When Simon saw the miracle, he fell at his knees, a position of humility and respect. In Simon's response he confessed that he was a sinner, and he could not be in the presence of the Lord.

Isaiah saw the Lord, and it brought him to a point of fear and confession as well. Isaiah 6:5, "So I said: 'Woe is me, for I am undone! Because I am a man of unclean lips, and I dwell in the midst of a people of unclean lips; for my eyes have seen the King, The Lord of hosts.'"

The Lord God cleansed Isaiah so that he could go and proclaim the message of God to the people. His message was a message of coming judgment upon the nation of Israel. Jesus cleansed the heart of Simon and the other disciples (John 15:3). Jesus, the Son of God, called these fishermen turned disciples, to take a new message to the people, a message of salvation.

Isaiah experienced the presence of God, and his life was changed, and he was immediately obedient. Isaiah said, "Here am I, send me" (Isa. 6:8). Simon and the others experienced the presence of God, and their lives were changed, and they were immediately obedient.

"They left everything and followed Him." These fishermen had just caught so many fish that they could not pull them in, and they left them. They left their boats, which they needed to do their work. They left everything and followed the Lord.

What have you left behind to follow Jesus?

Notes

LEADER'S GUIDE—SOJOURNER BIBLE STUDY

Week 36: The Beatitudes
Matthew 5:1-12

Key verse: *"Blessed are you when men revile you, and persecute you, and say all kinds of evil against you falsely, on account of Me." (Matthew 5:11)*

LEADER'S NOTE

The Beatitudes walk us through the salvation and sanctification process.

Help the students see the process. It begins by recognizing that our spirit is poor; something is missing. The Beatitudes conclude with the fact that persecution will come to those who follow Jesus.

Each state of being within the process grows from the preceding state. This is the sanctification process. We come to Christ from a poor spirit, we grow to be like Christ, and then we suffer for Christ.

CONTEXT

The Gospel of Matthew was written to a primarily Jewish audience. This is the beginning of what is known as the "Sermon on the Mount."

When Jesus went up on a mountain, the Jewish people would recall when Moses went up the mountain in the Exodus account. However, when Moses went up the mountain the people could not come near the mountain or they would die. Here, in the Matthew account, we see Jesus go to the mountain and the people were able to be near Him.

Moses came down with the Law of God. Jesus is the fulfillment of the Law, and now He is telling everyone how they can know God.

OPEN UP

What is persecution?

THINK ABOUT

Have you ever been persecuted because you follow Jesus? Why or why not?

READ

Verse 1: Why are the multitudes coming to Jesus? (You may want to review chapter 4:23-25.)

Verse 2: What is happening?

Verses 3-11: Look at each verse. What is the cause of the blessing, and what is the result? Can you see the spiritual growth in these verses from poor in spirit to the point of persecution?

Verse 12: Why should we rejoice when persecuted? Who does Jesus compare us to in our suffering?

FOCUS

> *"Blessed are you when men revile you, and persecute you, and say all kinds of evil against you falsely, on account of Me." (Matthew 5:11)*

Some translations use the word "blessed," and some use the word "happy." What is the Lord Jesus telling us? Is there really a happiness to be counted worthy to suffer for the Lord? We don't see it until the disciples begin to suffer for preaching the Gospel.

> *The apostles left the high council rejoicing that God had counted them worthy to suffer disgrace for the name of Jesus. (Acts 5:41)*

Do you think it would be easy to be happy about being persecuted for your faith? There is a difference in suffering for our faith, and suffering because we did something bad.

> *For what credit is it if, when you sin and are beaten for it, you endure? But if when you do good and suffer for it you endure, this is a gracious thing in the sight of God. (1 Peter 2:20)*

If you do something bad, and you get in trouble, you are not suffering for Jesus.

TALK

- What is this teaching me about God?
- What is this teaching me about people?
- Why is this important to me today?

CONNECT THE GOSPEL

This is the Gospel: "For what I received I passed on to you as of first importance: that Christ died for our sins according to the Scriptures, that he was buried, that he was raised on the third day according to the Scriptures" (1 Corinthians 15:3-4 NIV).

The "good news" of Jesus Christ is that we have been forgiven, and we have new life. The Beatitudes show us what this new life looks like. As we grow in our faith, we also grow closer to the Lord to the point of sharing in His suffering. Have you accepted Christ as your Lord based on the Gospel, and are you living what you believe?

SO WHAT?

Why are the Beatitudes important to me today? They are a great way to evaluate where you are in your faith. Do you claim to be a follower of Christ? If so, where are you in this process?

Are you poor in spirit because you know you are separated from God? Are you mourning over your lostness? Are you a gentle person or always angry or a bully? Go through the list. Where are you? Test yourself.

> *Examine yourselves to see whether you are in the faith; test yourselves. Do you not realize that Christ Jesus is in you—unless, of course, you fail the test? (2 Corinthians 13:5)*

SERVE

This would be a great time to help your friends come to know Jesus better. Talk to them this week about this lesson. Help them understand where they are and where you are in your relationship with Christ.

DIG DEEPER

> *Blessed are you when men revile you, and persecute you, and say all kinds of evil against you falsely, on account of Me. (Matthew 5:11)*

We have discussed in this lesson how the Beatitudes teach us the progression of recognizing the poverty of our spirit, mourning over our lostness, humbling ourselves, desiring God's righteousness, and how this recognition results in a change in our lives by the way we become merciful towards others through a pure heart, which leads us to be peacemakers by bringing others to a point of peace with God, and this will bring persecution because some people will be offended by the truth of the Gospel. We all have sinned and fallen short of the glory of God (Rom. 3:23).

Of course, this new life will lead to persecution. It may be something minor such as being mocked by friends or not being invited to parties or outings. It may result in people making accusations against you because you are not doing what they do. Even in the first century Peter understood this; First Peter 4:4, "Of course, your former friends are surprised when you no longer plunge into the flood of wild and destructive things they do. So, they slander you."

This new life may also create hardships for you. You may not be able to get a promotion or a job because you follow Jesus. In some countries, you may not be able to meet with other believers.

If any of these things describes you, consider yourself blessed of God!

Jesus constantly reminded people that following Him was not easy. John 15:18-19, "'If the world hates you, remember that it hated me first. The world would love you as one of its own if you belonged to it, but you are no longer part of the world. I chose you to come out of the world, so it hates you.'"

Jesus prayed in His priestly prayer, John 17:14, "'I have given them your word. And the world hates them because they do not belong to the world, just as I do not belong to the world.'"

Remember the word "blessed" can also mean "happy." The disciples rejoiced to be counted worthy of this suffering. When Paul and Silas were in prison, they were able to praise God in their singing and prayers. "About midnight Paul and Silas were praying and singing hymns to God, and the other prisoners were listening to them" (Acts 16:25).

> *We can rejoice, too, when we run into problems and trials, for we know that they help us develop endurance. And endurance develops strength of character, and character strengthens our confident hope of salvation. (Romans 5:3-4)*

In Paul's second letter to Timothy, and our last known letter from Paul, he warned Timothy of the persecution and suffering that comes when we live for Jesus. It has a price. "Yes, and everyone who wants to live a godly life in Christ Jesus will suffer persecution" (2 Tim. 3:12).

Jesus gave us the Beatitudes in the beginning of His ministry, and He gave us hope at the end of His life. John 16:33, "These things I have spoken to you, that in Me you may have peace. In the world you will have tribulation; but be of good cheer, I have overcome the world."

Notes

Week 37: Jesus Calms the Storm
Matthew 8:23-27

Key verse: *"The men were amazed and asked, 'What kind of man is this? Even the winds and the waves obey him!'" (Matthew 8:27)*

LEADER'S NOTE

Our Bible studies are attempting to show how God moves and works throughout the Scriptures, from Genesis to Revelation. During our study of the Gospel Era, we want the students to see how Jesus reveals Himself as God in the flesh, and we want the students to understand that Jesus is the Gospel. He is the "good news" of God's plan to save us.

In this lesson Jesus shows His power over nature. Jesus is the One Who created the sea, so of course, He can control it (Genesis 1:6-10).

CONTEXT

The Synoptic Gospels all tell of this event. Jesus has been teaching and healing. He has just finished the Sermon on the Mount, and now He is taking His disciples to the other side of the lake, or the Sea of Galilee. When they reach the other side, Jesus will heal a demon-possessed man. In between these events, we see the humanity of Jesus. He was tired, so He slept, and He slept well.

We don't know everyone in the boat. It may or may not have been all twelve of the disciples.

OPEN UP

What's the most amazing thing you have ever seen in your life?

THINK ABOUT

When was the last time you were afraid? What did you do?

READ

Verses 23-24: What is the significance of the actions we see in these two verses? Think about Jesus, the disciples, and the storm.

Verses 25-26: What did the disciples say, and what did Jesus say?

Verse 27: Describe the feeling of the men.

FOCUS

> *The men were amazed and asked, "What kind of man is this? Even the winds and the waves obey him!" (Matthew 8:27)*

What happened that made the disciples ask this question? Why would they ask that?

The Greek word here for "kind" is *po-tapos*. It is an adjective, so they are looking for a way to describe the One Who controls the storm.

How do you think someone would describe this event if they didn't believe in God? What would you say to them?

TALK

- What is this teaching me about God?
- What is this teaching me about people?
- Why is this important to me today?

CONNECT THE GOSPEL

This is the Gospel: "For what I received I passed on to you as of first importance: that Christ died for our sins according to the Scriptures, that he was buried, that he was raised on the third day according to the Scriptures" (1 Corinthians 15:3-4 NIV).

The "good news," the Gospel of Jesus Christ, is all about how God made a way for us to be in a right relationship with Him by covering our sin.

Jesus was tired, so He slept. We see that He is human like us. When Jesus calms the storm, He is showing us His power over nature. This God Who controls the natural world has the ability to bring us into a relationship with Him.

Only Jesus as a man could take our sin. Only Jesus as God can overcome death for us.

SO WHAT?

If Jesus does not have power over nature, then He is not the One Who created it. If He is not the One Who created it, then He is not God. However, here we see Him speak, and the storm obeyed.

In Genesis chapter 1, God spoke and each part of creation came into being. It is no surprise that He would speak here to control His creation.

SERVE

Do you know people who don't believe in God? This week, think about ways to talk to them about the power of God in creation. Maybe during a rainstorm or other weather event you can share with them that God is in control.

DIG DEEPER

The men were amazed and asked, "What kind of man is this? Even the winds and the waves obey him!" (Matthew 8:27)

How would you describe the One who can calm a storm? We can think of big descriptive words such as "amazing," "awesome," and "powerful," but are they complete in their description?

In the chronology of Jesus' miracles, the catch of fish that we studied in our last lesson occurred before this miracle. We do not know how much time had passed between the two miracles.

Theologians tell us that the next miracle after the miraculous catch of fish was when Jesus healed the man with leprosy (Mat. 8:1-4), then the Centurion's servant (Mat. 8:5-13), then the paralytic who came through the roof (Mat. 9:1-8), then the withered hand (Mat. 12:9-14), and then the widow's son (Luke 7:11-17).

Now our text tells us that the disciples were in the boat on the lake in a storm, and they were afraid that they were about to die. Matthew 8:25, "Save us, Lord; we are perishing." Matthew, Mark, and Luke give us different responses from the disciples, but they are all in agreement: the disciples were afraid of dying, and they were amazed at the power of Jesus' word.

After the disciples had seen all these previous miracles, what were they expecting Jesus to do? Judging by their reaction they were not expecting Him to calm the storm!

Genesis 1:9, "And God said, 'Let the waters under the heavens be gathered together into one place, and let the dry land appear.' And it was so." God spoke, and the waters obeyed.

God gave Job a lesson in Who He is also, "Can you call out to the clouds, so that abundant water drenches you? Can you command the lightning, so that it goes forth and calls to you, 'Look at us!'" (Job 38:34-35)

David knew this God, and His power, Psalm 65:5-8,

> *By awesome deeds you answer us with righteousness, O God of our salvation, the hope of all the ends of the earth and of the farthest seas; the one who by his strength established the mountains, being girded with might; who stills the roaring of the seas, the roaring of their waves, the tumult of the peoples, so that those who dwell at the ends of the earth are in awe at your signs. You make the going out of the morning and the evening to shout for joy.*

What would you say if you were there when the disciples asked, "What kind [type] of man is this that even the winds and the waves obey him?" Would you say, "This is the Lord God Almighty, the Creator of Heaven and Earth?" This is God as a Man. This is Jesus the Messiah.

Notes

LEADER'S GUIDE—SOJOURNER BIBLE STUDY

Week 38: Feeding the 5,000 (Optional: Use Easter lesson)
John 6:1-14

Key verse: *"After the people saw the sign Jesus performed, they began to say, 'Surely this is the Prophet who is to come into the world.'" (John 6:14)*

LEADER'S NOTE

If you choose to teach the Easter lesson here, you may want to review the Good Friday/Crucifixion lesson in Week 46.

If your students have been in church any amount of time, they are familiar with the mass feeding events. This lesson is not going to go deeply into the meal. We want the students to see what happens after a miracle. What was the result? In this case, the people respond in belief that this is the Prophet who was to come into the world.

After a miracle or a life-changing event, do we see Jesus for Who He is? There is always a lesson to learn and a life that is changed.

CONTEXT

In John chapter 5, Jesus has healed the lame man at the pool of Bethesda. This created a stir among the religious leaders because it was on a Sabbath. This led to Jesus explaining to them that they did not understand who is this Jesus.

Chapter 5 closes with Jesus telling them that if they believed the writings of Moses, then they would believe in Him. In Deuteronomy 18:15, Moses said, "The LORD your God will raise up for you a prophet like me from among you, from your fellow Israelites. You must listen to him."

So, this predominantly Jewish audience on the mountain is asking if this is the Prophet that Moses had said was coming. Yes, He is. They believed that Moses had fed everyone in the wilderness with bread from heaven during the trip from Egypt to Canaan, so when Jesus feeds this large group, they see the similarity to Moses.

OPEN UP

What is the most amazing thing you have ever experienced?

THINK ABOUT

What would you think if you saw a miracle happen?

READ

Verse 1: After what things? Summarize chapter 5, especially verses 46 and 47.

Verses 2-3: What happened?

Verse 4: Why is this important to know?

Verses 5-6: What is the situation?

Verses 7-9: What solution do the disciples have?

Verses 10-11: What happened?

Verses 12-14: What happened to the people and what did they think?

FOCUS

After the people saw the sign Jesus performed, they began to say, "Surely this is the Prophet who is to come into the world." (John 6:14)

Who is the Prophet the people are talking about? Read Deuteronomy 18:15.

Read John 5:46, and compare these three passages. Jesus is the Prophet whom Moses spoke of, and He has just done a great miracle. Whenever we see a miracle, it is important to see what happens after the miracle. What is the result?

More than people being fed, they recognized that this is the One they were waiting for. When Jesus calmed the storm in the last lesson, we saw the disciples ask, "Who is this?"

When Jesus performs a miracle, there is a life changed and a lesson to learn. Now we see Jesus revealing Himself to the multitude. The best way to see Jesus is to see Who He is by what He does.

TALK

- What is this teaching me about God?
- What is this teaching me about people?
- Why is this important to me today?

CONNECT THE GOSPEL

This is the Gospel: "For what I received I passed on to you as of first importance: that Christ died for our sins according to the Scriptures, that he was buried, that he was raised on the third day according to the Scriptures" (1 Corinthians 15:3-4 NIV).

When Paul said that Christ died according to the Scriptures, he was talking about the Old Testament. Here we see Jesus reveal Himself to be the Prophet that Moses had talked about in the fifth book of the Old Testament, Deuteronomy. The Jewish audience would have recognized this miracle because it was similar to God feeding the Hebrews when they came out of Egypt.

The Gospel is "good news" for the Jews as well as for us. God became a Man and revealed Himself to us, and we can know Him. Do you need a miracle to believe in Jesus, or will you believe in faith based on what the Bible tells us?

SO WHAT?

Just as Jesus fed the 5,000, He will feed you. All of these people were filled, but they would be hungry again for regular food. The greatest thing Jesus does for anyone is to provide us with the spiritual food we need. Only He can fill us.

SERVE

Find someone to feed this week, and when you do, help them know that Jesus will fill them. Talk about how He fed the multitude.

DIG DEEPER

After the people saw the sign Jesus performed, they began to say, "Surely this is the Prophet who is to come into the world." (John 6:14)

This mass feeding in an open field would have reminded the people of the stories that had been passed down in their history. The twelve baskets of leftovers that were picked up would have been a reminder of the twelve tribes of Israel and the ministry of Elisha (explained later).

The feeding would remind the people of how the Lord God used Moses to bring the people out of bondage in Egypt and into a new land. Along the way, the people complained about being hungry for the food in Egypt. The Lord sent food from heaven, a type of bread and quail (Exodus 16).

Before Moses died, he spoke to the people. He reminded them of all that they had been through and all that they had seen the Lord God do for them. The Lord God promised that He would not abandon His people.

Deuteronomy 18:15, Moses said, "The LORD your God will raise up for you a prophet like me from among you, from your fellow Israelites. You must listen to him."

And the Lord God spoke through Moses, "I will raise up for them a prophet like you from among their brothers. And I will put my words in his mouth, and he shall speak to them all that I command him" (Deut. 18:18). The ancient Jews understood this passage to be a reference to the Messiah.

However, Moses was not the only one to participate in a mass feeding event. In 2 Kings 4:42-44, during a famine, a man came to Elisha with twenty loaves of bread and some grain. There were a hundred prophets with Elisha, but his servant said that it was not enough. Elisha responded, "Give them to the men, that they may eat, for thus says the Lord, 'They shall eat and have some left.'"

Again, in 2 Kings 7, during the time of Elisha the prophet, the land of Samaria was under siege by the Assyrians. There was a great famine in the land, and the people were eating their own children. Elisha brought the word of the Lord to the king and told them that it would change in a day. The king's guard said, "If the Lord himself should make windows in heaven, could this thing be?" (2 Kings 7:2). It happened just as the prophet had said it would.

> *After the people saw the sign Jesus performed, they began to say, "Surely this is the Prophet who is to come into the world." (John 6:14)*

In the first century, the men in Acts 3:22-26 concluded that Jesus was this Prophet and the true Messiah.

> *Moses said, "The Lord God will raise up for you a prophet like me from your brothers. You shall listen to him in whatever he tells you. And it shall be that every soul who does not listen to that prophet shall be destroyed from the people. And all the prophets who have spoken, from Samuel and those who came after him, also proclaimed these days. You are the sons of the prophets and of the covenant that God made with your fathers, saying to Abraham, 'And in your offspring shall all the families of the earth be blessed.' God, having raised up his servant, sent him to you first, to bless you by turning every one of you from your wickedness."*

We have studied the prophets, the messengers of God. We know that they were rejected, and their message was rejected.

Now, in this text, the people are asking if this is the Prophet God promised. What sign do you need to see that Jesus is who He said He is? Can you say, "Surely this is the Prophet who is to come into the world?"

Notes

Week 39: The Promise of a Helper
John 14:15-29

Key verse: *"If you love me, you will keep my commandments." (John 14:15)*

LEADER'S NOTE

We want the students to see that being saved isn't something you do now to guarantee eternal life in the future. We want them to see that the Holy Spirit with us now means that eternal life starts now. We can't live for Jesus without Him living in us. Jesus gave us something hard to do, but He has also given us help.

Following Jesus will be the hardest thing these students will ever do in their lives. It's impossible to do this without help. If we say we love Jesus, we need to do what He tells us, and we can't do that without the Helper.

CONTEXT

Jesus has told the disciples that He is leaving them. He assures them that He will not leave them as orphans. An orphan has lost their parents. We are not losing Jesus if we follow Him.

In verses 16 and 26, Jesus tells us that we need this Helper, the Holy Spirit, to follow Him, to keep His commandments.

OPEN UP

What's the hardest thing you ever had to do? Did you have help?

THINK ABOUT

How can we do what Jesus told us to do? Can you follow Jesus without His help?

READ

Verse 15: What is the "if this/then this" statement in this verse?

Verses 16-17: What does Jesus tell us about this Helper?

Verses 18-20: What are the promises here?

Verse 21: What is the difference between verses 15 and 21?

Verses 22-24: What do we need to do to show our love for the Lord?

Verses 25-29: What are the promises found here?

FOCUS

> *If you love me, you will keep my commandments. (John 14:15)*

Do you love your parents? If yes, do you do what they tell you to do? If we love Jesus, then we should do what He tells us to do. That isn't easy, but it's not impossible either. If you begin to live for Jesus, actually live for Him every day, what do you think will happen? How do you think your friends will respond?

When we begin to truly follow Jesus and keep His commandments, we begin to look differently from the world around us. This may mean that we need to leave some of our friends and stop hanging out with them. You may have a girlfriend or a boyfriend that you need to break up with.

It is not easy to take these steps to follow Jesus. In this lesson, we want to follow Jesus, and we need the help of the Helper, the Holy Spirit.

TALK

- What is this teaching me about God?
- What is this teaching me about people?
- Why is this important to me today?

CONNECT THE GOSPEL

This is the Gospel: "For what I received I passed on to you as of first importance: that Christ died for our sins according to the Scriptures, that he was buried, that he was raised on the third day according to the Scriptures" (1 Corinthians 15:3-4 NIV).

The "good news" about Jesus, that He died and rose again to cover our sins and give us new life, isn't "good news" if it's temporary. The promise of the Holy Spirit means that He is always with us. If He is always with us, then He will give us the ability to follow His commandments.

Then the "good news" is really "good news" because we can live for Jesus. We will be a new creation.

SO WHAT?

What's the big deal about the Holy Spirit? Why is this something we need to think about now in the twenty-first century?

It has everything to do with us today. When the disciples walked with Jesus, He did everything and taught them everything. However, Jesus never planned to stay here forever.

The Holy Spirit is the Spirit of God in us who enables us to know Him. The only way to walk with Jesus, the only way to know Him, is to allow the Holy Spirit to work in our lives. If we will abide in Him, He will abide in us (John 15:4-11). The promise of the Holy Spirit is the promise that the presence of God is always with us.

SERVE

How can you serve this week based on the promise of the Holy Spirit? Are you afraid of talking to people about Jesus? Is it hard for you to start a conversation with people about the Bible or about church?

This week, ask the Holy Spirit to give you the ability to follow Jesus and the boldness to talk to people about Jesus. Ask Him to help you invite someone to church this week.

DIG DEEPER

If you love me, you will keep my commandments." (John 14:15)

In our effort to Dig Deeper here, let's consider some of the Greek words in this verse. First, "love" is from the Greek word *agapao*. This is a very deep love for someone. It is more than the love we would have for a friend or a food.

Then the word "keep." In the Greek, this word is "tereo." It has the meaning of following, to attend to carefully, take care of, to guard, to observe.

This is a paraphrase of John 14:15: "If you love me deeply, more than friends and your stuff, you will pay attention to my commands, and you will take care of my commands, and guard them, and observe them."

In context, John 14, is the beginning of the last words that Jesus would have for His followers. This sermon was given the night before His arrest. This was given to encourage the followers. Jesus told His followers to take heart, He told them that He would prepare a place for them and return, and He told them that the Holy Spirit would comfort them. This chapter reveals the love Jesus had for His disciples, and the love of God for us.

Several times in today's verses Jesus made a conditional statement, "If you love me." Were there some who followed Him but did not love Him deeply?

In Matthew 7:21-23, Jesus knew that some were only following for what they could get. "Not everyone who says to me, 'Lord, Lord,' will enter the kingdom of heaven, but only the one who does the will of my Father who is in heaven. Many will say to me on that day, 'Lord, Lord, did we not prophesy in your name and in your name drive out demons, and in your name perform many miracles?' Then I will tell them plainly, 'I never knew you. Away from me, you evildoers!'" For anyone to do the will of the Father involves them being in a loving relationship with Him.

What did Jesus command? Did He mean that we must keep the Ten Commandments? Did He mean that we need to follow the Levitical laws? If that were the case, then we would not be saved by grace (Eph. 2:8-9). The only work we are called to do is to believe in the One sent from God (John 6:28).

Fortunately for us, someone asked Jesus about these commandments. Matthew 22:36-40, "Teacher, which is the greatest commandment in the Law?" Jesus replied: "'Love the Lord your God with all your heart and with all your soul and with all your mind.' This is the first and greatest commandment. And the second is like it: 'Love your neighbor as yourself.' All the Law and the Prophets hang on these two commandments."

In all the Bible, the key is to love God deeply. Follow His word, guard His word, and take care of His Word; tend to it the way a farmer tends his garden with the hope that it will produce a great crop. "Keep my commandments."

Everything we are called to do as Christ followers can be summed up in this: love God and love people. If we love God, then our love for people will flow from our relationship with God the Father.

John 15:13-14, "Greater love has no one than this: to lay down one's life for one's friends. You are my friends if you do what I command." Jesus laid down His life for every one of us because of love, and all we must do is follow Him in obedience.

So, something to think about: Jesus said, "If you love me, you will keep my commandments." Would the converse be true? If we do not keep His commandments, does it mean we do not love Him?

Notes

LEADER'S GUIDE—SOJOURNER BIBLE STUDY

Week 40: Jesus Walks on Water
Mark 6:45-52

Key verse: *"For they all saw Him and were frightened. But immediately He spoke with them and said to them, 'Take courage; it is I, do not be afraid.'" (Mark 6:50)*

LEADER'S NOTE

We have seen Jesus feed the five thousand, and we have talked about how He calmed the storm. We are only looking at seven verses this week, so it may seem like a short lesson. However, we want to draw some Old Testament Scripture into the lesson and help the students see what is happening. When Jesus walked on water, He showed once again His deity.

The act of Jesus walking on water is definitely a miracle, but there is more to it than that. The disciples were frightened. Verse 52 tells us that the disciples didn't learn anything from the feeding of the five thousand but they had hard hearts.

If the disciples were walking with Jesus every day, and they still had hard hearts after seeing so much, what about us? We have the entirety of Scripture in front of us, and we have seen people whose lives have been changed. Do we know Jesus?

CONTEXT

Just prior to Jesus walking on the water, He had fed five thousand men plus women and children with five loaves of bread and two fish. After they picked up the extras, Jesus told His disciples to go across the lake.

Verse 45 tells us that Jesus sent the people away after the disciples left, and then Jesus went up on the mountain to pray. When Jesus finished praying, the boat and the disciples were out on the lake, and Jesus walked out to them.

OPEN UP

If you saw a man walking on water, would you be afraid?

THINK ABOUT

How many miracles have you read about in the Bible? What are some miracles that Jesus has done? Is it hard for you to believe that Jesus is God?

READ

Verses 45-46: What did Jesus do in these two verses?

Verses 47-48: What did Jesus see, and what did He do?

Verse 49: What did the disciples think?

Verse 50: What happened?

Verses 51-52: What was the reaction of the disciples, and what was their problem?

FOCUS

> *For they all saw Him and were frightened. But immediately He spoke with them and said to them, "Take courage; it is I, do not be afraid." (Mark 6:50)*

They all saw Him, and they were afraid. Why? Because, as verse 52 tells us, they hadn't learned anything from the mass feeding event that had just happened, and their hearts were still hard.

If they had recognized the power of God to bring bread to the people just as He did for the Israelites in the wilderness, then they should have rejoiced when He walked out to them.

The first time we saw the Lord God on the water is in Genesis 1:2, "and the Spirit of God was hovering over the waters." Then, the idea of God "passing by" comes from Exodus 34:6: "And he passed in front of Moses, proclaiming, 'The Lord, the Lord, the compassionate and gracious God, slow to anger, abounding in love and faithfulness, maintaining love to thousands, and forgiving wickedness, rebellion and sin. Yet he does not leave the guilty unpunished; he punishes the children and their children for the sin of the parents to the third and fourth generation.'"

Moses had asked to see the glory of the Lord, and the Lord revealed Himself as He passed by. Now, here in the middle of the sea, the Lord reveals Himself to His disciples and they are frightened and they don't understand. How does God need to reveal Himself to you so that you will not be afraid to follow Him?

TALK

- What is this teaching me about God?
- What is this teaching me about people?
- Why is this important to me today?

CONNECT THE GOSPEL

This is the Gospel: "For what I received I passed on to you as of first importance: that Christ died for our sins according to the Scriptures, that he was buried, that he was raised on the third day according to the Scriptures" (1 Corinthians 15:3-4 NIV).

The "good news" of the Gospel is that God has come to us, so that we can be with Him. Here in Mark chapter 6, God, in Christ, came to His disciples. Jesus met the disciples in the middle of their struggle and joined them.

Let's take courage knowing that Jesus has come to us in order for us to join Him. We can have faith in what He has done for us by taking the penalty for our sin.

SO WHAT?

Did Jesus walk on water or not? If He did, then He is greater than nature. If He did not, then this story is a lie. We all have to decide what to do with this story. If this story isn't true, why would so many people verify it? The disciples witnessed it. Are you prepared to believe it and accept that Jesus is God?

SERVE

How can you serve this week as your faith in Jesus is growing? What can you do to help others understand this Jesus?

DIG DEEPER

> *...for they all saw Him and were frightened. But immediately He spoke with them and said to them, "Take courage; it is I, do not be afraid." (Mark 6:50)*

(Each of the Gospels records the miracle of Jesus walking on the water except Luke. Theologians believe that because Luke was not an eyewitness to the event, he chose not to write about it. Matthew and John were eyewitnesses, and Mark recorded Peter's account.)

> *Shortly before dawn Jesus went out to them, walking on the lake. When the disciples saw him walking on the lake, they were terrified. "It's a ghost," they said, and cried out in fear. (Matthew 14:25-26)*
>
> *...they saw Jesus approaching the boat, walking on the water; and they were frightened. But he said to them, "It is I; don't be afraid." (John 6:19-20)*

The focus of our lesson is not whether Jesus walked on water. Our focus is why were the disciples afraid?

Mark tells us it is because they had not understood about the loaves. We talked about the miracle of the loaves in our Week 38 lesson. The miracle revealed to the people that Jesus was the One that God had promised Moses. Jesus is the Messiah, the Savior. This should have been enough for the disciples to expect Jesus to walk on water, not be surprised that He did it.

The miracle of the loaves, especially with the twelve baskets of leftovers, should have been a clear indication that God was among them. Only God can bring bread from Heaven. Only God can walk on water, Job 9:8, "who alone stretched out the heavens and trampled the waves of the sea." Instead of seeing God, they thought it was a ghost.

Ignorance of God and His Word prevents us from knowing Him and recognizing Him.

In Daniel 2, Nebuchadnezzar had a dream. His wise men could not interpret it. They did not know God, so they did not see His work. They even said, "No one can reveal it to the king except the gods, and they do not live among humans" (Daniel 2:11).

In John chapter 3, Jesus was explaining to Nicodemus the work of the Holy Spirit, but Nicodemus did not understand. Therefore, Nicodemus did not realize Who he was talking with (John 3:9-15).

In John 4:10, Jesus was speaking to the Samaritan woman at the well, and she did not understand. "Jesus answered her, 'If you knew the gift of God and who it is that asks you for a drink, you would have asked him and he would have given you living water.'"

After Jesus' resurrection, He met two of the disciples on the road to Emmaus, but they didn't recognize Him. "He said to them, 'How foolish you are, and how slow to believe all that the prophets have spoken! Did not the Messiah have to suffer these things and then enter his glory?' And beginning with Moses and all the Prophets, he explained to them what was said in all the Scriptures concerning himself" (Luke 24:25-27).

Job himself, after seeing God in His Words and His work, Job made the good confession.

> *Then Job replied to the Lord: "I know that you can do all things; no purpose of yours can be thwarted. You asked, 'Who is this that obscures my plans without knowledge?' Surely I spoke of things I did not understand, things too wonderful for me to know. You said, 'Listen now, and I will speak; I will question you, and you shall answer me.' My ears had heard of you, but now my eyes have seen you. Therefore, I despise myself, and repent in dust and ashes." (Job 42:1-6)*

Luke goes on to tell us in chapter 24 that after this Bible study, their eyes were opened when Jesus broke bread, and they recognized Him. Do you know enough about Jesus to recognize Him? Would you recognize Him if He came to you? Jesus spoke to the disciples, "It is I." Would you recognize His voice?

Notes

11: THE GOSPEL ERA

Week 41: The Good Samaritan
Luke 10:25-37

Key verse: *"And behold, a certain lawyer stood up and put Him to the test, saying, 'Teacher, what shall I do to inherit eternal life?'" (Luke 10:25)*

LEADER'S NOTE

The story of the Good Samaritan is one that most of your students should be familiar with. In this lesson, we want the students to consider the question in verse 25. We will explore this deeper in the Focus section.

We are more than half-way through the school year. This may be a good time to talk about, "What is love?"

CONTEXT

In Luke chapter 10, Jesus begins with a prayer for laborers in the harvest field. He sends out seventy of His disciples to go ahead of Him to the places He was intending to visit. They return with great news, but Jesus tells them the best thing is knowing Him.

This discussion brings this question about eternal life. So many religions have things to do to be right with their deity, but Jesus flips the script.

Jesus tells them it's about love. This love is total, complete, sold-out love that puts God first and then others before us.

OPEN UP

Who do you love the most?

THINK ABOUT

What's the best way to tell people that we love Jesus, with our words or our actions? Or both?

READ

Verse 25: What is the question? (What shall I DO?)

Verse 26: What does Jesus ask? What Law is Jesus talking about?

Verse 27: What does the man quote? Deuteronomy 6:5 and Leviticus 19:18.

Verses 28-29: What is the man struggling with?

Verses 30-35: What is the point of the story?

Verses 36-37: How does Jesus' response answer the question from verse 25?

FOCUS

> *And behold, a certain lawyer stood up and put Him to the test, saying, "Teacher, what shall I do to inherit eternal life?" (Luke 10:25)*

Many religions are based on works, things that must be done to be right with their deity or god. Christianity is different. Christianity is all about Jesus.

The lawyer asked what did he have to do? And Jesus said, "love." We use the word *love* for many things. In the story of the Good Samaritan, Jesus helps us understand this type of love, and He helps us understand who to love. This type of love involves sacrifice. It is just like Jesus sacrificing Himself, so that we can be in a relationship with Him.

Who is easier to love like this: someone we like or someone we don't like? Someone like us or someone different?

TALK
- What is this teaching me about God?
- What is this teaching me about people?
- Why is this important to me today?

CONNECT THE GOSPEL

This is the Gospel: "For what I received I passed on to you as of first importance: that Christ died for our sins according to the Scriptures, that he was buried, that he was raised on the third day according to the Scriptures" (1 Corinthians 15:3-4 NIV).

Romans 5:10 tells us that we were enemies of God, but He still gave us His Son. This is the Gospel, and this is the picture of love. Jesus loves the unlovable like us.

What must we do to have eternal life? Love like Jesus.

SO WHAT?

This type of love is hard to understand, and it is very different from what we see every day in a world that teaches us to love ourselves. If you are not interested in eternal life, then how you love and who you love is not important. But, if you want to follow Jesus, then we must follow His example and love as He did.

SERVE

Spend time this week praying for people in your life who are hard to love. Ask the Lord to show you how to show them the love of Christ.

DIG DEEPER

And behold, a certain lawyer stood up and put Him to the test, saying, "Teacher, what shall I do to inherit eternal life?" (Luke 10:25)

The intention of the question was to test Jesus. The man who asked the question was a lawyer, so he would have been knowledgeable of God's laws. Jesus asked the lawyer for his interpretation, "He answered, 'Love the Lord your God with all your heart and with all your soul and with all your strength and with all your mind', and, 'Love your neighbor as yourself'" (Luke 10:27).

Jesus approved his response, and then Jesus said, "Do this and you will live." Jesus' response made the two commands one. "Do this…" He did not say do these.

The command to love the Lord God came in Deuteronomy 6:4-6, "Hear, O Israel: The Lord our God, the Lord is one. Love the Lord your God with all your heart and with all your soul and with all your strength. These commandments that I give you today are to be on your hearts." The commands of God begin in the heart. They should guide us to a heart relationship with Him.

It appears that Jesus was not concerned about being tested. Even in Jesus' response, He revealed the love of God.

Micah 6:8 gives us this in other words, "He has shown you, O mortal, what is good. And what does the Lord require of you? To act justly and to love mercy and to walk humbly with your God." We can only show justice and mercy to others if we are walking humbly with our God. We can only walk humbly with our God when we love Him the way He commanded: with our heart, mind, soul, and strength.

Something to think about:

Jesus said that these are the greatest commandments. Then in John 13:34-35, He gave us a "new commandment." "A new command I give you: Love one another. As I have loved you, so you must love one another. By this everyone will know that you are my disciples, if you love one another."

Jesus did not change the commands in Luke 10:27. Here, Jesus told His disciples to follow His example of love: love as He loved. Jesus showed us how to love the Father, and He showed us how to love people.

The love of God that is complete never fails to produce in us a love for others, regardless of who they may be. In our lesson, once again, it is not about work or an activity; it is about love. We should believe in the One God has sent, and we should love in the way He has shown. He loved the world He created so much that He gave His life for His creation (John 3:16).

Notes

LEADER'S GUIDE—SOJOURNER BIBLE STUDY

Week 42: The Prodigal Son
Luke 15:11-32

Key verse: *"And the son said to him, 'Father, I have sinned against heaven and in your sight; I am no longer worthy to be called your son.'" (Luke 15:21)*

LEADER'S NOTE
We want to encourage you to use last week's lesson to lead into this lesson.

Just as Jesus said to love the Lord and to love our neighbor, use this lesson to explain the importance in seeking forgiveness and restoration.

CONTEXT
The story of the Prodigal Son is one part of a three-part parable that Jesus told the religious leaders. There was a lost sheep, a lost coin, and a lost son. In Luke 15:2, these religious leaders were "grumbling" because Jesus was eating with tax collectors and sinners.

The parable ends with the grumbling son who never left his home, but pouted when his brother was welcomed back. "And he didn't grasp the heartache and loss of his brother's departure or the significance of his return" (KnowableWord.com).

In the first two, the sheep and the coin, there was searching, restoration, and rejoicing. With the prodigal son, there was a sinner who turned from his sin, returned to his father, and was restored.

OPEN UP
What's the difference between being sorry for doing something and being sorry for being caught doing something?

THINK ABOUT
When we are children, and we do something bad, our parents tell us to "say you're sorry." Most of the time we really are not sorry, but we say it anyway. Are you still like that?

READ
Verses 11-13: What did the son do, and what did the father do?

Verses 15-17: What happened to the son? Do you think he was in a desperate situation?

Verses 18-19: What is the son planning to do, and what does he hope will happen?

Verse 20: What did the father do?

Verse 21: What is the son's confession? Who or what did he sin against?

Verses 22-24: What does the father do?

Verses 25-30: What does the brother do? Have you seen people in church act like this when something good happens to someone else? Have you acted like this?

Verse 31-32: What does the father say to the brother?

FOCUS

And the son said to him, "Father, I have sinned against heaven and in your sight; I am no longer worthy to be called your son." (Luke 15:21)

Many times, in church, we hear the word *repentance*. Do you understand it? It's the idea of turning away from what you are doing and turning toward Jesus. Think about it as re-orienting yourself on the things of God.

A lot of people, when they do something bad, are sorry about being caught, but not truly sorry for their actions.

In today's lesson, the Prodigal Son recognized his sin, and the Bible says, "he came to his senses" and realized that he had sinned against heaven and against his father. Do we realize that when we sin, we are sinning against heaven and someone?

As in the parable, when we turn and seek true forgiveness, we will find true restoration with our Father in heaven.

TALK

- What is this teaching me about God?
- What is this teaching me about people?
- Why is this important to me today?

CONNECT THE GOSPEL

This is the Gospel: "For what I received I passed on to you as of first importance: that Christ died for our sins according to the Scriptures, that he was buried, that he was raised on the third day according to the Scriptures" (1 Corinthians 15:3-4 NIV).

The Gospel is all about the forgiveness of God when we turn to Him by trusting in the Son Whom He sent to us. Jesus came to seek and to save the lost, like us. We are lost, but God has made a way for us to be found.

SO WHAT?

If we never ask for forgiveness from those we hurt, we are living in sin. This will eat our souls like a cancer, and we will never know perfect fellowship with our Father.

SERVE

How can you serve this week by applying this lesson? Is there someone you need to ask to forgive you? This is a great time to be restored in broken relationships.

DIG DEEPER

And the son said to him, "Father, I have sinned against heaven and in your sight; I am no longer worthy to be called your son." (Luke 15:21)

Luke chapter 15 contains three parables about something and someone who was lost. The shepherd lost one sheep, and he went to find it and bring it home. The sheep did nothing, but the shepherd did everything. The shepherd even showed his ownership of the sheep: "I have found my lost sheep."

The woman lost a coin. Scholars believe it was one of ten worn around a woman's head to show her marital status. The loss of one coin was a problem. In the parable, Jesus described how diligently she searched for this one coin, her coin. "I have found my lost coin." The coin did nothing to restore itself.

Then the parable of the lost son. The son showed brokenness and repentance. The son turned from his life, and he returned to his father. It does not say that the son returned to his town or his home, but to his father. "I will set out and go back to my father" (Luke 15:18). The son returned to the one he knew loved him. The son did not seek to be restored to the family; he only wanted a place with the workers.

Luke 15:20, "But while he was still a long way off, his father saw him and was filled with compassion for him; he ran to his son, threw his arms around him and kissed him." The father was waiting for the son, perhaps looking for him since he saw him a long way off. And the father ran to the son.

We looked at the Beatitudes a few lessons ago, and we learned about being broken over sin. Matthew 5:3, "Blessed are the poor in spirit, for theirs is the kingdom of heaven." This son was poor in spirit, and he was welcomed to his father's kingdom.

The problem in chapter 15 was the hard-hearted view of the religious leaders. They did not associate with people who were not "religious," and they were not happy that Jesus welcomed "sinners." Luke 15:1-2, "Now the tax collectors and sinners were all gathering around to hear Jesus. But the Pharisees and the teachers of the law muttered, 'This man welcomes sinners and eats with them.'"

The truth of repentance and the love of God has existed since the days of the Old Testament.

After David sinned with Bathsheba and God convicted him, he was broken. Psalm 51:17, "My sacrifice, O God, is a broken spirit; a broken and contrite heart you, God, will not despise."

God the Father is seeking after us. In fact, He came to seek and to save the lost (Luke 19:10). He is waiting for us to turn to Him. First John 1:9, "If we confess our sins, he is faithful and just and will forgive us our sins and purify us from all unrighteousness."

Come to the Father and experience His open arms.

Notes

Week 43: The Greatest Commandment
Mark 12:28-34

Key verse: *"And when Jesus saw that he had answered intelligently, He said to him, 'You are not far from the kingdom of God.' And after that, no one would venture to ask Him any more questions." (Mark 12:34)*

LEADER'S NOTE

This lesson is very similar to Week 41, and the Good Samaritan. This week we want you to point out the difference between head knowledge and heart knowledge. There is a big difference between knowing about Jesus and knowing Him in a way that changes your life.

CONTEXT

In the beginning of chapter 12, Jesus told a parable about a land owner. It's about God, the Land Owner. The land is a reference to Israel and the people He has used to care for His land, the prophets. The prophets were rejected, and eventually God sent His Son, and the Son was killed. When Jesus finished the parable the religious leaders recognized that Jesus was talking about them.

The religious leaders were angry, and so they tried to trap Jesus. They asked about taxes, and then they asked about marriage in heaven.

Each of Jesus' responses revealed the fact that the religious leaders did not understand the Scriptures (vs. 24). That brings us to the question of the scribe. What is the greatest commandment?

They couldn't trap Jesus with the tax question and the Roman laws, so they asked Him if there is a commandment that is greater than others. In essence, would He disregard the Law of Moses by putting one above the others?

OPEN UP

Can you obey God without loving Him?

THINK ABOUT

Can you obey your teachers without loving them?

READ

Verse 28: What is the question?

Verses 29-31: What does Jesus say? Where can you find these commandments?

Verses 32-33: What does the scribe say about these commandments?

Verse 34: Do you think the man was saved because he knew this?

FOCUS

And when Jesus saw that he had answered intelligently, He said to him, "You are not far from the kingdom of God." And after that, no one would venture to ask Him any more questions. (Mark 12:34)

The scribe gave an intelligent answer. He knew that these commands were better than offerings and sacrifices. It looks like he knows the Word of God, and he is really smart.

But, Jesus said, "You are not far from the kingdom of God." What's the problem? If you are "not far" from home, are you home?

Do you think he possessed this love that Jesus is talking about? If he is trying to trap Jesus, does he love Jesus?

TALK

- What is this teaching me about God?
- What is this teaching me about people?
- Why is this important to me today?

CONNECT THE GOSPEL

This is the Gospel: "For what I received I passed on to you as of first importance: that Christ died for our sins according to the Scriptures, that he was buried, that he was raised on the third day according to the Scriptures" (1 Corinthians 15:3-4 NIV).

Jesus is the Love of God. In Jesus we see perfect love, and therefore we see perfect obedience. When Jesus died for us, He showed His love for us and His obedience to God the Father by paying for our sins.

The love of Jesus is the Gospel.

SO WHAT?

Why is this important? This lesson is an opportunity to do some self-reflection. Have you been coming to church for a long time or a short time? Do you have Bible verses memorized? Do you know the Bible stories?

Do you have all of this "church knowledge," but still don't love God or other people?

SERVE

Why do we serve people? Do we serve so that people will say good things about us or because we have love for them?

Spend time this week in prayer. Ask God to show you who or what you love the most?

DIG DEEPER

> *And when Jesus saw that he had answered intelligently, He said to him, "You are not far from the kingdom of God." And after that, no one would venture to ask Him any more questions. (Mark 12:34)*

In the lesson for week 41, the question was about how to inherit eternal life. In that lesson, we talked about loving God and loving people. Today the question is about the greatest commandment. The questions are different, but the response is the same: love God and love people as yourself.

In today's reading, we are focusing on the fact that the man was "not far from the kingdom of God."

In Mark 12:33, the scribe had also said, "To love him with all your heart, with all your understanding and with all your strength, and to love your neighbor as yourself is more important than all burnt offerings and sacrifices." This man knew that God desired love more than sacrifice. He knew the answer, but it appears that he did not know this type of love.

When Saul disobeyed the command of God, God took the kingdom from Saul. Saul had done a great thing in defeating the Amalekites, but he failed in being obedient. "But Samuel replied: 'Does the Lord delight in burnt offerings and sacrifices as much as in obeying the Lord? To obey is better than sacrifice, and to heed is better than the fat of rams'" (1 Sam. 15:22). Obedience is a response to love.

This scribe knew this, and he knew the Word of God, and yet he was not saved. He was still outside of the Kingdom. The scribe knew the Word of God, but he did not have a relationship with the God of the Word.

As Jesus closed the Sermon on the Mount, He warned the people that there would be some who claimed to do the work of God, but Jesus said, "Not everyone who says to me, 'Lord, Lord,' will enter the kingdom of heaven, but only the one who does the will of my Father who is in heaven. Many will say to me on that day, 'Lord, Lord, did we not prophesy in your name and in your name drive out demons, and in your name perform many miracles?' Then I will tell them plainly, 'I never knew you. Away from me, you evildoers!" (Mat. 7:21-23).

There are many people who profess to be Christians or believers in God, but that doesn't mean they are saved. The key to salvation is in an obedient relationship through faith in Jesus. John 6:28-29, "Then they asked him, 'What must we do to do the works God requires?' Jesus answered, 'The work of God is this: to believe in the one he has sent.'"

Let's go a little deeper here, too. It is one thing to say you believe, but does your belief result in obedience?

Consider two things: James 2:19, "You believe that there is one God. Good! Even the demons believe that—and shudder." The demons believe in God, but they are not saved.

John 14:15, "If you love me, keep my commands." This brings us back to the question, which is the greatest? Love the Lord God with every part of your being, love your neighbor as yourself, and the new command that Jesus gave His disciples, "love one another as I have loved you" (John 13:34).

Saving faith is an active faith, and it requires action, not just information. Are you living in a way that shows your faith in Jesus? Are you living in obedience, or will He say, "You are not far from the kingdom of God"?

Notes

LEADER'S GUIDE—SOJOURNER BIBLE STUDY

Week 44: Judas Betrays Jesus
Luke 22:19-23, 47-48

Key verse: *"But behold, the hand of the one betraying Me is with Me on the table." (Luke 22:21)*

LEADER'S NOTE

The lessons on the Good Samaritan, the Prodigal Son, and the Greatest Commandment, we hope, have helped the students to see the picture of God's love. We have been told to love the Lord God and to love our neighbor, and we have seen the repentant heart of the Prodigal Son and the Father's love for him.

In this lesson we want to look at how it is possible to look like a Jesus follower, but not love Jesus.

We will discuss the Last Supper in our next lesson.

CONTEXT

In Luke chapter 22, we have arrived in Jerusalem for the Passover. Jesus is completing His work and preparing for the Cross. The disciples have gathered with Jesus to eat the "last supper."

Jesus knows that He is about to be betrayed, and He still shares a meal with Judas. Jesus has been in control of His life from the beginning. Jesus told His disciples several times about these events so that they would remember what He had told them (John 16:4).

OPEN UP

Why do you come to church and Sunday school?

THINK ABOUT

Do you think that everyone who comes to church truly follows Jesus? Why do you say that?

READ

Verses 19-20: What did Jesus do?

Verses 21-22: What is Jesus saying? Was the death of Jesus pre-determined?

Verse 23: What are the disciples thinking?

Verse 47: What did Judas do? Why did he do this?

Verse 48: What did Jesus say? What does He mean by this? Maybe: *Judas, are you showing fake love to the one you have turned against?*

FOCUS

> *"But behold, the hand of the one betraying Me is with Me on the table." (Luke 22:21)*

Think about the situation of the Passover Feast. Jesus is about to die. His blood is going to be shed to cover our sins. Jesus is eating with His followers. How long have these men been with Jesus? How did these men come to know Jesus? He called them.

Judas has been with Jesus, and he has seen the miracles. In verse 23, the disciples were confused because they didn't know who could betray Jesus. This shows us that even the other eleven disciples didn't suspect Judas.

How do you think Judas acted while he was with them? Do you think he was just like the others? Do you think he looked different?

Just because people say they follow Jesus, doesn't mean they really do. We need to be aware that some people come to church and do church things for different reasons.

TALK

- What is this teaching me about God?
- What is this teaching me about people?
- Why is this important to me today?

CONNECT THE GOSPEL

This is the Gospel: "For what I received I passed on to you as of first importance: that Christ died for our sins according to the Scriptures, that he was buried, that he was raised on the third day according to the Scriptures" (1 Corinthians 15:3-4 NIV).

The "good news" is that Jesus died for us. He died for Judas too, but Judas turned away from Him. This is very different from the Prodigal Son who walked away from his father, but he repented and came back to his father.

The Gospel is "good news" for everyone who will accept it, but it is more than just saying we believe it. If we truly believe what Jesus has done for us then our lives will look different.

SO WHAT?

Why is this lesson important? It's important because we all need to decide which of the sides we are on. We are almost finished with this Bible study year, and you will begin a new study, or you will walk away from church. This is a good time to ask ourselves if we truly love Jesus, or are we following Him hoping He will give us something?

SERVE

Let's spend this week thinking about what it means to follow Jesus. Are we loving other people because of our love for Him?

DIG DEEPER

But behold, the hand of the one betraying Me is with Me on the table. (Luke 22:21)

Last week we talked about how it is possible to know the Word of God but still be outside the kingdom of Heaven. Today we are looking at Judas, the betrayer. He knew Jesus and lived with Him, but He was not saved. Judas lived with Jesus for three years. Think of it as being in church every day for three years.

We know a few things about Judas. Jesus chose Judas to be a disciple in Matthew 10:4. In John 12, when Mary anointed Jesus with very expensive perfume, it was Judas who complained that the perfume was wasted and should have been sold. John also gave us a little more information regarding Judas' intention: "But one of his disciples, Judas Iscariot, who was later to betray him, objected, 'Why wasn't this perfume sold and the money given to the poor? It was worth a year's wages.' He did not say this because he cared about the poor but because he was a thief; as keeper of the money bag, he used to help himself to what was put into it" (John 12:4-6).

The Gospel of Matthew also recorded that Judas went to the chief priests looking for some type of payment if he would lead them to Jesus. Matthew 26:14-16, "Then one of the Twelve—the one called Judas Iscariot—went to the chief priests and asked, 'What are you willing to give me if I deliver him over to you?' So, they counted out for him thirty pieces of silver. From then on Judas watched for an opportunity to hand him over."

Also, in Luke 22:4-6, "And Judas went to the chief priests and the officers of the temple guard and discussed with them how he might betray Jesus. They were delighted and agreed to give him money. He consented, and watched for an opportunity to hand Jesus over to them when no crowd was present."

If Jesus is truly God, and we believe He is God, then why would He choose Judas? There has been a lot of speculation about this, and we will not discuss speculation. It is important to consider Scripture in the light of Scripture.

The Gospels reveal to us that Jesus knew what was going to happen:

Matthew 17:22, "When they came together in Galilee, he [Jesus] said to them, 'The Son of Man is going to be delivered into the hands of men.'" "Delivered" means that someone would hand Him over to the authorities.

> *"We are going up to Jerusalem," he said, "and the Son of Man will be delivered over to the chief priests and the teachers of the law. They will condemn him to death and will hand him over to the Gentiles." (Mark 10:33)*

Our focus verse today is Luke 22:21, and if we read further, Jesus gave us more information: "'The Son of Man will go as it has been decreed. But woe to that man who betrays him!'"

Jesus knew who would betray Him. Nothing happened in Jesus' life outside the will and plan of God the Father, and this includes being betrayed. In Luke 24:27, "And beginning with Moses and all the Prophets, he explained to them what was said in all the Scriptures concerning himself." The Old Testament told us this would happen, so when Jesus was betrayed by one of His own people, it would be one more sign of Him being the Messiah of God.

The intent of the Apostle John in his Gospel was to show the deity of Jesus. In the Gospel of John, chapter 13 verse 18, "'I am not referring to all of you; I know those I have chosen. But this is to fulfill this passage of Scripture: "He who shared my bread has turned against me."'"

John was pointing the reader back to David in the Psalms. David was a prophet and a king. He wrote much about the coming Messiah, approximately a thousand years before the birth of Jesus. Psalm 41:9, "Even my close friend, someone I trusted, one who shared my bread, has turned against me."

When Jesus said, "But behold, the hand of the one betraying Me is with Me on the table," He knew the plan.

In the "Let's Focus" section, we made the comment, "Just because people say they follow Jesus does not mean they really do. We need to be aware that some people come to church and do church things for different reasons." We need to test the spirits: "Dear friends, do not believe every spirit, but test the spirits to see whether they are from God, because many false prophets have gone out into the world" (1 John 4:1).

A true Jesus follower will point people to Jesus and not seek their own gain.

Notes

Week 45: The Last Supper
Luke 22:7-20

Key verse: *"And having taken some bread, when He had given thanks, He broke it, and gave it to them, saying, 'This is My body which is given for you, do this in remembrance of Me.'" (Luke 22:19)*

LEADER'S NOTE

Last week we introduced the Lord's Supper as we discussed the betrayal of Judas. This week we want to focus on the significance of the Supper event and the reason we continue to participate in the Lord's Supper. We want the students to understand that every time we do this, we are told to remember the body of Jesus which was broken for us.

All around the world, Christians participate in the Lord's Supper. A cracker or bread, and a small cup of juice may seem like a little thing, but it's a powerful reminder to us of what Jesus did for all of us. Note also that Jesus gave His body; it was not taken.

> *"No one has taken it away from Me, but I lay it down on My own initiative. I have authority to lay it down, and I have authority to take it up again. This commandment I received from My Father." (John 10:18)*

In verse 16, Jesus said He would not eat it again with us until it is fulfilled in the kingdom of God. Many believe that event is the marriage supper of the Lamb in Revelation 16:9.

CONTEXT

Matthew, Mark, and Luke give us the events of that night. Luke records Jesus as saying that the cup is the New Covenant.

The Old Covenant was given to Moses, and it was sealed with the blood of bulls and lambs. This New Covenant is sealed in Jesus' blood. He is the last sacrifice.

> *For by one sacrifice he has made perfect forever those who are being made holy. The Holy Spirit also testifies to us about this. First, He says: "This is the covenant I will make with them after that time, says the Lord. I will put my laws in their hearts, and I will write them on their minds." Then he adds: "Their sins and lawless acts I will remember no more." And where these have been forgiven, sacrifice for sin is no longer necessary. (Hebrews 10:14-18)*

Jesus and His disciples are celebrating the Passover meal on the night in which Jesus would be betrayed and arrested. This Passover meal began in Exodus when God brought the children of Israel out of Egypt with great signs, the last of which was the death of the first born of the Egyptians. We discussed the Passover event in Week 11.

In the Passover, a spotless lamb was killed and his blood placed on the doorposts to save the people from the death angel. Now Jesus is about to die, the Spotless Lamb of God, and His blood will save everyone who puts their faith in Him.

OPEN UP

How do you remember important events in your life?

LEADER'S GUIDE—SOJOURNER BIBLE STUDY

THINK ABOUT
Has there been a time in your life when someone did something for you that you never want to forget?

READ
Verse 7: What is the significance of the Day of Unleavened Bread? It is the day when the Jewish people would get everything out of their homes that had leaven in it. Leaven was a picture of sin; therefore, this day was a picture of the removal of sin.

Verses 8-14: What do these verses show us? Was there ever a point in Jesus' life when He wasn't in control?

Verses 15-16: What is Jesus saying in these statements? This is the last time He will eat as a family until He establishes the family again (Revelation 16:9).

Verses 17-20: What does the cup represent? What does the blood represent? Read Ezekiel 31:31-34.

FOCUS
> *And having taken some bread, when He had given thanks, He broke it, and gave it to them, saying, "This is My body which is given for you, do this in remembrance of Me." (Luke 22:19)*

Now think about the process in this verse. What did Jesus have in His hand? What did He do with it first? What did He do after He gave thanks? What did He do after He broke it?

In John 6:35, Jesus said that He was the Bread of Life. If He is the Bread of Life, think about what He did.

Jesus took unleavened bread; the picture of sin being removed. He gave thanks. Jesus knew that He was about to be crucified, and He still gave thanks for what He had. Jesus broke the bread, and His body was about to be broken. Then He gave this bread, this symbol of His broken body, to the people who followed Him.

What does Jesus tell us to do? He tells us to remember His body which was broken for us.

TALK
- What is this teaching me about God?
- What is this teaching me about people?
- Why is this important to me today?

CONNECT THE GOSPEL
This is the Gospel: "For what I received I passed on to you as of first importance: that Christ died for our sins according to the Scriptures, that he was buried, that he was raised on the third day according to the Scriptures" (1 Corinthians 15:3-4 NIV).

The Passover, now the Last Supper, is a picture of the Gospel. It is Jesus being broken, taking away the sin, for us. Every time we take the Lord's Supper we are presenting the Gospel.

SO WHAT?
Why have we taken an entire lesson talking about this? Why is it important? It's important because we don't want to take it in the wrong way, with the wrong attitude in our heart.

Paul wrote in 1 Corinthians 11:27-29, "So then, whoever eats the bread or drinks the cup of the Lord in an unworthy manner will be guilty of sinning against the body and blood of the Lord. Everyone ought to examine themselves before they eat of the bread and drink from the cup. For those who eat and drink without discerning the body of Christ eat and drink judgment on themselves."

SERVE

This is a good time to think about the Lord's Supper. Think about how you will prepare for the next time it is served in church. Will your heart be prepared to accept what Jesus has done for you? Or, will you take it so that no one will think anything bad about you?

DIG DEEPER

And having taken some bread, when He had given thanks, He broke it, and gave it to them, saying, "This is My body which is given for you, do this in remembrance of Me." (Luke 22:19)

In Exodus chapter 12, Moses recorded the first Passover. A common thread throughout the Bible is how God Himself comes into the lives of His people to save them from bondage. In the time of Exodus, the people of God were in bondage in Egypt. Today, we all are in bondage to sin. John 8:34, "Jesus replied, 'Very truly I tell you, everyone who sins is a slave to sin.'"

"Obey these instructions as a lasting ordinance for you and your descendants. When you enter the land that the Lord will give you as he promised, observe this ceremony. And when your children ask you, 'What does this ceremony mean to you?' then tell them, 'It is the Passover sacrifice to the Lord, who passed over the houses of the Israelites in Egypt and spared our homes when he struck down the Egyptians.'" Then the people bowed down and worshiped. The Israelites did just what the Lord commanded Moses and Aaron.

At midnight the Lord struck down all the firstborn in Egypt, from the firstborn of Pharaoh, who sat on the throne, to the firstborn of the prisoner, who was in the dungeon, and the firstborn of all the livestock as well. Pharaoh and all his officials and all the Egyptians got up during the night, and there was loud wailing in Egypt, for there was not a house without someone dead. (Exodus 12:24-30)

The first Passover was a picture of how God saved the people who were obedient to do what He commanded. They needed a spotless lamb (Exodus 12:5), then the lamb was to be killed (Exodus 12:6), then the blood of the lamb was to be painted on the doorframe (Exodus 12:7). The people were told to remember this event and celebrate it annually.

Then the day came when the Passover Lamb stepped into humanity, and His own people did not recognize Him (John 1:11). However, John the Baptist did recognize Jesus and His role in the redemption of all people. John 1:29, "The next day John saw Jesus coming toward him and said, 'Look, the Lamb of God, who takes away the sin of the world!'"

On the night that Jesus celebrated the Passover with His disciples, He did not quote from Exodus 12; instead, He said something different. Jesus identified Himself as the Passover Lamb. "This is my body, which is given for you." No longer would there be a need for an annual sacrifice for sin.

In Exodus 12, when the unblemished lamb was killed, its death provided a way for the people to have new life in freedom. When Jesus, the unblemished Lamb of God, was killed, He provided a way for us to have new life in freedom from the bondage of sin.

In Exodus 12, the people who believed the Word of God and went under the blood were saved. When we take the cup of juice or wine, we remember that the blood of Jesus was shed for our own salvation.

So when we take the Lord's Supper, what are we doing? We are remembering that God became a man to take away our sin so that we could have a relationship with Him. We have been redeemed, and it was not anything we did, but Jesus paid it all.

> *For you know that it was not with perishable things such as silver or gold that you were redeemed from the empty way of life handed down to you from your ancestors, but with the precious blood of Christ, a lamb without blemish or defect. (1 Peter 1:18-19)*

Next time you participate in the Lord's Supper, remember what Jesus did for you.

Notes

Week 46: Good Friday/Crucifixion
Luke 23:32-49

Key verse: *"We are punished justly, for we are getting what our deeds deserve. But this man has done nothing wrong."* (Luke 23:41)

LEADER'S NOTE

As we have studied the Gospel Era, we have looked at John the Baptist and the teachings of Jesus. We have seen along the way that God has revealed Himself to us in the Person of Jesus the Messiah.

In this lesson our key verse is the statement of one of the two criminals who were crucified with Jesus. The criminal recognized that he was a sinner in the presence of an innocent Man.

You may also want to point out the statement made by the centurion in verse 47. The centurion praised God and also proclaimed Jesus' innocence.

It is our hope that your students will recognize where they stand in their relationship with Jesus the Messiah.

CONTEXT

Each of the Gospel accounts describes the trial and crucifixion of Jesus. Only in Luke's account do we see Jesus forgive those responsible for His death.

Jesus was crucified according to the plan of God (Acts 2:23). However, for those in Jesus' day, it appeared that Jesus had offended the Jewish religious leaders and the Roman government. That's why they put the sign above Him that read, "King of the Jews." Anyone who claimed to be a king was a threat to the Caesar.

And this brings us to Golgotha, and three crosses, and a picture of what we all are facing. First, we need to decide if an innocent Man died for us. Then we need to recognize that this truth needs to be told to others.

OPEN UP

Have you ever been punished for doing something wrong or something bad?

THINK ABOUT

Do you want to be punished for all of your sins, or do you want someone to take the punishment for you?

READ

Verses 32-33: What is happening?

Verse 34: What did Jesus do?

Verses 35-38: What are the people doing?

Verse 39: What did the man say? Are you prepared to be mocked for following Jesus, especially when you are struggling to do what is right?

Verses 40-42: Explain what this man is saying.

Verse 43: What did Jesus say to the criminal?

Verses 44-46: What happened? Who was in control?

Verse 47: What did the centurion say? The first Gentile to praise God for what Jesus did.

Verses 48-49: Can you describe the two groups and their actions?

FOCUS

We are punished justly, for we are getting what our deeds deserve. But this man has done nothing wrong. (Luke 23:41)

The Bible tells us that this man was a criminal. We don't know his crime, but it was worthy of the death penalty. We also don't know how he came to know that Jesus was innocent.

What does the man say about himself and the other criminal? Are they getting what they deserve? Do we want the punishment we deserve?

What does the man say about Jesus? Did this man believe that Jesus is the Messiah? Look at his request in verse 42. Based on his request, he must know Who Jesus is.

TALK

- What is this teaching me about God?
- What is this teaching me about people?
- Why is this important to me today?

CONNECT THE GOSPEL

This is the Gospel: "For what I received I passed on to you as of first importance: that Christ died for our sins according to the Scriptures, that he was buried, that he was raised on the third day according to the Scriptures" (1 Corinthians 15:3-4 NIV).

The "good news" of the Gospel was first pictured in Genesis chapter 3, when innocent blood was shed to cover the sins of the guilty. This theme or idea of the innocent dying for the guilty continues throughout the Old Testament and the system of sacrifice.

Now, here at the cross, innocent blood is being shed, and the innocent Man, the spotless Lamb of God, is taking the punishment for the sins of the world. This is the Gospel.

SO WHAT?

What's the big deal? So what if a criminal who was dying recognized Jesus as being innocent? Why is that important two thousand years later?

It's important because when Jesus died, He died one time for all people.

For Christ also suffered once for sins, the righteous for the unrighteous, that he might bring us to God, being put to death in the flesh but made alive in the spirit. (1 Peter 3:18)

This means He died for us. Some will believe and have eternal life. Some will reject Jesus and have eternal death.

SERVE

Use this week to think about what Jesus has done for us. How can you tell other people that they can be forgiven?

Do people make fun of you when you talk about Jesus? Pray for opportunities to tell people about the hope you have in Jesus. At the same time, we need to live in such a way that people see that we are different because we are living for Jesus.

DIG DEEPER

We are punished justly, for we are getting what our deeds deserve. But this man has done nothing wrong. (Luke 23:41)

In our last lesson, we discussed the Last Supper. We know that Jesus was the unblemished Lamb of God. This means that He was without sin.

In today's lesson we read about the two men who were crucified with Jesus. They were criminals. They knew they were criminals, and one even recognized his guilt in the presence of Jesus' innocence.

In the beginning of verse 41, the man made the comment "we are getting what we deserve." Everyone has sinned except this Lamb of God. Romans 3:23, "...for all have sinned and fall short of the glory of God."

Sin has a price. This was seen first in the Garden of Eden in Genesis chapter 3. If anyone disobeys God, the punishment is death, separation from God, who is the source of Life.

The Lord God spoke through Ezekiel, "The one who sins is the one who will die. The child will not share the guilt of the parent, nor will the parent share the guilt of the child. The righteousness of the righteous will be credited to them, and the wickedness of the wicked will be charged against them" (Ezek. 18:20).

For the wages of sin is death, but the gift of God is eternal life in Christ Jesus our Lord. (Romans 6:23)

Now what about this second criminal? He recognized his sinfulness in the presence of Jesus. Sound familiar? When Simon Peter recognized that he was in the presence of the Lord, he too recognized his sin nature, "He fell at Jesus' knees and said, 'Go away from me, Lord; I am a sinful man!'" (Luke 5:8)

Do we recognize who we are when we "see" Jesus for who He is? Some people do not believe they are sinners. Others think that they are not as bad as "some people."

If the cost of sin is death, which results in eternal separation from our Creator, do we really want to pay that price? We can pay it, or we can accept what Jesus has done for us. Second Corinthians 5:21, "He made Him who knew no sin, to be sin on our behalf, that we may become the righteousness of God."

The criminal on the cross recognized his sin, he recognized Jesus' sacrifice, and he asked for salvation. Luke 23:42, "Then he said, 'Jesus, remember me when you come into your kingdom.'"

Two men died with Jesus that day, a picture of the choices we all have today: accept Him or reject Him. One man rejected Jesus, and he is eternally separated from God the Father. The other man accepted Jesus, cried out to Him, and was saved, and is in the eternal presence of God the Father.

Jesus answered him, "Truly I tell you, today you will be with me in paradise." (Luke 23:43)

Notes

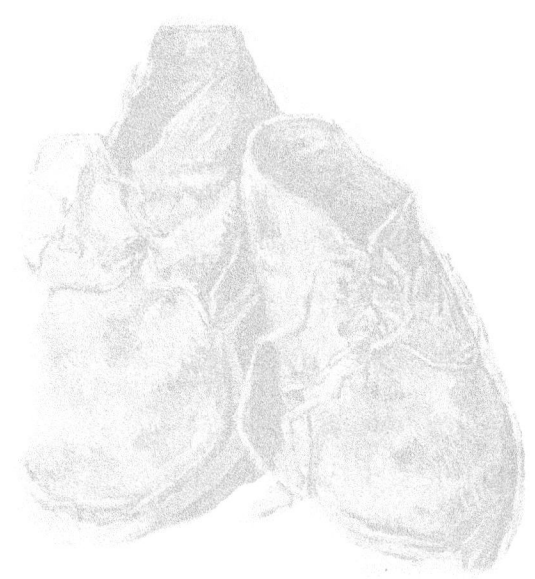

12:
The Church Era

12: THE CHURCH ERA

Week 47: Pentecost
Acts 2:36-47

Key verse: "And Peter said to them, 'Repent, and let each of you be baptized in the name of Jesus Christ for the forgiveness of your sins; and you shall receive the gift of the Holy Spirit.'" (Acts 2:38)

LEADER'S NOTE

We have had an overview of the Old Testament, and we have looked at the work of Jesus as He called people to Himself and revealed Himself along the way. Now we are transitioning our study to the Church Era. We are in the Church Era now. It began in the first century, and it continues today.

We want the students to understand that the Bible is not a history book, although it contains historical events. The Bible, the Word of God, is what points us to God's plan in Christ Jesus, and it connects believers around the world.

Jesus has risen. How now shall we live? Help the students to understand that we are saved in the same way as this group was in Acts 2. We repent, we turn from our way to the way of Christ, and we get baptized to show that we are accepting what Christ has done for us.

We are NOT teaching that baptism saves, but that it is a sign of obedience and belief in what God has done for us in Christ Jesus.

CONTEXT

The name *Pentecost* comes from the Greek word for *fiftieth*. In the time of Acts 2, many Jewish people were in Jerusalem for the Feast of Weeks. This Jewish harvest festival was held seven weeks and one day after the Passover Feast of Unleavened Bread.

In Jewish tradition, the Feast of Weeks is celebrated fifty days after the first grain harvest. Interesting to connect it to Jesus being raised as the "First Fruit," according to Paul in 1 Corinthians 15:20-28. Now, here in Acts 2, we see a picture in this Harvest Festival of those who will follow Jesus.

OPEN UP
How did you first hear about Jesus?

THINK ABOUT
What does it mean to repent?

READ

Verse 36: What did Peter say about Jesus? What did Peter say that the people had done?

Verse 37: What happened to the people?

Verses 38-40: What did Peter tell the people to do? What is the promise in verse 39?

Verse 41: What happened? What did Jesus tell His followers in Matthew 28:18-20?

Verses 42-47: How did the Church grow? What did they do? Who added to their numbers? How were they a community of believers?

LEADER'S GUIDE—SOJOURNER BIBLE STUDY

FOCUS

And Peter said to them, "Repent, and let each of you be baptized in the name of Jesus Christ for the forgiveness of your sins; and you shall receive the gift of the Holy Spirit." (Acts 2:38)

In the beginning of chapter 2, Luke tells us that there was a group of people gathered together in one place. The Holy Spirit descended like "tongues of fire" and enabled people to speak different languages.

Then Peter explained what was happening, and he used Old Testament references to help the people understand that this was a work of God. He told them that Jesus was the Promised One, and then Peter told the people that they had crucified the Lord's Christ.

At this point the people felt conviction for their sins. Their first question was, in verse 37, "what must we do?" When God, through the power of the Holy Spirit, makes us aware of our sin, we need to respond in a way that will restore our relationship with Him.

If you have been baptized once, you don't need to be baptized again, but we do need to repent and turn to Jesus every time we sin. This is evidence of the Holy Spirit working in our lives.

What will you do?

TALK

- What is this teaching me about God?
- What is this teaching me about people?
- Why is this important to me today?

CONNECT THE GOSPEL

This is the Gospel: "For what I received I passed on to you as of first importance: that Christ died for our sins according to the Scriptures, that he was buried, that he was raised on the third day according to the Scriptures" (1 Corinthians 15:3-4 NIV).

The Gospel is the story of God's love for us. Jesus died for us because of our sin. This lesson is about what we need to do if we believe that we have sinned against God and desire to be restored. Our sin is the reason Jesus was crucified so that we could be restored to our Heavenly Father.

SO WHAT?

There are people who believe that Jesus died for their sins, but they have never repented and turned to follow Jesus. It doesn't matter what you believe if that belief has not resulted in action.

The people in Acts 2 believed what Peter said, and they took action. They repented, and then they were baptized to show publicly that they had turned to Jesus.

SERVE

How can you apply this lesson to your life this week? Have you believed in what Jesus did for you? Have you repented and turned to follow Him? Have you been baptized? If you can say "yes" to all of these, then share this message with people you know. Ask people to tell you how they heard about Jesus and what they did after they heard.

DIG DEEPER

And Peter said to them, "Repent, and let each of you be baptized in the name of Jesus Christ for the forgiveness of your sins; and you shall receive the gift of the Holy Spirit." (Acts 2:38)

12: THE CHURCH ERA

In our last lesson, we discussed the choices that everyone has of accepting or rejecting what Jesus has done for us. As our study enters the Church Era, we see the people asking what they must do to be saved.

It is important for us to understand what is happening here. The events of Acts 2 took place less than two months after Jesus was crucified and resurrected. Acts 1:3 tells us that Jesus appeared to people over a period of forty days. So that means that the events in Acts 2, the Feast of Pentecost, is about ten days after Jesus gave the disciples the instructions in Acts 1:8, "But you will receive power when the Holy Spirit comes on you; and you will be my witnesses in Jerusalem, and in all Judea and Samaria, and to the ends of the earth."

Now, in Acts 2:4, it has happened; the Holy Spirit has come in power. The believers were gathered together in one place, and "All of them were filled with the Holy Spirit and began to speak in other tongues as the Spirit enabled them." This was not an unknown language as some denominations teach. The believers spoke in languages that were understood by the people who were in the city from other areas. Acts 2:11, "we hear them declaring the wonders of God in our own tongues!" The ability to speak another language is a gift that should be used to express the wonders of God to people who may never hear it (Romans 10:17).

This gift of the Holy Spirit that Jesus promised in Acts 1:8 gave Peter and the others the ability to be witnesses for Christ among people from all over the Roman Empire. However, this work of the Holy Spirit was not a random event.

Peter quoted from Joel 2:28-32 as he explained to the people what they were seeing. Peter also quoted from Psalms 16 and 110. God was fulfilling His promises once again. This event got the attention of the people, and they were willing to hear Peter's message. We know this by their response to what Peter said last in verse 36, "Therefore let all Israel be assured of this: God has made this Jesus, whom you crucified, both Lord and Messiah" (Acts 2:36).

This bold statement, that God has made Jesus "Lord and Messiah," means that it was God's work to make Jesus the Son, the Master, and the Savior. This word "Lord" is the Greek word "kyrios," which means master, Lord or God.

In the lesson from Week 46, we saw the criminal on the cross ask Jesus to remember him when Jesus entered the kingdom. He was seeking to be made right. These people in Acts 2 recognized the truth of the Gospel, and they were pierced to the heart and they asked how they could be made right. "When the people heard this, they were cut to the heart and said to Peter and the other apostles, 'Brothers, what shall we do?'" (Acts 2:37)

Peter's message to the people was simple, and it applies to every one of us today: turn away from your sin, turn to Jesus, and then be baptized to show obedience to Jesus. The gift of the Holy Spirit is for everyone who believes.

> *I will ask the Father, and He will give you another Helper, that He may be with you forever; that is the Spirit of truth, whom the world cannot receive, because it does not see Him or know Him, but you know Him because He abides with you and will be in you. (John 14:16-17)*

The power of the Holy Spirit gives every believer the ability to declare the wonders of God, and may we encourage people to repent and be saved.

Notes

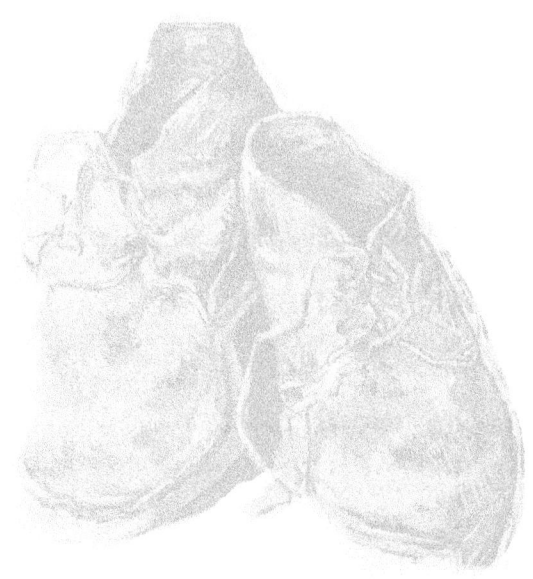

13:
The Mission Era

Week 48: Paul and Barnabas Sent
Acts 13:1-52

Key verse: "And the word of the Lord was being spread through the whole region." (Acts 13:49)

LEADER'S NOTE

We understand that this is a very long chapter for this lesson. You may want to condense the reading this week. We will be discussing the Mission Era this week and next week, so we wanted to focus on Paul and Barnabas today.

In this chapter we see how they were selected, how they worked, how they were persecuted, and how they rejoiced.

The key verse is our reminder of what happens when the people of God are faithful to do what the Lord has called them and equipped them to do.

CONTEXT

Paul met Barnabas in Acts 9, after Paul had his salvation experience on the road to Damascus. Many new believers were struggling to accept Paul's conversion, but Barnabas took Paul to meet the church leaders, and he testified about Paul's conversion.

We don't meet them again until chapter 13. Here in chapter 13, the Church was meeting in Antioch, and the Lord called out Barnabas and Paul (Saul) to be set apart for His work. The chapter begins with them being set apart for the mission, and it ends with affirmation of the mission.

Until now, we have seen the Gospel in Jerusalem, Judea, and among the Samaritans and God-fearing Gentiles. Now, beginning in chapter 13, the Gospel will begin its journey to the ends of the Earth.

This chapter is the only sermon that Luke recorded from Paul's synagogue visits. Theologians believe that this was the same message he preached in every synagogue. He began with Moses, then David, then showed that Jesus was the descendent of David, and then Jesus' death and resurrection by connecting Old Testament prophecy.

OPEN UP

How did the Gospel of Jesus Christ get to you?

THINK ABOUT

Will the Gospel stop with you, or will it continue to spread?

READ

Verses 1-3: Who was there? Where were they, and what were they doing?

Verse 4: Who sent them? Why is this important?

Verses 5-8: What happened?

Verses 9-12: What happened? What was the result of the miracle?

Verses 13-15: Who left? Do we know why? Where are they now?

Verses 16-41: Can you outline Paul's sermon?

Verses 42-44: What was the result of the sermon?

Verses 45-47: Was everyone happy about the sermon and its affect?

Verses 48-49: Who heard the Word? Who got the glory? What did they do with the Word?

Verse 50: What happened?

Verses 51-52: What happened?

FOCUS

And the word of the Lord was being spread through the whole region. (Acts 13:49)

If you read the beginning of the book of Acts, you see that Jesus told His disciples to go to the nations with His teaching and be witnesses for Him. However, the disciples didn't really leave Jerusalem until chapter 8, after the death of Stephen. Until the death of Stephen, they had been sharing the Gospel in their area only.

Now, in chapter 13, how is the Word of God beginning to spread? Have you ever thought about how the Gospel got to your country, your state, your city, your family, and you?

Is every Christian faithful to share the Gospel with people who have not heard it? No. Why not? What are some reasons why the Gospel isn't spreading today?

TALK

- What is this teaching me about God?
- What is this teaching me about people?
- Why is this important to me today?

CONNECT THE GOSPEL

This is the Gospel: "For what I received I passed on to you as of first importance: that Christ died for our sins according to the Scriptures, that he was buried, that he was raised on the third day according to the Scriptures" (1 Corinthians 15:3-4 NIV).

The Gospel is the promise of God to redeem His Creation. The promise is fulfilled in Jesus. Some people will reject the Word of God, but we are not responsible for how people respond. We are only responsible for sharing the Gospel. Matthew 28:18-20 and Acts 1:8 are commands not options.

SO WHAT?

So what if the Gospel was being spread? How does that affect you today? You have heard about Jesus and how you can be saved by grace through faith in Jesus, so, who cares if it spreads or not?

As a follower of Christ, we should all care about the spread of the Gospel. If the Gospel saves, and if people need to hear it to be saved (Romans 10:14), then it's important that the Gospel is spread.

At the time of this writing, there are over three billion people who have not heard the Gospel (Joshua Project). They haven't rejected Christ; they just haven't heard of Him. If they never hear the Gospel, they won't have any hope of being saved.

Maybe you don't want to talk about Jesus, but you can at least pray for the Lord to send laborers to tell people about Him (Luke 10:2).

SERVE

We asked this question during our Focus time, and now let's finish with this question: Is every Christian faithful to share the Gospel with people who have not heard it? No. Why not? Will the Gospel continue to spread because of you, or will it stop because of you?

Pray this week for people to share the Gospel with, and pray for boldness to share the "good news" of Jesus.

DIG DEEPER

And the word of the Lord was being spread through the whole region. (Acts 13:49)

In our last lesson, we saw the birth of the early Church during the Feast of Pentecost. The Holy Spirit came in power, and He equipped the believers to proclaim the wonders of God in a way that people understood the Gospel and wanted to be saved. They wanted to be made right with God.

Why is it important to share the Gospel? The first reason, of course, is because Jesus told us to, but it is more than that. Did the idea of people coming to saving faith begin in the first century? No.

We will take a short look at some examples in the Old Testament of God's plan of salvation for all people. In Genesis 17:4, God gave this promise to Abraham: "As for me, this is my covenant with you: You will be the father of many nations." The word for "nations" means "ethnic groups" or "people groups."

Naturally Abraham could not reach every people group on the earth. God would use his descendants to help people know the God of Creation.

From Abraham would come Jacob, renamed Israel. God would use the descendants of Israel to bring all people to Himself, most importantly, the Messiah was a descendant of Judah of Israel.

> *And now the Lord says—he who formed me in the womb to be his servant to bring Jacob back to him and gather Israel to himself, for I am honored in the eyes of the Lord and my God has been my strength— he says: "It is too small a thing for you to be my servant to restore the tribes of Jacob and bring back those of Israel I have kept. I will also make you a light for the Gentiles, that my salvation may reach to the ends of the earth." (Isaiah 49:5-6)*

In Luke 2:29-32, Simeon said that the baby Jesus was the light to the nations.

Now, in Acts chapter 13, we see the fulfillment of God's plan to bring the nations to Himself. The beauty of it all is that He allows us to be a part of it, just as He did the early believers.

If you have a map of the Eastern Mediterranean Sea, Turkiye, and Israel, you can follow the Gospel movement. It is very helpful to look at a map when you study the Bible.

In Acts chapter 13, we have already talked about how the first mission team was selected and sent. As we dig deeper, let's look at how the Word spread throughout the region. The region being southern Turkiye and the Island of Cyprus.

Acts 13:3 tells us that it began with fasting and prayer. This is crucial before we begin any work, especially mission work (Mat. 17:21). Fasting and prayer brought them into fellowship with the Holy Spirit. Verse 4 tells us that the Holy Spirit guided their path.

They traveled across the whole Island of Cyprus. The Holy Spirit was with them, and lives were changed. Then they sailed to Perga and on to Pisidian Antioch, present day Antalya, Turkiye.

They used the same mission method everywhere they went. They entered the synagogue first because the Gospel was always for the Jew first and then the gentile (Rom. 1:16). These missionaries could speak to the Jews in their own cultural context because Paul and Barnabas had been Jews. This gave them a common place to begin with the Gospel. Acts 13:46 tells us that they spoke the Word of God "boldly."

The Key Verse is our reminder of what happens when the people of God are faithful to do what the Lord has called them and equipped them to do. Paul and Barnabas trusted the Holy Spirit to use them. We know from the end results that the Word spread. Acts 19:10 tells us that all the Jews and Greeks in the province of Asia heard the Word of the Lord. How far will the Word of God go if we trust the Holy Spirit to use us and guide us?

Notes

13: THE MISSION ERA

Week 49: The Antioch Meeting
Acts 15:1-31

Key verse: *"But we believe that we are saved through the grace of the Lord Jesus, in the same way as they also are." (Acts 15:11)*

LEADER'S NOTE

This chapter mentions circumcision and fornication. You know your students, so use your discretion as to how much time you want to spend on these subjects.

The point of the lesson is that we are all saved the same way—through the grace of the Lord Jesus, and verse 9 says that our hearts are cleansed by faith.

You may want to connect Ephesians 2:8-9 in the lesson.

CONTEXT

Acts 14 closes with Paul and Barnabas in Antioch. They had completed a mission trip, and they were reporting to the Church in Antioch that God had opened a door of faith to the Gentiles.

In Acts chapter 15, there is a problem of some Jewish leaders who had converted to Christianity, teaching the non-Jewish (Gentiles) that they needed to be like the Jews before they could follow Jesus. This was a very big event in the early church because non-Jewish people were coming to faith in Christ. In the early days of the Church, most of the new believers were Jews who had decided to follow Jesus.

Now, some of these Jewish converts were misleading the new believers who came from non-Jewish backgrounds. The Jewish converts were adding a "work" to be saved. However, our salvation comes from our faith alone.

The church leaders met together, they discussed the situation, and then they issued a statement to the Church in Antioch. Simply put, the statement told the new believers to not live like the unbelievers around them.

OPEN UP

What does it mean to "be saved"?

THINK ABOUT

If you believe that you are saved and are right with God, what did you do to be saved?

READ

Verse 1: What is the problem?

Verses 2-4: How do you see unity?

Verse 5: What's the problem? In Matthew 23:4, Jesus warned that the Pharisees were putting heavy burdens on the people and not helping them.

Verse 6: What did the leaders do? Is this important?

Verses 7-11: What did Peter say about salvation?

Verse 12: What did the people do?

Verses 13-18: What did James say? Who does he quote? (Amos 9:11-12).

Verses 19-21: What did they decide?

Verse 22: Why are they sending this delegation?

Verses 23-29: Did the council tell them how to be saved?

Verses 30-31: What happened? How did the people react?

FOCUS

> *But we believe that we are saved through the grace of the Lord Jesus, in the same way as they also are. (Acts 15:11)*

Do you know people who are not saved, people who are not living for Jesus? What do you think about them? Do you wish they would change and then follow Jesus? Do we need to be perfect before we can follow Jesus? Have you ever heard someone say that you need to do something in order to be saved?

TALK

- What is this teaching me about God?
- What is this teaching me about people?
- Why is this important to me today?

CONNECT THE GOSPEL

This is the Gospel: "For what I received I passed on to you as of first importance: that Christ died for our sins according to the Scriptures, that he was buried, that he was raised on the third day according to the Scriptures" (1 Corinthians 15:3-4 NIV).

The "good news" of Jesus Christ is that anyone can be saved by faith alone in Christ alone. This may be a good time to read John 3:16 and Ephesians 2:8-9.

SO WHAT?

Why is this a big deal, and why did we spend an entire lesson on it?

Because there are many religions and cults in the world today who are teaching that you must do something to be right with God or to get to heaven. We want you to know that you are saved the same way Abraham was saved, by faith.

> *Abram believed the Lord, and he credited it to him as righteousness. (Genesis 15:6)*

SERVE

This week find ways to tell people about Jesus. Tell people that they can be right with God by their faith in Him. They don't need to do anything. Find ways to serve someone, and this will open the door for a conversation.

DIG DEEPER

> *But we believe that we are saved through the grace of the Lord Jesus, in the same way as they also are. (Acts 15:11)*

In Acts 2, we saw the Church grow in an amazing way during the Feast of Pentecost. In Acts 13, we saw the message spreading across regions. Anywhere the church goes, it will grow. Anytime the church grows, there will be growing pains. Acts chapter 15, shows us how the early church handled these early growing pains.

From the time of Abraham, God has had a plan for every ethnic group. Genesis 12:3, "I will bless those who bless you, and whoever curses you I will curse; and all peoples on earth will be blessed through you."

In Exodus 9, God used the nation of Israel and their captivity to make Himself known to Pharoah and the Egyptians. "But I have raised you [Pharoah] up for this very purpose, that I might show you my power and that my name might be proclaimed in all the earth" (Exodus 9:16).

The Old Testament gave us examples of Gentiles who came to know God: Melchizedek, Jethro, Balaam, Rahab, and Ruth. Jonah went to Ninevah, a Gentile city.

The Jewish people were so hard-hearted in the days of Jesus that He reminded them of the salvific work of God among Gentiles in the days of Elijah and Elisha, long before He arrived.

> *"Truly I tell you," He continued, "no prophet is accepted in his hometown. I assure you that there were many widows in Israel in Elijah's time, when the sky was shut for three and a half years and there was a severe famine throughout the land. Yet Elijah was not sent to any of them, but to a widow in Zarephath in the region of Sidon. And there were many in Israel with leprosy in the time of Elisha the prophet, yet not one of them was cleansed—only Naaman the Syrian." (Luke 4:24-27)*

Here in Acts chapter 15, Paul and his team returned to Jerusalem to share their mission report with James and the council. Some of the new believers who had been Jewish thought that everyone had to go through the Jewish rituals before being baptized into faith in Christ. The concept of grace was difficult for them to grasp, and it is difficult today as well for many people.

Paul wrote to the church at Ephesus, "It is by grace you have been saved, through faith, and that not of yourselves, it is a gift of God, so that no one can boast" (Eph. 2:8-9). Webster's dictionary defines "grace" as "unmerited divine assistance given to humans for their regeneration or sanctification."

The prophet Isaiah wrote seven hundred years before the time of Jesus. Isaiah gave this word, which referred to the Messiah of Israel: "It is too small a thing for you to be my servant to restore the tribes of Jacob and bring back those of Israel I have kept. I will also make you a light for the Gentiles, that my salvation may reach to the ends of the earth."

After much discussion, the council used the Scripture to arrive at a decision, "The words of the prophets are in agreement with this" (Acts 15:15). As a result, they did not put a burden on the Gentiles.

Acts 15:20, "Instead we should write to them, telling them to abstain from food polluted by idols, from sexual immorality, from the meat of strangled animals and from blood." Now, to us, this may seem like a burden or some work that had to be done to be saved. We need to remember the cultural context in which it was written. In the first century, in the Roman Empire among pagan cultures and idol worship, the Christians had to be separate from that life. Instead of the Council saying, "You must be like us," they said, "Don't be like the culture around you."

It is the same today. "If any man be in Christ, he is a new creation: behold, the old has gone and the new has come" (2 Cor. 5:17). If we are going to live for Jesus, then our lives must be different from the culture around us. If we are doing the same thing that everyone else is doing, then are we really saved?

When people are allowed to come to Jesus just as they are, they will celebrate the freedom in Christ. Acts 15:31, "The people read it and were glad for its encouraging message."

Notes

14: The End of Time Era

14: THE END OF TIME ERA

Week 50: The Revelation
Revelation 5:1-14

Key verse: *"And they sang a new song, saying: 'You are worthy to take the scroll and to open its seals, because you were slain, and with your blood you purchased for God persons from every tribe and language and people and nation.'" (Revelation 5:9)*

LEADER'S NOTE

As you bring this Sunday school year to a close, we want the students to know that our hope is in Christ. We can have that hope now, as we go through these days, and we have hope in eternity.

That is what Revelation shows us amidst all of its imagery and veiled language. Jesus came as a Lamb to be slain. He came in weakness, humility, and poverty. He will return as a Lion, as a King in power, in glory, and with all the wealth of heaven.

We chose chapter 5 because it shows that Jesus is worthy to be worshiped by the angels and by people from every ethnic group.

We have studied the Word of God for fifty-two weeks. We have done our best to connect the Gospel in each lesson for the purpose of getting the students to this point. We are not wasting time telling people about Jesus, because we know that one day there will be a lot of people with us worshiping the King of kings.

CONTEXT

The Revelation of Jesus Christ to the Apostle John is apocalyptic literature. It has no parallel. It was written to Christians in the first century who were suffering immense persecution.

Genesis and the Revelation serve as bookends for all of the Bible. Where Genesis is the beginning with the Creation narrative, Revelation is the new beginning with a new creation of a new heaven and new earth.

What was broken during the fall of the first man and woman will be restored by the Son of Man. Satan lied and brought a curse, but the time will come when there won't be any lies, and the curse will be broken.

At the end of Genesis chapter 3, the man and woman were driven away from the presence of God. In Revelation 22:4, we will see His face.

OPEN UP

What is the purpose of the Bible?

THINK ABOUT

Why did God send Jesus to die?

READ

Verses 1-2: What is the situation? Who is holding it, and who can open it?

Verses 3-5: Why did John weep, and what was he told? What references are used to describe the One Who is worthy?

Verse 6: What did John see? Who is this? How is He described? (Genesis 49:9-10; Isaiah 11:10). The seven horns are a sign of omnipotence, and the seven eyes are a sign of omniscience (Zechariah 4:10).

Verses 7-10: What happened? What does the song tell us about the work of Christ?

Verses 11-13: Who is singing, what are they singing about, and who are they pointing to in their song?

Verse 14: What should be the natural response when we see God?

FOCUS

> *And they sang a new song, saying: "You are worthy to take the scroll and to open its seals, because you were slain, and with your blood you purchased for God persons from every tribe and language and people and nation." (Revelation 5:9)*

Do you remember what "redemption" means? What do we see here in the song of verse 9? Who is worthy to take this scroll? Only one person was worthy? And, what made Him worthy?

Only Jesus could do this. He paid the redemption price with His blood, He did the work by being slain, His work resulted in us being restored to God the Creator, and His work was enough to bring people to Him from all over the world.

TALK

- What is this teaching me about God?
- What is this teaching me about people?
- Why is this important to me today?

CONNECT THE GOSPEL

This is the Gospel: "For what I received I passed on to you as of first importance: that Christ died for our sins according to the Scriptures, that he was buried, that he was raised on the third day according to the Scriptures" (1 Corinthians 15:3-4 NIV).

The purpose of the Gospel is that we may know what God has done in Jesus to bring us back to Himself in a right relationship. Here in Revelation chapter 5, we see the culmination of the Gospel. People from every tribe, tongue, and nation are worshiping the Lord. Because of what Jesus has done, we have been redeemed, purchased with His blood, and now are a part of His Kingdom.

SO WHAT?

The big "so what?" If you are living for Jesus, and if you have been trying to tell people about Jesus then you know that sometimes you may feel discouraged and wonder if you are making a difference. Here in the book of Revelation is the answer to the question, "Am I making a difference when I tell people about Jesus?" The answer is "yes."

When we read the book of Revelation, we get to see the end of the story. This should encourage us to keep telling people about Jesus. Some of the people we talk to will get saved.

SERVE

If you know that people from every ethnic group will be worshiping Jesus one day in heaven, do you think it's important to tell people from different ethnic groups about Jesus? How will they hear about Jesus if someone doesn't tell them? How will they be saved if they never hear?

We all have an opportunity to help people to be a part of Revelation chapter 5.

DIG DEEPER

> *And they sang a new song, saying: "You are worthy to take the scroll and to open its seals, because you were slain, and with your blood you purchased for God persons from every tribe and language and people and nation." (Revelation 5:9)*

In order to understand how powerful this event is, we need to know something about the "scroll" and the One who was slain to purchase, or redeem, people with His blood.

From the very beginning of the Bible, in Genesis chapter 1, we saw that we have been created in the image of God with the command to multiply that image. When sin entered the world through disobedience, the image was ruined. However, God provided a way to cover the sinners and restore the image. Genesis 3:21, "The Lord God made garments of skin for Adam and his wife and clothed them." Some animal must have died in order to use its skin. From that point on, we see the pattern of the innocent dying on behalf of the guilty.

We have talked about the substitutionary sacrifice in Genesis 22:8, when Abraham told Isaac that "God himself would provide the lamb." We have talked about the statement of John the Baptist when he saw Jesus, "Look, the Lamb of God, who takes away the sin of the world" (John 1:29).

We talked about redemption and the kinsman-redeemer in our study of Ruth. Jesus is our Redeemer, and He has redeemed us, purchased us from the bondage of sin, "For you know that it was not with perishable things such as silver or gold that you were redeemed from the empty way of life handed down to you from your ancestors, but with the precious blood of Christ, a lamb without blemish or defect" (1 Peter 1:18-19).

But what about this scroll?

We need to go back to the time of Daniel and the prophecies that were given to him from God:

> *At that time Michael, the great prince who protects your people, will arise. There will be a time of distress such as has not happened from the beginning of nations until then. But at that time your people—everyone whose name is found written in the book—will be delivered. Multitudes who sleep in the dust of the earth will awake: some to everlasting life, others to shame and everlasting contempt. Those who are wise will shine like the brightness of the heavens, and those who lead many to righteousness, like the stars for ever and ever. But you, Daniel, roll up and seal the words of the scroll until the time of the end. Many will go here and there to increase knowledge. (Daniel 12:1-4)*

We do not know how many years will pass between Daniel sealing the scroll and Jesus opening it, but we know that there is only One who is worthy to open the scroll. Who is this?

Revelation 5:5, "Then one of the elders said to me, 'Do not weep! See, the Lion of the tribe of Judah, the Root of David, has triumphed. He is able to open the scroll and its seven seals.'" This is Jesus, the Lion of the tribe of Judah.

Who is this? Revelation 5:6, "Then I saw a Lamb, looking as if it had been slain, standing at the center of the throne." This is Jesus the Lamb of God.

Why is He worthy? He is worthy because He was slain, and He paid the price with His blood. That payment "purchased for God persons from every tribe and language and people and nation."

Just think about that: This means that people from every ethnic group will be "purchased for God." Ephesians 1:7a, "In him we have redemption through his blood, the forgiveness of sins." Forgiveness of sins is what we all need to be restored to God our Creator. Now we are His.

"He replied, 'Go your way, Daniel, because the words are rolled up and sealed until the time of the end. Many will be purified, made spotless and refined, but the wicked will continue to be wicked. None of the wicked will understand, but those who are wise will understand'" (Daniel 12:9-10). May we be among those who are wise and understand the plan of God to redeem people to Himself.

Daniel was overwhelmed when the Lord God revealed the end to him, but Daniel was promised his eternal inheritance (Daniel 12:13).

Will you be a part of this heavenly choir? Revelation 5:9, "And they sang a new song, saying: 'You are worthy to take the scroll and to open its seals, because you were slain, and with your blood you purchased for God persons from every tribe and language and people and nation.'"

Notes

Week 51: The Gospel in Christmas
Luke 2:1-20

Key verse: *"And the shepherds went back, glorifying and praising God for all that they had heard and seen, just as had been told them." (Luke 2:20)*

LEADER'S NOTE

We talked about the angelic announcement to Mary in Week 32. In that lesson we focused on Mary and her faithfulness in her role.

In this lesson, we want to look at the announcement to the shepherds and how they responded. You may decide that you want to teach Week 32 and this lesson back-to-back.

The Christmas story has been repeated for two thousand years, and we are not attempting to rewrite the narrative.

CONTEXT

Matthew and Luke give us information about the birth of Jesus. Luke gives us the details of the night and morning of the birth, whereas Matthew tells us about the angelic messenger to Mary and Joseph, and then he tells us about the visit of the Magi. There could be as much as a two-year gap between Matthew chapters 1 and 2.

Luke gives us the information we need to place the event during the reign of Caesar Augustus. Most theologians place the date near 4 B.C.

OPEN UP

What is the main thing people talk about during the Christmas season?

THINK ABOUT

When was the last time you told someone how to find Jesus?

READ

Verses 1-3: What is a decree? Why is a census important?

Verses 4-5: Why did Mary and Joseph have to travel?

Verses 6-7: What happened? Why would Luke tell us that this is Mary's first-born son?

Verses 8-9: Who visited whom? When is another time when an angelic messenger visited someone to make an announcement about Jesus?

Verses 10-12: What did the angel say? Who has been born? A Savior who is Christ the Lord.

Verses 13-14: What happened? What does this mean?

Verses 15-16: What did the shepherds do? What words in these verses indicate that the shepherds felt like this was important?

Verses 18-20: What actions by the people are identified here? Those who heard it wondered. Mary treasured and pondered. The shepherds glorified and praised God.

LEADER'S GUIDE—SOJOURNER BIBLE STUDY

FOCUS

And the shepherds went back, glorifying and praising God for all that they had heard and seen, just as had been told them. (Luke 2:20)

The shepherds received the birth announcement in a very special way. They could have ignored the angels and stayed in the field, but they didn't. They believed what they were told by the messengers of God, and they took action.

What did they do first? They went to see. What did they do after they had seen Jesus? They told about how they heard about Jesus. What did the shepherds do after the word and the witness had been confirmed? They glorified and praised God because it was true.

How often do you hear people talk about how to find Jesus during the Christmas season?

TALK

- What is this teaching me about God?
- What is this teaching me about people?
- Why is this important to me today?

CONNECT THE GOSPEL

This is the Gospel: "For what I received I passed on to you as of first importance: that Christ died for our sins according to the Scriptures, that he was buried, that he was raised on the third day according to the Scriptures" (1 Corinthians 15:3-4 NIV).

We can't get to the Gospel if Jesus had not been born. He had to be born and live a perfect life, so that He could be the perfect sacrifice for our sins.

Here we have the beginning of the fulfillment of Genesis 3:15, that the Seed of the woman would have to crush the serpent. Jesus was born to fulfill the promise God made in Genesis 3, so that His death would crush Satan and the power of death forever.

SO WHAT?

Why do we need to study the actions of some sheep herders? Why is this important?

When the shepherds were the first to come to Jesus, it showed that Jesus came for everyone, regardless of class or status.

We see in verse 4 that they went to the city of David because they were in David's family line. We see in verse 11 that Jesus was born in the city of David. David was a shepherd before he was a king. Here we see the first people to visit the King of kings are shepherds not kings.

SERVE

Christmas is a season with a lot of activities and parties. It can be a time of joy or a time of stress. This week, find ways to help people see the joy of Christ's birth. Can you help them see Jesus the way you see Him, so that they too will go home glorifying and praising God?

DIG DEEPER

And the shepherds went back, glorifying and praising God for all that they had heard and seen, just as had been told them. (Luke 2:20)

As we go deeper today, let's look at the holy messengers, the message, and the audience. Hebrews 1:6 tells us that the angels would worship the Son of God, "And again, when God brings his firstborn into the world, he says, 'Let all God's angels worship him.'"

So this heavenly multitude, who were sent from God, worshiped the Son of God. In their worship of the Son of God, they told others, the shepherds, about this Savior.

What was the message? "A Savior has been born to you; he is the Messiah, the Lord" (Luke 2:11). This is the message the people had been waiting for since the days of Moses. In Exodus 3, God told Moses that He had seen the suffering of His people, and He would come to rescue them. The picture of the coming Savior (Ex. 3:8). Here in the birth of the Christ Child is God's rescue mission for His people.

The angels of God were sent to shepherds, not to the chief priests. These shepherds were plain men like Jacob (Gen. 30:29). The angels of God met the shepherds where they were, out in the field. The angels spoke to them in the language they understood, and the shepherds responded to the Word of God, which was delivered by His messengers.

Then the shepherds went to see this Savior. "When they had seen him, they spread the word concerning what had been told them about this child." These shepherds had now become messengers of God. They had a message to share, and they did.

This message is the greatest message anyone could hope to hear. God has come to save us to Himself. He has given us His Holy Spirit to enable us to tell others this message. Acts 1:8, "But you will receive power when the Holy Spirit comes on you; and you will be my witnesses in Jerusalem, and in all Judea and Samaria, and to the ends of the earth."

The power of God came to the shepherds where they were and in their language. "The glory of the Lord shone round about them" (Luke 2:9). Now the power of God has come to us in the Holy Spirit.

We have the glory of God with us. These shepherds were the first witnesses of the Savior, the Messiah of God. If we have seen this Savior, then should we not go "glorifying and praising God for all that they had heard and seen," just as it has been told to us?

Notes

LEADER'S GUIDE—SOJOURNER BIBLE STUDY

Week 52: The Gospel in Easter
Matthew 28:1-10

Key verse: *"He is not here, for He has risen, just as He said. Come, see the place where He was lying." (Matthew 28:6)*

LEADER'S NOTE

In Week 45 we saw the Last Supper, in Week 46 we saw the betrayal of Judas, and in Week 47 we saw the crucifixion. You may want to bring in this lesson after Week 47. Of course, Easter Sunday is different every year, which means these lessons may not line up well on the church calendar.

Once again, we ask you to use your discretion on this and any other lesson.

All four Gospels have an account of the events of Resurrection Day. There are similarities, and there are differences. We want to make the point that, "He is not here, He is risen." We also want to follow that truth with, "come and see / go and tell."

CONTEXT

According to Leviticus 23, the Day of First Fruits was the first day after the Sabbath after the Feast of Unleavened Bread. That means that the Sunday after Jesus was crucified was the Day of First Fruits. The Apostle Paul confirms this another way in 1 Corinthians 15:20: "But Christ has indeed been raised from the dead, the first fruits of those who have fallen asleep."

For the Jewish people who believed in the resurrection account, this would have been significant. For the followers of Jesus, it was the first day that they could go to the tomb to anoint His body because of the Sabbath restrictions.

So, that is where we begin today. On the first day of the Jewish week, with the women going to the tomb first. It's interesting that Jesus' birth was announced to lowly shepherds who were the first to see Him. Then, His resurrection was first observed by women, also from a lower place in society in the first century.

OPEN UP

Did Jesus do what He said He was going to do? (Luke 9:22).

THINK ABOUT

What does the resurrection of Jesus prove to us?

READ

Verse 1: What day is the Jewish sabbath?

Verses 2-4: What happened?

Verse 5: How does the angel describe Jesus? Why is this important?

Verse 6: What three things does the angel say about Jesus? What does the angel tell them to do first? Come and see.

Verse 7: What does the angel tell the women to do next? Go and tell. What is the message?

Verse 8: What did the women do? Why don't we go quickly to tell people about Jesus?

Verses 9-10: What did the women want to do? What did Jesus tell them?

14: THE END OF TIME ERA

FOCUS

He is not here, for He has risen, just as He said. Come, see the place where He was lying. (Matthew 28:6)

Think about what the angel is telling the women. He began by telling them to not be afraid. Then he goes on to state three facts. He's not here, He rose, and He told you He was going to do this. Why do you think the angel needed to remind them that Jesus had said He would rise?

TALK

- What is this teaching me about God?
- What is this teaching me about people?
- Why is this important to me today?

CONNECT THE GOSPEL

This is the Gospel: "For what I received I passed on to you as of first importance: that Christ died for our sins according to the Scriptures, that he was buried, that he was raised on the third day according to the Scriptures" (1 Corinthians 15:3-4 NIV).

The Gospel is not "good news" if Jesus didn't rise from the grave. The resurrection means that Jesus conquered death. It means our sin debt is paid because the cost of sin is death. (Romans 3:23, and the gift of God is eternal life in Christ Jesus.)

The angel told the women that Jesus rose as He said. Paul said that it happened according to the Scriptures. Because it was foretold, and because it happened as Jesus had promised, this means that His Word is true. We can trust what He tells us. He also told us that He will come again (John 14), so we can believe that He will.

SO WHAT?

What does this mean to me today that Jesus is risen, His tomb is empty, and it happened the way He said it would? It means we have hope today in our own resurrection and eternal life.

> *But Christ has indeed been raised from the dead, the first fruits of those who have fallen asleep. For since death came through a man, the resurrection of the dead comes also through a man. For as in Adam all die, so in Christ all will be made alive. But each in turn: Christ, the first fruits; then, when he comes, those who belong to him. (1 Corinthians 15:20-23)*

SERVE

If you believe that Jesus has risen as the Bible says, then why don't you go and tell people that He has gone ahead and we will see Him? Why don't you go quickly?

Find a way to serve today and this week. Find people to tell because this will change their life.

DIG DEEPER

He is not here, for He has risen, just as He said. Come, see the place where He was lying. (Matthew 28:6)

What is the significance of Jesus' resurrection? The resurrection of Jesus is one of the foundations of our faith, and the resurrection of Jesus is our hope. "And if Christ has not been raised, your faith is futile; you are still in your sins" (1 Cor. 15:17).

Matthew chapter 28 gives us four proofs of the resurrection. You will want to read the rest of the chapter, but here they are in brief.

Proof number one: The angel testified to the fact of the resurrection. This is our focal verse today. "He is not here, He is risen."

Proof number two: Jesus appeared to the women. "Suddenly Jesus met them. 'Greetings,' he said. They came to him, clasped his feet, and worshiped him" (Mat. 28:9).

Proof number three: The soldiers who had been at the tomb reported His resurrection. Matthew 28:11, "While the women were on their way, some of the guards went into the city and reported to the chief priests everything that had happened."

Proof number four: The resurrected Jesus appeared to His disciples in Galilee. Matthew 28:16-17, "Then the eleven disciples went to Galilee, to the mountain where Jesus had told them to go. When they saw him, they worshiped him; but some doubted."

The disciples had been taught that the Messiah would die and rise again. For example, in Matthew 12:40, Jesus connected His resurrection to the story of Jonah.

Hosea had prophesied of the effect of a third day salvation: "After two days he will revive us; on the third day he will restore us, that we may live in his presence" (Hosea 6:2).

The Matthew Henry Commentary speaks of this perfectly: "He assures them of the resurrection of Christ; and there was enough in that to silence their fears; He is not here, for he is risen. To be told He is not here, would have been no welcome news to those who sought him, if it had not been added, He is risen" (Excerpt from the Blue Letter Bible, Matthew Henry Commentary on Matthew 28).

What should our response be to the fact of the resurrection? It should be in line with the command the angel gave to the women, "Then Jesus said to them, 'Do not be afraid. Go and tell my brothers to go to Galilee; there they will see me'" (Mat. 28:10). The women were obedient. Then the disciples were obedient to go to Galilee, where they would also see the risen Lord Jesus.

Then the disciples were given a command to go, after they had been told to come and see.

> *Then Jesus came to them and said, "All authority in heaven and on earth has been given to me. Therefore, go and make disciples of all nations, baptizing them in the name of the Father and of the Son and of the Holy Spirit, and teaching them to obey everything I have commanded you. And surely, I am with you always, to the very end of the age." (Matthrew 28:18-20)*

Jesus has risen. What proof do you need of His resurrection? He invites all of us to come and see. If you have seen Him in His word, then go and tell.

Notes

CLOSING WORDS FROM HEBREWS 13:20-21

"Now may the God of peace, who through the blood of the eternal covenant brought back from the dead our Lord Jesus, that great Shepherd of the sheep, equip you with everything good for doing his will, and may he work in us what is pleasing to him, through Jesus Christ, to whom be glory for ever and ever. Amen."

SCRIPTURE CITATION INDEX

The Berean Standard Bible
The Holy Bible, Berean Standard Bible, BSB is produced in cooperation with Bible Hub, Discovery Bible, OpenBible.com, and the Berean Bible Translation Committee. This text of God's Word has been dedicated to the public domain.

Ruth 2:20

English Standard Version (ESV)
The Holy Bible, English Standard Version. ESV® Text Edition: 2016. Copyright © 2001 by Crossway Bibles, a publishing ministry of Good News Publishers.

Gen. 1:11, 5:29, 11:2,4,8
Deut. 11:25
Isa. 25:8
Josh. 2:9,11
Judges 2:2
2 Kings 4:43, 7:2
Ezra 7:10
Job 9:8
Psalm 65:5-8
Math. 1:5
Mark 12:28-31
Luke 2:32, 5:11
John 2:15,29
Acts 2:1-11, 3:22-26, 13:47
Rom. 16:20
Philippians 2:8
Heb. 11:7,31
James 2:25
1 Peter 2:20, 3:18
Rev. 7:9, 12:9-10

International Standard Version (ISV)
Copyright © 1995-2014 by ISV Foundation. ALL RIGHTS RESERVED INTERNATIONALLY. Used by permission of Davidson Press, LLC.

Job 38:34-35

King James Version (KJV)
Public domain

Neh. 1:4
Luke 2:9
John 3:3,5

New American Standard Bible (NASB)
New American Standard Bible®, Copyright © 1960, 1971, 1977, 1995, 2020 by The Lockman Foundation. All rights reserved.

Gen. 1:1, 2:17,24, 3:19,21,24, 6:8, 12:3, 22:18
Ex. 3:6, 9:16, 19:5, 36:23
Deut. 6:12-13
Josh. 4:23-24
Judges 2:6-8
2 Sam. 7:13,16
1 Kings 12:24
2 Kings 19:35
2 Chron. 7:1
Psalms 14:1, 119:130
Prov. 1:7
Isa. 6:8, 7:14, 49:5-6, 56:8
Dan. 2:11,22
Math. 5:3,11,44, 7:21-23, 9:36, 10:28, 12:50, 28:6
Mark 6:50, 12:34, 15:10
Luke 1:16-17, 2:20,30-32, 5:8, 10:25, 13:34, 15:21, 18:38, 19:10, 22:19,21
John 1:11,12-13,14, 4:19-21, 10:18, 14:15,16-17, 16:33, 17:20-21
Acts 2:38, 4:12, 13:49, 15:11
Rom. 1:16, 3:23, 6:23, 8:1
1 Cor. 14:33
2 Cor. 5:21
Eph. 2:8-9
Col. 3:17
Heb. 1:1-2
James 1:15
1 John 2:12, 4:17-18

SCRIPTURE CITATION INDEX

New International Version (NIV)

Holy Bible, New International Version®, NIV® Copyright ©1973, 1978, 1984, 2011 by Biblica, Inc.® Used by permission. All rights reserved worldwide.

Gen. 3:8-9,15, 4:26, 6:13, 12:2-3, 14:4, 15:6, 22:8, 28:11-14, 35:11-12, 48:15-16, 50:20

Ex. 3:7-10, 4:22-23, 6:6-8, 7:5, 9:16,20-21, 12:13,24-30, 14:4,31, 20:2, 23:4-5, 25:22, 34:6

Lev. 19:18

Deut. 6:4-6, 18:15,18, 25:17-19

Judges 2:10

1 Sam. 3:1,7,19,20,21, 13:14, 15:3,20-21,22

2 Sam. 7:16

1 Kings 11:13, 18:37

2 Kings 1:8

2 Chron. 6:4-6, 36:15,16

Ezra 7:6

Neh. 1:6-7

Job 11:13-15, 12:23, 19:25, 42:1-6

Psalms 22:6,27-28,31, 41:9, 47:7-9, 51:17, 116:12-13, 137:5-6, 139:16

Prov. 1:7, 18:10, 20:22

Ecc. 12:13-14

Isa. 7:14, 9:6,7, 40:3, 52:14, 55:10-11

Jer. 18:8,10, 31:31, 33:14-17

Ezek. 18:20,32, 36:25-27, 37:22-28

Dan. 1:8, 2:11,21, 12:1-4,9-10

Hosea 6:2

Jonah 3:10

Micah 6:8

Mal. 2:15, 3:1,17, 4:4

Math. 1:1,7, 4:17, 5:4,45, 6:33, 7:21-23,29, 8:25,27, 12:36-37,42, 13:52, 14:25-26, 17:22, 26:14-16, 27:35,39, 28:9,10,11,16-17,18-20

Mark 1:4-6,14-15, 8:33, 10:33, 12:30-31,33,34

Luke 1:3,4,17,31-33,35,68, 2:11,17, 3:16, 4:24-27, 6:32-36, 10:27, 15:1-2,18,20-21, 16:16, 19:9, 22:4-6,20,22, 23:41,42,43, 24:25-27

John 1:18,23,29, 2:15, 3:3-6, 4:10, 6:14,19-20,28-29, 8:34, 12:4-6,31,32, 13:18,27,34-35, 14:25, 15:13-14, 17:20-21, 19:11

Acts 1:8, 2:4,11,36-41, 7:2-4, 15:15,20,31, 16:25, 17:24,26

Rom. 5:9-10, 6:22-23, 7:7, 8:1-4,28, 10:9-11, 12:4-5

1 Cor. 3:16, 11:27-29, 15:3-4,17,20-23

2 Cor. 13:5

Gal. 3:6-9,28, 4:4-7, 5:22-23

Eph. 1:7, 2:10, 5:30-32

Col. 1:15,16, 21-23, 3:1-4

2 Tim. 2:1-2,4

Heb. 9:22, 10:1-4,8-10,14-18, 11:19, 13:20-21

James 1:5, 2:19, 3:9-12

1 Peter 1:6-9,10-12,18-19

1 John 1:9, 2:3-6, 4:1

Rev. 5:5,6,9, 21:1,3-5, 22:20-21

New King James Version (NKJV)

Scripture taken from the New King James Version®. Copyright © 1982 by Thomas Nelson. Used by permission. All rights reserved.

Gen. 1:3,9, 3:15, 6:22, 35:7

Ex. 9:16-17, 40:34

2 Chron. 5:14

Isa. 6:5

Mark 1:2

Luke 5:5

John 13:34

Gal. 3:24

Philippians 2:7-8

2 Peter 3:9

New Living Translation (NLT)

Holy Bible, New Living Translation, copyright © 1996, 2004, 2015 by Tyndale House Foundation. Used by permission of Tyndale House Publishers, Inc., Carol Stream, Illinois 60188. All rights reserved.

Num. 23:19

Isa. 49:6

Jer. 31:31

Luke 2:30-32

John 15:18-19, 17:14

Acts 2:23, 5:41

Rom. 5:3-4

2 Tim. 3:12

1 Peter 4:4

www.ingramcontent.com/pod-product-compliance
Lightning Source LLC
Chambersburg PA
CBHW081919170426
43200CB00014B/2768